Rita Soulahian Kuyumjian

# Archeology of Madness

## Komitas, Portrait of an Armenian Icon

Gomidas Institute
London

This publication was made possible by a grant from the
Armenian General Benevolent Union.

Illustration Credits
Komitas Archives, Charents Museum of Literature and Art, Yerevan (pp. 23, 31, 32, 34, 42, 43, 45, 46, 48, 50, 51, 58, 59, 60, 65, 73, 78, 81, 83, 87, 89, 104, 108, 155, 175); Matevos H. Muratian and Kevork Keotagian, eds. *Agnarg Hay Yerazheshdutian Badmutian*, (Yerevan: ARMSSR Academy of Sciences, 1963) (pp. 25, 27); AGBU Nubarian Library, Paris (p. 211); Simone Denis Torkomian, Paris (p. 152); Dr. Léon Gilbert of SERHEP (pp. 175, 177); Archives of l'Hôpital Villejuif, France (pp. 171, 188, 193); Harutyune Boyadjian (p. 15); Jirair Kuyumjian (pp. 41, 151, 209)

Published by Taderon Press by arrangement with the Gomidas Institute



ISBN 978-1-903656-21-1

For comments and inquiries please contact:
Gomidas Institute
42 Blythe Rd
London W14 0HA
England

Email: *books@gomidas.org*

But, you know, I feel more fellowship with the defeated than with saints.
Heroism and sanctity don't really appeal to me, I imagine.
What interests me is being a man.

ALBERT CAMUS
*The Plague*

# Table of Contents



ILLUSTRATIONS

# Acknowledgments

This book represents several years of labor in a variety of fields. The work was carried out with the advice and assistance of a great many people, to whom I wish to express my gratitude.

Dr. Paul Ginestet of the Villejuif Asylum in Paris graciously allowed me to consult the hospital's archives and to make copies of Komitas's medical file. The research I completed with Dr. Ginestet's kind permission formed one of the cornerstones of this work.

*La société d'études et de recherches historiques en psychiatrie* (SERHEP) responded quickly and comprehensively to my inquiries by sending me a collection of documents from the file kept on Komitas during his years at the Ville-Évrard asylum near Paris, as well as much useful information about the asylum itself.

Phillipe Guillouard of the Interior Ministry of France helped me with the translation of the various legal and medical documents in Komitas's file. In so doing he provided me with crucial elucidation of France's *Code de la Santé Publique* and the laws governing the practice of psychiatry in France in the early part of this century.

Mrs. Knarig Grigorian and Henrik Pakhchinyan of the Charents Museum of Literature and Art in Yerevan offered invaluable assistance in compiling a file of letters, manuscripts, photographs, and other biographical materials. Artsvi Pakhchinyan, Gourgen Gasbaryan and Marine Mousheghyan of the Museum of Literature and Arts made it possible to scan original pictures from the Komitas archives in Yerevan.

A large and varied group of people helped me to locate sources and references the world over. Among them were Raymond Kevorkian of the Nubarian Library in Paris; Father Vahan of the Mkhitarist Congregation in Vienna; Father Vartan Demirjian of the Antilias book depository; Mrs. Zvart Tanielian of the Haygazian College in Beirut; and the librarians of St. Mary's Hospital in Montreal.

Dr. Robert Bull of Montreal and Aris Sevag of New York generously offered their advice and comments on the early versions of the manuscript.

Ms. Hasmik Injejikian, a Montreal musicologist, guided me patiently through the history of Armenian music.

Professor Vahakn Dadrian, author of *The History of the Armenian Genocide*, gave me excellent advice in finding source materials on the Genocide in both Armenian and non-Armenian literature.

Nourhan Ouzounian of Montreal offered his enthusiastic assistance in translating certain official documents from Turkish into Armenian, as well as translating the Armenian poetry of Baruyr Sevag into English. He also helped with the editing of an earlier version of the manuscript.

Constructive criticism of the initial manuscript, as well as valuable advice on how to direct the work to a wider audience, was given by Mr. Manoog Young of the National Association of Armenian Studies and Research in Belmont, Massachusetts, Edward Alexandre of Bethesda, Maryland and Dr. Elizabeth A. Gregory of Boston.

Professor James Russell kindly offered editorial comments on the first version of the manuscript. The anonymous readers of the Gomidas Institute provided useful comments, for which I am grateful.

Dr. George Pollock of Chicago provided me with steadfast support and encouragement regarding the worthiness of this project.

My assistant Brian Lynch helped me enormously with the finer points of English syntax, and worked closely with me to restructure the book so that it would appeal to audiences both within and outside the psychiatric profession. I am likewise grateful to Ms. Sara Blackburn for carefully editing the text.

Members of McGill University student book club Marina Todorova, Antonio Sorge, Dolfen Addeh, Arman Kuyumjian, Annette Reed, and Carolina Mingarelli read the manuscript and offered their useful observations.

This book could not have been produced without the unwavering support and patience of the many colleagues and friends who listened carefully to the various working hypotheses that I developed over the ten years of work on this project. I would especially like to thank Anoush Agnerian, Hourig Attarian, Viken Attarian, and Hagop Khacikian.

Of course, I owe my greatest debt of gratitude to my husband Dr. Jirair Kuyumjian, and to my son Arman, whose encouragement and faith never flagged during the many periods of exhaustion and despair that I experienced in producing this work and bringing it to publication.

Finally, I would like to thank Mrs. Louise Simone for her abiding interest in this project and for her steadfast support, and the Armenian General Benevolent Union for a generous grant that made this publication possible.

# Introduction

It is hard to find an Armenian who has never heard the name Komitas Vartabed. Despite the passing of more than six decades since his death in 1935, his work still occupies a central place in almost any concert program of classical Armenian music. And yet he is virtually unknown to those who live outside the Armenian communities scattered around the globe.

Komitas Vartabed was never a child prodigy like Mozart, and his output was relatively modest: roughly eighty songs and choral pieces, seven dances for the piano, an unfinished arrangement of the Armenian Mass, and a handful of theoretical sketches. How, then, did his name come to be imprinted on the psyche of every Armenian?

Armenian musicologists regard Komitas as the father of contemporary Armenian classical music on the basis of his ethnomusicological field studies, his career as a teacher, his beautiful baritone voice, and his many lectures on the history of ecclesiastical and folk music. But I believe that it was Komitas's tireless efforts in organizing mixed choirs and conducting performances of his songs and choral works that won him a special place in the hearts of Armenian people. With the choirs he organized in Tbilisi, Baku, Constantinople, Smyrna, Alexandria, Cairo, Paris, Lausanne and Geneva, he performed pieces of music that he had fashioned from millennium-old materials and polished to jewel-like brilliance, imbuing them with his deep sense of their cultural significance. Through this process, the works came to serve as beloved connections for great numbers of Armenian youths that grew up far from their homeland, severed from their cultural roots. Komitas touched these young people personally, enriched them emotionally, challenged them artistically, and reconnected them to their cultural heritage.

Two great strands of human life are interwoven in the Armenian psyche: suffering and art. In profound ways, Komitas's life is one of the clearest manifestations of this psychic trait. Armenians conceive of suffering as a national phenomenon, for suffering has served them as a people: it has strengthened their determination to survive. But it continues to exact terrible costs. With the loss of their ancestral homelands and an enormous part of their population, many Armenians continue to inflict unconscious painful psychological wounds upon themselves, identifying themselves with their wounded nation. For this reason, Komitas, a man who became mad under the pressures of unacknowledged, unhealed trauma, has taken on extraordinary symbolic importance.

It is significant that Komitas's life as an artist represented a process of healing his own psychic wounds. His relentless pursuit of musicological precision, which he hoped would save from oblivion not only the modest pieces of folk music left to him by his parents, but also the musical heritage of his nation, served him well. He enjoyed immense professional success and, most importantly, won the love and admiration of his people—a love that provided an invaluable substitute for the love he had lost when he became an orphan.

Komitas's music still has a profound healing effect on listeners, Armenian and non-Armenian alike. His songs, so often laden with a deep sense of melancholy, regularly draw audiences to their feet. This is where art and suffering unite. This is where Komitas and the nation that gave birth to him become one.

Survivors of the Armenian Genocide have recognized Komitas's prolonged suffering as a symbol of their own personal and collective anguish, and ranked him among Armenian martyrs. Indeed, members of the Armenian Apostolic Church have recently proposed his canonization. Given that mental illness usually disqualifies a candidate for sainthood, such a recommendation offers further evidence of his profound importance to Armenians.

The nature of Komitas's illness has been a mystery for many that have taken an interest in him—myself included, despite my years of experience as a practicing psychiatrist. Early in 1987, I began rereading my copy of *Anlreli Zankagadun* [The Ever-Ringing Belfry], a collection of verse about Komitas by the eminent Armenian poet Baruyr Sevag. I was overcome by a deep and painful sense of the inner turmoil that Komitas had endured over the last twenty years of his life, first in the 1915 Turkish camp where he was incarcerated and then in psychiatric hospitals in Turkey and France. I wondered at the immensity of the tragedies that had desiccated his imagination and alienated him from the world of the living. What a loss to humanity, I thought; what a waste to have been silenced in this way at the age of forty-five. How could this proud and talented man overcome the humiliation of being abused and treated like a criminal? How could such an artist endure the torture inflicted on the very people around whom his work and indeed his whole world revolved?

These reflections led to more questions: what affliction lay behind all of the puzzling symptoms that he displayed over the years? Had anyone researched his illness thoroughly? Had anyone seriously examined the possible relationship between his experience in the death-camp and his symptomatology?

After reading Sevag's book, I devoted myself to answering these questions. It was not only a matter of arriving at certain psychiatric conclusions about Komitas's own symptoms (many of which suggested that he had developed a condition now referred to as Posttraumatic Stress Disorder, or PTSD), but of unearthing the very roots of the psychological trauma inflicted on victims of the Armenian Genocide. I wanted to treat Komitas's experience as a case study, in the same way that it has been employed by writers and artists to symbolize the sufferings of his people as a whole.

In 1988, I began my search for an accurate diagnosis of Komitas's illness by contacting Hôpital Villejuif, the institution on the outskirts of Paris where he spent the last thirteen years of his life. Given that the patient in question had been dead for nearly fifty-three years, I knew that uncovering his medical file might be difficult, even impossible. The records—if they existed at all—might have been filed under any one of the many other names that Komitas assumed during his lifetime. My fears proved to be unfounded. In November 1988, six months after I had begun my letter-writing campaign, I received a reply from a Professor Ginestet at the hospital, informing me that Komitas's records still existed and that I was welcome to consult them if I wished.[1] A week later I was in Paris.

I was surprised by the strength of my emotions when I arrived at Professor Ginestet's office and saw Komitas's medical file on the corner of his desk. Suddenly I began to doubt whether I was prepared to confront what had been written there. It was as if the file, with "Gomidas" (the French transliteration of his name) inscribed in calligraphy on its greenish cover, was a sacred relic left behind by the powerful figure whom I had been hearing about since childhood. Surprisingly thin and worn, the folder had been gathering dust in the hospital's archives for decades; I hoped it would be the archaeological treasure that held the solution to the mysteries of Komitas's suffering.

I opened the file and began leafing through it with a mixture of curiosity and the guilt of an intruder, feelings one might have upon entering a forbidden attic in the house of an ancestor who had died under enigmatic circumstances. What I discovered, however, was a seemingly random collection of papers: lists of clothing and visitors, certificates of committal and death, records of minor surgery, transfer requests—in short, the detritus of administrative procedure, all of it bureaucratic and yet strangely intimate. The enchantment of handling these forgotten pieces of

Armenian cultural history soon began to give way to disappointment. Nowhere in the records was there mention of a diagnosis or psychiatric treatment with which my training had made me familiar. I felt I had entered *terra incognito*. Evidently, finding answers to my questions would require deeper investigation.

Today more than ever, I believe that providing an accurate diagnosis for Komitas's suffering will help demolish the wall of silence and misunderstanding that has so far prevented psychiatrists and others from advancing their discussions of the traumatic effects of the Armenian Genocide.

Only recently have discussions of the psychological consequences suffered by survivors begun to appear in the vast literature otherwise devoted to the Armenian Genocide, a literature comprised mostly of eyewitness accounts.[2] The reasons for this delay have much to do with political history. The Armenian Republic, which came into existence shortly after the Genocide, lasted a mere two years (1918–1920), far too brief a period for embarking upon any sort of rigorous study of the calamities of the preceding years. In the decades following the collapse of the Republic Armenia fell into the hands of the Soviets, who had no interest in pursuing a matter that might jeopardize the tenuous but politically important relationship between Moscow and the Genocide's perpetrators, the Turkish government.[3]

The problem was further complicated by attitudes in the surviving Armenian communities themselves, many of which were scattered over the Middle East, Europe, and the Americas. Armenian professionals who grew up in the decades following the Genocide, most notably the Armenian psychologists and psychiatrists of these generations, seemed deeply reluctant to discuss the traumatic effects of the Genocide on survivors, including themselves and their families. Why this silence on the part of the victims and their descendants? Perhaps it is yet another instance in which denial has been used to cope with enormous tragedy: many Armenian expatriates tried simply to erase their memories of what had been inflicted on them, in the hope that the anguish they felt would also disappear, and that their children would be free of it. Moreover, in attempting to integrate themselves into new social and professional realms (especially that of Western academia, where the concept of "trauma" has until recently remained marginal and politically controversial), survivors and their descendants have felt compelled to distance themselves from the socially embarrassing stereotype of "the starving Armenians."[4]

Komitas Vartabed is considered by many to be the pioneer of contemporary Armenian classical music. The quality and quantity of his work can be compared to those of other great ethnomusicologists of the late nineteenth and early twentieth centuries, such as Bela Bartok. His innovative compositions and musicological research played a crucial role in introducing the unique musical heritage of Eastern cultures to the West. "Komitas's work," writes musicologist Robert Atayan

> came as a culmination of the efforts of earlier Armenian composers and as a supreme expression of the yearnings of his contemporaries. He raised the standard of art music in Armenia to a level where it could create international interest, and, basing his work on Armenian material, he was able at the same time to write music in line with contemporary Western developments. . . .Taken as a whole, Komitas's *oeuvre* is a vast gallery of Armenian images and a musical epic of national life.[5]

What follows in this book explores Komitas's illness from both a biological and a psychoanalytic-psychological perspective. Most psychiatrists no longer feel bound to subscribe to views of human psychology and behavior that are based exclusively on either nature or nurture, genetics or environment; they now believe that one need not preclude the other. I hope that this book will allow general readers to understand this complex approach as part of a compelling story of a life lived under dramatic historic circumstances, while providing professionals with a rich and telling case of trauma-related mental illness. I hope, too, that it will explain why Komitas became the icon of a grieving people.

As I moved towards the completion of my work, I felt as though a heavy burden was being lifted from my shoulders, a burden placed on me by the traumas that haunted my own childhood and early adulthood. As a child I watched my father struggle to rebuild his life, which had been shattered by the horrific events of 1915. By working my way through the suffering endured by Komitas, I feel that, however inadvertently, I have also worked through the tragedies that plagued my family. It is as though I have been healed by proxy. I hope this understanding allows my readers, Armenian and non-Armenian, to achieve a similar sense of inner understanding and harmony.

My ultimate wish for this book is that it will help alleviate the sense of guilt many Armenians still feel about Komitas's tragic fate, and encourage dialogue that pays homage to all those who suffered in the Genocide of 1915. The subject acquires greater relevance with every passing year, as we attempt to find more effective and compassionate ways to treat the victims of genocidal campaigns the world over.[6]

Notes to Introduction

1. Louise Hovanissian Fauve was one of the first to request permission to review Komitas's medical file at Villejuif. As she was not a member of his family, however, she was prevented from doing so by the confidentiality rules in place at the time. Eventually, she was successful in gaining permission: she accomplished this by acquiring the written consent of the Catholicos of the Armenian Church, Vasken I, who was considered a member of Komitas's adoptive "family," the Church.

2. Exceptions to this general state of affairs are becoming more common. In 1988, the Armenian-American Society for Studies on Stress and Genocide was formed. Research conducted by one of its members (Dr. Anie S. Kalayjian, a New York psychologist specializing in traumatic stress disorders) was published in *The Journal of Traumatic Stress*. See: "Coping with Ottoman Turkish Genocide: An Exploration of the Experience of Armenian Survivors," *Journal of Traumatic Stress* 9, no. 1 (1996): 87–97.

3. In 1968, full fifty-three years after the fact, a memorial to the victims of the Genocide was finally erected in Yerevan. The monument is called "Dzidzernagapert."
4. This issue is addressed throughout Peter Balakian's excellent memoir, *The Black Dog of Fate: A Memoir* (New York: Basic Books, 1997).
5. Robert Atayan, "Komitas," in *New Grove Dictionary of Music and Musicians,* edited by Stanley Sadie (New York: Groves Dictionaries of Music, 1980): 167.
6. Throughout this book I have used the Western Armenian pronunciation to transliterate Armenian words and terms (see Thomas J. Samuelian, *Armenian Dictionary in Transliteration*, New York: Hippocrene, 1993). The only exceptions to this use are a few names, which I have spelled according to the preferences of the persons themselves. The most prominent exception is that of Komitas himself: here I have avoided the Western transliteration ("Gomidas") in favor of the spelling that he himself used.

# 1

# Orphanhood and its Aftermath 1869–1881

In the year eighteen-hundred and sixty-nine
What was the yield of our vine?
How much fruit did our orchards grow?
It's hard to know!

Perhaps on that day
—Though unknown to mankind—
Mother Nature, almighty and wise,
Was jubilant,
For she knew whom she had begotten,
And she could already hear
A myriad of sweet melodies
Of the Armenian heartland!

—Baruyr Sevag[1]

By the late nineteenth century, Armenians living in the small city of Kütahya in western Turkey had endured decades of officially sanctioned discrimination. They did their best to lead conventional lives, considering themselves peaceable subjects of the vast Ottoman Empire, no different from the Turks and Greeks with whom they lived and did business. After all, Armenian culture had been a part of the city's history for seven hundred years: Armenians had first come to Kütahya in the twelfth century, migrating from the Armenian homelands that lay between the Black and Caspian Seas hundreds of miles to the east. These settlers established the pottery trade for which Kütahya became famous, and built their homes on the southern slopes of the round-topped mountains that encircled the city.[2] The community prospered over the centuries, and its members saw themselves as natives of the city.

But this view was not shared by the Ottoman government in Constantinople, two hundred miles to the northwest. Like the millions of Armenians living elsewhere in the Empire, the Armenians of Kütahya were part of a scattered but culturally coherent minority: they were ardent Christians, clinging (dangerously, in the opinion of the government's Muslim elite) to their legacy as the world's oldest Christian nation.[3] They had not been politically autonomous since the collapse of the last Armenian kingdom in the fourteenth century, but they had survived as a people, with their distinct language and their ancient church intact.[4] Consequently, Ottoman rulers regarded them as an alien element and afforded them a second class status.

Even though Komitas's parents spoke only Turkish, their lives were radically different from those of their non-Armenian neighbors in Kütahya. Because Kevork and Takuhi Soghomonian were Armenian by birth and Christian, they were subject to the socially crippling proscriptions imposed on all Ottoman Armenians: special taxes, prohibitions against providing legal testimony in courts, possessing firearms, and even restrictions against speaking the Armenian language outside of religious ceremonies.

It was into this environment that Komitas was born on September 26, 1869. Three days later he was christened Soghomon Soghomonian ("Komitas Vartabed" is the name he took many years later when he joined the Armenian clergy).[5] He would remain the family's only child.

According to the autobiographical sketches that Komitas wrote as a young man, the fortunes of the family fluctuated greatly in the years before his birth:

> My father, Kevork Soghomonian, was originally from Kütahya,[6] and my mother, Takuhi Hovhanessian, from Bursa. They were both . . . from the Zog tribe, and had immigrated at the turn of the century from the province of Koghtn, village of Tseghna. The Soghomonians were a prominent family until my birth, when they became almost bankrupt . . . .[7]

Takuhi was a beautiful and talented young woman of only sixteen when she gave birth to Komitas.[8] She wove carpets, composed and sang songs, and wrote poetry. Her devoted husband Kevork, a shoemaker by trade, was a good-natured man who loved music.[9] Their marriage (which was tragically short-lived, as we shall see) flourished in an atmosphere of intense creativity. Music was an integral part of their daily life: Kevork and his brother Harutyune sang at St. Theodoros Church in Kütahya, and often played the stringed folk instruments of the *kusans,* the folk minstrels of the Caucasus. From his earliest days, Komitas was immersed in the blend of traditional musical forms—ecclesiastic and popular, spiritual and worldly—that would become the consuming passion of his life.

According to Margaret Babaian, who would later become Komitas's closest friend, the two distinct facets of his personality—jovial and somber—were the legacy of his parents' contrasting temperaments. Kevork was reputed to be the most cheerful person in Kütahya, while Takuhi suffered episodes of deep melancholia. Because these sketchy descriptions of the Soghomonians were most likely given to Margaret Babaian by Komitas himself, they are as close as we can come to the truth about their personalities.

The modest, musical family was soon stricken by tragedy. Komitas was only six months old when, in March of 1870, his mother died at the age of seventeen. Komitas was left in the care of Kevork's sister-in-law, who was at that time nursing a child of her own.[10] The cause of Takuhi's death remains unknown, but it is not surprising that among the few surviving anecdotes about Komitas's early life there is evidence that the loss left deep and painful scars. For example, when Komitas returned to Kütahya in 1892 after an absence of ten years, he went to the room in which he had spent his childhood and sobbed at the sight of the nail in the wall on which his mother's picture used to hang.[11]

One of Komitas's biographers, Isabela Yolian, states that his paternal grandmother Mariam took care of him after his mother died.[12] This is supported by Komitas's autobiographical sketches, in which he refers to his grandmother as his "second" mother; he makes no mention of his father's sister-in-law in his writings.[13] But the adequacy of the care he received as a child becomes questionable when we read other accounts. One of his childhood friends remembers him as

> a thin, malnourished, serious and kind little boy. He was poorly dressed, and would come to school in the stormy winter weather frozen blue. He would warm up his hands with his breath. . . .We had pillows on which we sat but Soghomon [Komitas] used to sit on his legs on the bare wooden floor. He used to shiver while reading. Very often he was hungry, and I used to share my breakfast with him.[14]

Details of Komitas's emotional life at this time are scarce, but we can draw certain conclusions by carefully interpreting what little we have. A poem he wrote many years later, for example, evinces the intense loneliness that enveloped him after the loss of his mother. While it is entitled "My Mother's Lullaby," it is not a rendition of the bedtime songs that his mother never had a chance to sing to him; rather, it represents a symbolic transformation of her memory into a protecting spirit:

When the sun of my second summer
Was caressing the young fields,
As my mother was breathing
The yellow spring of the west,
She flew and went to the altar
Like a dove of the sky
Leaving me alone, and lonely
Her spirit as a shelter.[15]

Here, with great tenderness, a son ponders his mother's death: his emotions are embodied in powerful religious imagery, through which he transmutes the mortal body of his mother into a divine bird, and her soul into a spiritual guardian. Curiously, he locates the period of her death—her "breathing" of "the yellow spring of the west"—in his "second summer": Komitas was born in September and his mother died the following March, at the beginning of his *first* summer. This anachronism can be read as an attempt to console him by denying the even earlier loss of his mother.

By the time he wrote this poem, Komitas had learned to confront and transform his losses by using his immense artistic powers. The work is an example of the inherently creative type of mourning that he practiced, in which suffering is metamorphosed on the "altar" of art and thereby sanctified. It was loneliness that he was attempting to transform here, the terrible feeling of abandonment that he experienced when his mother vanished from his childhood. Near the conclusion of the poem he encapsulates this feeling in a single Armenian word: *menavorig* (translated above as "lonely," with considerable loss of impact), a coupling of the adjective *menavor*, meaning "solitary," with the diminutive suffix, –*"ig"*. The result expresses both hermit-like isolation and childlike helplessness. Variants of the word appear frequently in Komitas's writings, particularly in those he produced during periods of great emotional stress.

> Children require a nurturing environment that instills them with a sense of physical well being and psychological security. Only in such an environment can a child achieve the state of "basic trust" in the world that is crucial to normal and healthy development.[16]

Whether or not a particular childhood event has had a lasting effect on character development can be determined only in retrospect. But it is certain that the death of a parent poses a serious threat to the normal development of a child's personality, and that the loss of both parents, whether by death, divorce, or abandonment, can be catastrophic. The traumatic effects are most severe if the child is in the particularly vulnerable stage of development that occurs between the ages of six months and six years. Such early losses of parental care, especially maternal care, inevitably have an enormous impact on the child's personality, and can render him or her susceptible to the onset of anxiety states or depressive illnesses later in life.

With the death of Takuhi, the infant Komitas lost the person who would have provided a sanctuary of stability to which he could return after each of his tentative explorations of the world around him. The fragmentary descriptions of Komitas's childhood show clearly that this loss placed his young and rapidly growing psyche in a precarious position. One of his biographers tells us that as a boy he would constantly hound his grandmother with the question: "Did anyone ask for me?"[17] This desperate searching for the irretrievably lost protector is typical of children who are suffering from the deep anxieties that set in after the death of a parent. Stricken by a powerful sense of insecurity, the despondent little boy was driven by the hope that his mother would simply reappear, that he would be "found" again by the figure that had vanished from his life forever.

Komitas could not turn to his father in the hope of finding another "powerful protector," as psychiatrist John Bowlby has called such a parent. Kevork, heartbroken by the death of Takuhi, had taken to drinking excessively, leaving the child to fend for himself.[18] The fact that as an adult Komitas avoided and despised alcohol suggests that this change in his father's behavior caused him great anguish and instilled deep resentments.

Kutahia, Turkey. The house where Komitas lived as a child

In 1880, four years after he had finished grade school in Kütahya, Komitas was sent by his father to Bursa, sixty miles away, where he was to continue his education. Komitas's maternal grandparents still lived in Bursa, and it is possible that the lonely ten-year-old stayed with them during this time. Even before he had had time to come to terms with this latest upheaval, disaster struck again: only four months after the move, Kevork died suddenly, and Komitas was sent back to Kütahya.

The reason for this forced return remains a mystery. Why was the newly orphaned child allowed to withdraw from the school in Bursa (the name of which, also remains a mystery) at the very moment that he was most in need of a structured environment? If he was boarding at the school, why was he prevented from staying on, given that his home in Kütahya now stood empty? And if he was indeed in the care of his grandparents in Bursa, why did they allow him to leave now that he was virtually alone in the world? Did an unthinkable act of rejection take place? These questions may never be answered, but it is clear that Komitas's fortunes did not improve with his return to Kütahya. As his childhood friend, N. Mildonian, remembers:

> His life was especially pitiful after his father's death. The child was virtually homeless. Often I met him on the streets hungry, crying. I brought him back home with difficulty. Acquaintances found him sleeping on the cold tiles of the laundry room, and would wake him up and bring him home.[19]

Komitas's cousin Marig states that he was adopted by his [paternal] uncle Harutyune.[20] Komitas might have been forced to withdraw from the school in Bursa because his cobbler uncle Harutyune was unable to pay for his education. Although Harutyune had adopted him officially, Komitas behaved as though he was homeless. Marig remembers that he "used to drift away . . . and sleep outdoors."[21] In any case it seems clear that by the time he was ten years old, Komitas's familial and social structure had collapsed.

Deprived of paternal care by Kevork's alcoholism and subsequent death, Komitas was again placed in circumstances that made him vulnerable to the mental illness he suffered later in life. Studies in developmental psychology show that if a child is to be spared further trauma following the death of a parent, the surviving parent must have the capacity to adapt to the sense of emptiness and disillusionment that comes with grieving. If the parent cannot achieve this while maintaining a nurturing and affectionate bond with the child, the child becomes susceptible to serious psychological and social problems.[22] The alcoholism and eventual death of his only parent helped set the stage for psychological tragedies that were still many years in the future.

By wandering compulsively, Komitas was fleeing his anguish by entering a state of dissociation, a psychological maneuver used by children and adults alike to escape the painful effects of trauma. Compulsive wandering (or "Fugue State") was first described comprehensively by Erwin Stengel in 1939. Stengel found that many of those who felt compelled to rove from place to place were persons who "had lost one or both parents during their childhood."[23] in later studies Stengel linked this form of compulsion with the mental states of escape or "fugue" that often develop in response to serious trauma.[24]

These elements encompass much of Komitas's tormented inner life: the boy who found that he could lose himself temporarily in his wanderings would spend many of his later years immersed, fully and irretrievably, in a world of his own making.

Notes to Chapter One: Orphanhood and its Aftermath

1. Baruyr Sevag, *Anlreli Zankagadun* [The Ever-Ringing Belfry] (Beirut: Sevan, 1960): 7–8.
2. Arnag, "Nisher Varbedin Gyanken" [Notes From Varbed's Life], *Amenun Daretsuytse* (Venice) (1924): 305.
3. Armenia adopted Christianity as its state religion in 301 A.D. In the year 2001, the Armenian Apostolic Church will celebrate its 1700th anniversary.
4. The Armenian people possess an identifiably distinct history that stretches back more than three thousand years. Since the fifteenth century, the Armenian plateau and its people have been subjugated by a series of powerful and often oppressive empires. By the time Komitas was born, the Ottoman Turks, except for the eastern sector, which had passed from Persian into Russian hands earlier in the nineteenth century, ruled most of Armenia. See: Richard Hovannisian, "The Historical Dimensions of the Armenian Question: 1878–1923," in *The Armenian Genocide in Perspective,* edited by Richard Hovannisian (Oxford: Transaction, 1986): 19.

5. For the sake of clarity, we will refer to our subject as "Komitas," though he went under the name "Soghomon" until 1895.
6. Here and elsewhere, Komitas spells the name of his native town "Gudina," the ancient name favored by Armenians.
7. Komitas, Autobiographical Papers, June 1908, Komitas Archives, Doc. 71, Charents Museum of Literature and Art, Yerevan. Koghtn is the province where the renowned group of songs and poems called the *Koghtan Yerker* originated. Having survived some twenty-five hundred years, they are the oldest pieces of Armenian literature.
8. K.N. Kasbarian, "Komitas: Gensakragan Agnarg" [Komitas: A Biographical Sketch], in *Zhamanagagitsnere Komitasi Masin* [Contemporaries on Komitas], edited by K.N. Kasbarian (Yerevan: Haybedhrad, 1960): 8.
9. Arnag, "Komitas Vartabed," *Hayrenik* (Boston), no. 3 (January 1936): 73.
10. S. Tashjian, "Was Soghomon (Komitas Vartabed) a destitute, miserable and abandoned child after his parents' death? Was he left with no family to care for him?" *Hem Yeramia* (New York) (July–September 1996): 15.
11. In the memoirs of Margaret Babaian quoted here, it is stated that Komitas's mother "died while giving birth to him." This is most probably inaccurate, given that most other accounts claim that she died six months after his birth. It does suggest, however, that her death is somehow related to post-partum complications. Such a theory also suggests that Komitas may have carried feelings of guilt for having "caused" her death.
12. Isabela Yolian, *Komitas* (Yerevan: ARMSSR Academy of Sciences, 1969): 14.
13. Komitas, Autobiographical Paper, 1.
14. Komitas Archives, 71–72, Notebook B. Charents Museum of Literature and Art, Yerevan.
15. Komitas Vartabed, *Knarerkutyunner* [Poetry], edited by Toros Azadian (Istanbul: Mêshaguyt, 1939): 19.
16. E.H. Erikson, *Eight Stages of Men in Childhood and Society* (New York: Norton, 1950): 219. By "basic trust," Erikson means the trust instilled in children by the sameness and continuity of their care providers. Any weakening of this trust may have consequences in adulthood; *e.g.*, stressful situations may trigger depression and withdrawal.
17. Tsitsilia Prudian, *Komitas* (Yerevan: Hayastan, 1969): 8.
18. Arnag, "Komitas Vartabed," 73.
19. *Komitas Archives*, 71–72, Notebook B. Charents Museum of Literature and Art, Yerevan.
20. Komitas himself later confirmed this. See: Toros Azadian, *Komitas Vartabed* (Constantinople: Gutenberg, 1931): 106.
21. S. Tashjian, Letter to Author, January 17, 1995, Sydney, Australia.
22. Karita M. Hummer and Arnold Samuels, "The Influence of the Recent Death of a Spouse on the Parenting Function of the Surviving Parent," in *Childhood Bereavement and its Aftermath*, edited by Sol Altschul (Madison, Conn.: International University Press, 1988): 38.

23. Erwin Stengel, "Studies on the Psychopathology of Compulsive Wanderings," *British Journal of Medical Psychology* 18 (1939): 251.
24. See: Erwin Stengel, "On the Aetiology of Fugue States," *Journal of Mental Sciences* 87 (1941): 572–599; American Psychiatric Association, *Diagnostic and Statistical Manual of Psychiatric Disorders,* 4th ed. (Washington, D.C.: American Psychiatric Association, 1994): 481–482. "Shell shock" is one widely known example of these states, all of which are now categorized as types of *dissociative fugue.* See *Diagnostic and Statistical Manual of Psychiatric Disorders.* Fourth ed. American Psychiatric Association, 1994, pp. 481–2.

# 2

# Adoption and Recovery 1881–1896

With the autumn of 1881 came a sudden and dramatic change in the fortunes of the grief-stricken boy. The primate of the Armenian Apostolic Church in Bursa, Kevork Vartabed Tertsagian, had been summoned to Etchmiadzin in Eastern Armenia, to the ancient abbey that houses the Holy See of the Armenian Apostolic Church,[1] where he was to be elevated to the office of bishop. Before departing, Tertsagian was asked by the Holy See to find a local orphan-boy with a strong singing voice, and to bring the child with him for enrollment in Etchmiadzin's prestigious Kevorkian Seminary.

One story has it that Komitas was selected for this honor by the luck of a draw, but it is more likely that his musical abilities had distinguished him from the other orphans of Kütahya: his clear, innocent voice and emotional performances were well-known among the townspeople. By the age of twelve, he had become an accomplished singer of Armenian ecclesiastical pieces and Turkish folk songs. Chosen to accompany Tertsagian into the heart of Eastern Armenia, he set out on the longest and most important journey of his young life. Accompanying Komitas were letters of recommendation from his teachers at his grade school and members of his church council. Both letters, directed to Kevork IV, emphasized his orphanhood wandering the streets and lack of opportunity to continue his education in Kutahya. They also explained that his knowledge base was poor for his age due to his helpless circumstances and his poverty. But he was worthy of further education.[2]

The Kevorkian Seminary had been founded in 1874 by Catholicos Kevork IV (*catholicos* is the title of the Church's highest-ranking official, roughly analogous to "pope"). By the standards of the time, the education it offered its students was highly comprehensive and rigorous: the first six years of study were roughly equivalent to the curriculum of present-day high school. Students who wished to join the clergy received an additional three years of religious instruction. Admissions were decided by a series of exams, and only the most promising applicants were accepted. The Seminary's total number of students rarely exceeded three hundred.

Despite its close ties to the ancient abbey, the Seminary cultivated an educational environment that was remarkably secular. Its students, many of whom were politically sophisticated and passionately committed to liberal and democratic principles, were quick to organize demonstrations against any policy they deemed regressive or unfair. This atmosphere of tolerance and open debate made the Kevorkian Seminary one of Armenia's richest sources of intellectual leadership. Indeed, the generations of graduates it produced during its forty-three years of operation formed the core of Armenian educational institutions, most notably Armenia's state university, which was founded during the very brief life span (from 1918 to 1920) of the First Armenian Republic.[3]

It was into this sphere of social opportunity and frenetic intellectual activity that Komitas was introduced in the autumn of 1881. Because he was unable to speak Armenian—the *lingua franca* of the abbey and its school—his arrival did not go unnoticed. Yet he quickly won the favor of the Catholicos, for he had inherited the gift of song from his parents, and the Seminary's venerable dean was a connoisseur of music.

Komitas as a novice at the
Kevorkian Seminary, 1890

To the scattered and often oppressed Armenian nation, Catholicos Kevork IV was a figure of towering importance: spiritually insightful, politically fearless, and deeply aware of the vital role that education, particularly musical education, played in the survival of Armenian culture. He recruited only the most highly accomplished teachers of music for his Seminary, and commissioned them to transcribe the sacred music of the church into the Armenian system of notation known as "Limonjian's method." He also founded the *Ararat* monthly review and oversaw the construction of the Etchmiadzin Museum and the House of Manuscripts, in which ancient artifacts, books, archival material, and rare manuscripts are preserved to this day.[4] The journey from Kütahya to Etchmiadzin lasted from September 7 to 31. On October 1, 1881 Komitas was presented to Catholicos Kevork IV.

Although Kevork IV seemed annoyed at first that the orphan from Kütahya could only speak Turkish, he quickly recognized

Komitas's great natural talent for music. After addressing the boy in Armenian (Komitas later remembered being "stupefied" by this), the Catholicos asked him to sing the hymn "Luys Zvart." The voice that the old man then heard ringing from the walls of the chamber was so clear and subtle that it seemed to illuminate the Armenian words from within, even though the little singer understood none of them. As Komitas would describe the occasion, the voice moved Kevork IV to tears, which "tumbled down [his] face and . . . white beard . . . [and were] lost in the folds of his habit."[5] From then on, a deeply nurturing relationship grew between Kevork IV and the fatherless child. The Catholicos gave Komitas a seat near his own chair and often asked him to sing the solos during celebrations of the Mass. "You should hear how he sings," he would say whenever Komitas was introduced to visitors.[6]

Tragically, this bond—invaluable to a boy in desperate need of love, security, and encouragement—was soon severed: in December 1882, only a year and two months after Komitas came to Etchmiadzin, Kevork IV died. The boy had lost his first great patron; it was as if he had become an orphan once more.

By this time, however, Komitas had begun to flourish in his new environment. If his first eleven years had been a series of psychological catastrophes, his adolescent years at the Seminary were a period of emotional and intellectual stability, a time of shelter. He was placed under the care of a "big brother," a fellow seminarian assigned to tutor him in Armenian. His sense of confidence grew with his proficiency in the language of his teachers and peers. Gradually, the kinship he found among them came to replace the lost relationships of his early childhood.

The privations of life in Kütahya were also blotted out, for he now had access to Etchmiadzin's storehouses of knowledge and culture: research libraries and archives, repositories of old manuscripts, journals and articles published by the monastery's own press, concerts organized by the Seminary and classes taught by prominent artists, writers, and philologists. Stirred by such richness, the creative instinct that his parents' folk songs and poetry had instilled in him was fully awakened, and became fueled by ambition. He grew to believe what had formerly been unthinkable, that he would attend university—that he would be a scholar, an artist of importance.

Magar Yegmalian

Komitas's new sense of self-esteem showed in the ease with which he moved among his classmates. He quickly gained a reputation as an impromptu comedian who could mimic the accents and even the folk dances of different regions.[7] He was modest, lively and popular. And he would never refuse a request to sing for his friends.

Music had become Komitas's passion. When he was not studying its theoretical subtleties in his classes, he was schooling himself in its popular forms: the music of the streets and fields, the songs of the pilgrims who made their way to Etchmiadzin from every corner of Armenia.

But the complex world of Armenian music into which he was now being formally initiated had been in a state of deep turmoil for decades. Armenia had entered the nineteenth century divided, its freedom and independence long lost. Eastern Armenia was under subsequent Persian and Russian occupation, and Western Armenia under the rule of the Ottoman Turks. As a result, organized musical culture did not exist in Armenia during the first half of the nineteenth century. There were no formal concerts, no professional composers or performers.[8]

Nevertheless, music, composed and disseminated orally, continued to flourish among the people, particularly among urban troubadours, village peasants, and the clerics of the Armenian Church.[9] Of these the troubadours (called *kusan*, *sazantar*, or *ashugh* in Armenian)[10] were perhaps the most influential. They drew large, enthusiastic crowds to the town squares and were rewarded with spontaneous donations for their performances. They were also invited into the homes of the townsfolk to play at family celebrations and weddings; no gathering was complete without their songs about love and work, natural disasters, and national heroes.

The songs of the Armenian peasantry, on the other hand, were typically improvised pieces reflecting the vicissitudes of rural life, or expressing the community's joy at a marriage or grief at a death. Many of these pieces were transcribed in the late nineteenth and early twentieth centuries, a task to which Komitas would devote much of his career. In the following decades they served as a fertile source of raw material for future Armenian composers,[11] among them Aram Khachadourian, whose ballet *Kayane* and Symphony No.2 contain important elements of folk melodies.

The liturgy and hymns of the Armenian Apostolic Church, which were traditionally performed only by deacons and priests, had been transcribed during the Middle Ages by means of a distinctly Armenian system of notation known as *khaz*,[12] which consisted of "neumes," or signs that indicated the varying pitches of a given chant.[13] These records were effectively useless, however, because the key to interpreting *khaz* notation had been lost for centuries. Consequently, the sacred music had been passed down

Kristapor Gara-Murza

orally, a process that left it vulnerable to the influence of neighboring musical traditions. As Komitas would later remark, the music of the Armenian Church "became a toy and a tool to express personal musical tastes of the choristers (*diratzu*)."[14] When performed, it had more in common with melodramatic and sentimental Turkish love songs than with the canticles and hymns of Armenia, which were intended to be sung in a somber and austere manner.

Thus, by the early nineteenth century, a consensus had been reached among Armenian musicians, scholars, and religious leaders that unless a way was devised of setting the music to paper, they were in danger of losing, entirely and forever, what was left of its authentically Armenian structure.[15] But whether to create a new system of notation or to adopt the European system remained a matter of debate.

At this point, in 1813, a self-taught Armenian musician from Constantinople, Limonjian Hampartsum, began laying the foundations for a uniquely Armenian system of notation based on the ancient neumes, assigning new values to symbols that had been meaningless for centuries. It was slow, painstaking work, and when Limonjian died in 1839 it remained unfinished. His students eventually completed it, however, and future generations of Armenian composers inherited an essential tool for transcribing the nation's musical heritage: the Divine Liturgy, the hymns, and the songs of the peasants.[16]

By the end of his first year of studies in Etchmiadzin, Komitas had begun using "Limonjian's method" avidly, having learned its intricacies from two of the Seminary's music teachers, Ghevont Vartabed Zhamararian and Sahag Vartabed Amaduni.[17] Indeed, according to the reminiscences of a classmate, mastering this system of notation led Komitas to discover one of his life's great passions. During the Easter holidays, which he spent at the house of this fellow student in the nearby village of Keorpalu, he watched with fascination as Armenian peasants improvised songs in honor of the religious festival—beautiful, moving songs that were forgotten almost as soon as they were performed.[18] These pieces, thought the young seminarian, should not be allowed simply to disappear. He decided to make transcriptions of the evanescent folk music of the villages and thus began his distinguished career as an ethnomusicologist. Over the course of his productive years, he would use Limonjian's method to set down hundreds of the songs he heard as he roamed the Armenian countryside, staying in the homes of villagers who affectionately dubbed him *Notaji Vartabed,* "the note-crazy priest."[19]

He soon realized that this pursuit had larger implications than collection and preservation. Working constantly with Limonjian's ingenious system, he gradually became convinced of the importance of recovering one crucial and long-lost element of

Armenian musical knowledge: the ability to read *khaz*. Achieving this would allow the canticles of the Armenian Church to be performed precisely as they had been in ancient times, before the centuries of exposure to Persian, Turkish, and Kurdish musical and cultural influences. It would mean distilling the essence of Armenian music thereby proving the existence of an authentically Armenian musical tradition stretching back to pagan times. Finding this "philosopher's stone" of Armenian musicology was to become one of the central goals of his career.

Komitas's next great musical mentor, Kristapor Gara-Murza (1853–1902), was a charismatic performer and teacher with a large and devoted following among the Armenian public. Born and raised in the Crimea, he had received his musical education in Europe. His careful studies of the ways in which European music had evolved from the classicism of Bach to the romanticism of Liszt and Chopin convinced him that the musical culture of Armenia had fallen far behind those of other nations. Thus he embarked on an intense, seventeen-year-long campaign of public education: traveling throughout Armenia, Georgia, and the Crimea, he gave hundreds of concerts, taught the rudiments of European music to students in Armenian schools, and organized more than ninety choirs based on the European principles of polyphonic harmonization. As a result he was nicknamed "The Moving School."[20]

In 1892, Gara-Murza came to teach at the Kevorkian Seminary, and his presence exerted a tremendous influence on the musical development of Komitas, who was now a young man of twenty-three. Although Komitas later seemed unwilling to appreciate the influence of Gara-Murza's work on his own, and even criticized the "folk songs" of his teacher for lacking authentically Armenian content,[21] Gara-Murza became one of the crucial links in the young man's musical education. It was from him that Komitas learned the innovative polyphonic choral structures around which he built his later musical achievements, as well as the importance of educating the public about Armenia's musical heritage. In many ways, Komitas's career can be seen as a continuation, an enhancement, of the work begun by his teacher.

Gara-Murza spent only a year teaching in Etchmiadzin and he was extremely popular with his students. His expulsion from the Kevorkian Seminary—the result of pressure exerted by the more conservative members of Etchmiadzin's clergy, who found his polyphonic renderings of traditional sacred pieces unsettling—caused large-scale protests and boycotts of classes. Seventeen years later, Komitas's employment as a music teacher at the Seminary would be terminated in a similarly dramatic manner.

After Gara-Murza's departure, Komitas was given the unenviable assignment of filling his old teacher's position, which he accepted with ambivalence—regretting the fate of his teacher, but elated by the unexpected opportunity. Komitas was stepping into an environment fraught with tension and resentment: many of the students clearly thought he had betrayed their lost mentor. Yet he felt that he had no choice but to comply with the orders of the Catholicos.

* * * * *

> Since childhood I was drawn to the spiritual life. The Kevorkian Seminary further nourished this love and as a sixth-year student . . . I pledged to become a celibate priest.

*—Komitas,* Autobiography, *1908*

The church had always been a sanctuary for Komitas, a society into which he fit securely even when his feelings of loneliness were most intense. He had always felt warm and safe inside a church's four walls, as if he had found the place to which he belonged. Now that life in the Seminary had helped him to mature and nurtured his creativity; his devotion to the Armenian Church was greater than ever. Shortly after graduating from the Seminary's senior classes he was ordained *apegha* (novice).

Garabed Gosdanian, the principle of Kevorkian Seminary, with whom Komitas kept regular correspondence

The ceremony was conducted by the newly-elected Catholicos, Khrimian Hayrig, a man with whom Komitas would develop a close, almost filial relationship, similar to the one he had had with Kevork IV, but deeper and more complex. For Komitas now needed more than the shelter and empathy he had been offered as an orphaned child: as an ambitious young artist living in a highly conservative environment, he needed the presence of someone who truly believed in his work, a father-figure who could offer unconditional support.

Khrimian Hayrig (*hayrig* is the Armenian word for "father," not in the clerical but the familial sense) was a handsome and imposing clergyman with deep blue eyes, a powerful and persuasive voice, and a penetrating mind. Before being elected Catholicos of the Armenian Church in 1892, he had been primate of several Armenian dioceses in the Ottoman Empire and had occupied the Armenian Patriarchal See of Constantinople. He had also spent two years under house arrest in Jerusalem: his popularity among Armenians had been perceived as a threat to the Ottoman authorities there. Wherever he worked, he commissioned the construction of academic or agricultural schools, founded scholarly journals, and set up printing presses. He even took up overtly political causes, leading successful protests against the heavy taxes levied on Armenians by the Ottoman government. It

Komitas in 1896, before going to Berlin to study

was in honor of his tireless work on their behalf that Armenian people everywhere began to refer to him as "Hayrig," a custom followed to this day.[22]

When the revered Catholicos officially welcomed into the clergy the intense and talented young man who had been baptized Soghomon Soghomonian, Khrimian followed church tradition by giving him a new name, "Komitas," after the seventh-century musician-Catholicos Komitas Aghayetsi. Two years later, in February 1895, he ordained Komitas as a *vartabed*, a celibate priest, the rank in the Church's hierarchy that Komitas would retain for the rest of his life.

Despite Komitas's powerful devotion to the Armenian Apostolic Church and its musical heritage, he soon clashed with many of his fellow clergymen. In 1895, he published on Etchmiadzin's press his first collection of transcribed folk music, *The Songs of Agn*, an anthology of twenty-five pieces that included wedding and love songs, lullabies, and dances.[23] A reactionary faction at the monastery immediately expressed its disapproval of the publication, charging that it was inexcusable for a priest sworn to celibacy to write, sing, or teach love songs. They referred to Komitas sarcastically as "the love-singing priest." Komitas's harassment by the "old school" clergy had begun. Rumors accusing him of sexual misconduct circulated in the Seminary, a form of unofficial persecution perpetrated by "brethren" that deeply wounded and confused the romantic young artist-cleric who was actually struggling to suppress his desire for romantic love. Confused, he vented his bitterness at the gossip in an August 1895 letter to one of his trusted superiors at the Seminary, the principal Garabed Gosdanian:

> I have endured long enough. If I do not speak, the stones will scream out. Enough of this torture! They all seem to be sworn to reinstate the medieval courts of Inquisition in order to judge a person for crimes he has not committed, to kill him and then defame him afterwards.[24]

The anger of his words suggests a man who felt that the privacy, the secrecy of his innermost self, had been breached. Tormented by fear, he now saw his opponents as "inquisitors" bent on doing him harm. Although the letter offers no direct evidence that he had come to doubt his vocation to the church, actions he took suggest that he may have been undergoing some sort of identity crisis. He was only twenty-six and already he was experiencing a clash between his major roles in life, the clerical and the artistic. The clash seemed to sway him towards his musical pursuits, which included obtaining a higher education in music and the arts. In early October 1895, hounded by angry rumors and encouraged by Khrimian Hayrig to further his education,

Komitas left Etchmiadzin for Tbilisi, a city to which he had made several visits with the Catholicos.

Tbilisi was Komitas's only real option at the time. Because it was nearby and had a rectory in which he could stay, the move required no major expense. More importantly, Tbilisi was the home of a man who would become his third great teacher, Magar Yegmalian (1856–1905).

Komitas group picture

Yegmalian was an extraordinarily gifted Armenian musician who had studied first in Etchmiadzin and then under Rimsky-Korsakoff in St. Petersburg. During his ten years as choirmaster of the Armenian Church in St. Petersburg, he began the task of transforming the rigidly monophonic Armenian Church liturgy into polyphonic form, a mammoth undertaking that he finished many years later while employed as a music teacher and choirmaster in Tbilisi. This polyphonic rendering of the liturgy—a masterpiece of majestic scope and spirit—remains the most widely used arrangement in Armenian churches.[25]

Once more the student of an ambitious and broadly educated mind, Komitas deepened his understanding of the principles of European harmony that Gara-Murza had taught him, and learned the methods Yegmalian used as a choirmaster working in the church and in the secular Nersessian College in Tbilisi.[26] Curiously, as with Gara-Murza, the painful events of Yegmalian's life foreshadowed Komitas's own destiny: from 1902 until his death in 1905, Yegmalian was stricken with mental illness, forcing him to leave many of his works unfinished. The degree to which Komitas's later hardships mirrored those endured by his great teachers—the suppression of Gara-Murza's work by the church, and the madness of Yegmalian—is startling.

During the six months Komitas spent with Yegmalian, he also prepared for the entrance examinations required by European music conservatories. Because there were no universities or conservatories in the region at the time, it was common for the most promising young Armenian students to pursue a higher education in Europe. Komitas, now twenty-six and firmly committed to a career in music, aspired to study in Berlin, despite the fact that such plans demanded large sums of money.

Help was not far off. At the request of Khrimian Hayrig, a wealthy Armenian oil explorer from Baku, Alexander Mantashian, agreed to pay Komitas's tuition for three years, a total of eighteen hundred rubles.[27] Komitas realized that the money would hardly be enough to cover his most basic expenses, but this was nevertheless a stroke of good fortune. It would do much to help him overcome the crises that were plaguing his identity.

## Notes to Chapter Two: Adoption and Recovery

1. The abbey remains the spiritual center of Armenian culture. The monastery was built on the ruins of a pagan temple in 301–303 AD, when Christianity was officially adopted as the state religion of Armenia. Legend has it that the site was revealed in a vision to the church's first bishop, Gregory the Illuminator. It remains one of the world's finest examples of the architecture of the early Middle Ages. See: Tz. B. Aghayan et al, eds., *Hay Zhoghoverti*

*Badmutyun* [History of Armenian People], vol. 2 (Yerevan: ARMSSR Academy of Science, 1984): 76.

2. Atamian A. "Nor Vaverakrer Komitasi Masin" [New Documents on Komitas] (Yerevan: Academy of Sciences, 1956) 9: 102.
3. The Seminary closed in December 1917, when the sociopolitical structure of the region changed dramatically in the aftermath of the First World War and the Armenian Genocide.
4. See: Tz. B. Aghayan et al, eds., *Hay Zhoghoverti Badmutyun* [History of Armenian People], vol. 2 (Yerevan: ARMSSR Academy of Science, 1984): 76.
5. Komitas, Autobiographical Papers, June 1908, Komitas Archives, doc. 71, Charents Museum of Literature and Art, Yerevan: 12.
6. Isabela Yolian, *Komitas* (Yerevan: ARMSSR Academy of Sciences, 1969): 16.
7. Hrachia Ajarian, "Husher Komitasi Masin" [Memories of Komitas], *Etchmiadzin* (Etchmiadzin) (1953): 18–20.
8. Matevos Muratian, "The Armenian Music Culture During the First Half of the Nineteenth Century," in *Agnarg Hay Yerazheshdutian Badmutian* [Overview of the History of Armenian Music], edited by Kristapor S. Kushnarian, Matevos H. Muratian, and Kevork Keotagian (Yerevan: ARMSSR Academy of Sciences, 1963): 73–78.
9. *Ibid.*, 78.
10. Hasmik Injejikian, "Sayat Nova and Armenian Ashugh Musical Tradition," Master's thesis, McGill University, 1990.
11. Matevos Muratian, "Hay Yerazheshdutyune XIX Tarum yev XX Tari Êsgezpum" [Armenian Music in the Nineteenth and Early Twentieth Centuries], in *Agnarg Hay Yerazheshdutian Badmutian.* [Overview of the History of Armenian Music], edited by Kristapor S. Kushnarian, Matevos H. Muratian, Kevork Keotagian (Yerevan: ARMSSR Academy of Sciences, 1963): 81.
12. "From the ninth and tenth centuries onwards however, we find in hundreds of sacred manuscripts a system of musical signs known in Armenian *as khaz,* which are written in above the text to mark the pitch, nuance, rhythm and cadence of various forms of recitative and plain song and of hymns employed in the Armenian liturgy and in religious ceremonies." Vrej Nersessian, ed., *Essays on Armenian Music* (London: Kahn & Averill, 1978): 7.
13. "The word *neume* derives from Greek and appears to have been first used in the West before the 4th century by the grammarian Cominianus . . . denoting a 'sign' or a 'gesture.'" Later on, in the 8th century, neumes became associated with ecclesiastical melodies. *New Grove Dictionary of Music and Musicians*, vol. 13, edited by Stanley Sadie (New York: Groves Dictionaries of Music, 1980): 128.
14. Komitas, "Hayots Yegeghetsagan Yerazheshdutyune Dasneinnerort Tarun" [Armenian Church Music of the 19th Century], in *Hotvatzner yev Usumnasirutyunner* [Articles and Studies] (Yerevan: Haybedhrad, 1941): 131.

15. Muratian, "Hay Yerazheshdutyune XIX Tarum yev XX Tari Êsgezpum," 82.
16. *Ibid.*, 82–85.
17. K.N. Kasbarian, "Komitas: Gensakragan Agnarg" [Komitas: Biographical Sketch], in *Zhamanagagitsnere Komitasi Masin* [Contemporaries on Komitas], edited by K.N. Kasbarian (Yerevan: Haybedhrad, 1960): 9.
18. Komitas, "Hay Keghchug Yerazheshdutyun" [Armenian Peasant Music], in *Hotvadzner yev Usumnasirutyunner* [Articles and Studies] (Yerevan: Haybedhrad, 1941): 15.
19. Kasbarian, "Komitas: Gensakragan Agnarg," 16.
20. Muratian, "Hay Yerazheshdutyune XIX Tarum yev XX Tari Êsgezpum," 124–133.
21. Matevos Muratian, ed., "Komitasi Andib Namagnere" [Unpublished Letters of Komitas], *Badmapanasiragan Hantes* 17 (Yerevan), no. 1 (1958): 248.
22. Arminé Keushgerian ed., *Khrimian Hayrig* (Montreal: Canadian Diocese of the Armenian Chursh, 1994): 29–30.
23. In Hovsep Janikian's book *Hnutyunk Agna,* also published in 1895, Komitas's work *Shar Agna Zhogovertagan Yerkeri* appears as an addendum.
24. Komitas, Letter to Garabed Gosdanian, doc. 15, Komitas Archives, Charents Museum of Literature and Art, Yerevan: 1.
25. Muratian, "Hay Yerazheshdutyune XIX Tarum yev XX Tari Êsgezpum," 138–144.
26. Komitas, Letter to garabed Gosdanian, doc. 17, Komitas Archives, Charents Museum of Literature and Art, Yerevan: 1.
27. Matevos Muratian, "Komitase yev Hay Tasagan Yerazheshdutyan Tsevavorume" [Komitas and the Formation of Armenian Classical Music], in *Haygagan Yerazheshdagan Mshaguyti Badmutiun* [History of Armenian Musical Culture], edited by Matevos Muratian (Yerevan: ARMSSR Academy of Sciences, 1970): 408.

# 3

# Repaying the Debt
# 1896–1905

Komitas arrived in Berlin at the beginning of June 1896, filled with visions of his future as a musical scholar and artist. He was twenty-seven and for the first time in his life he was enjoying a sense of relative autonomy. To him Europe was not only an open field of possibilities, but also a haven of the privacy he had been denied in the tightly-woven community in Etchmiadzin. He could freely walk on Unter den Linden Boulevard and admire Berlin's architecture. He could attend the opera house which was just facing his university. He could stroll through the parks, the bookstores, and the libraries.

There were difficulties, however. He had come to Berlin without having been accepted by any of the city's universities—a problem compounded by the fact that he spoke no German. Merely finding his way through this bustling new environment would have been daunting had it not been for a group of Armenian friends studying in Berlin, who showed him the city and found an apartment for him.

The problem of finding the European education he had desired for so long was not so easily solved. In July he wrote to Garabed Gosdanian and described his weeks of arduous travel in search of a teacher:

> I have not written to you because my situation was uncertain. . . . I had to go to Dresden; that did not work out. In Zurich I presented myself to . . . [Joseph] Joachim . . .[1]

Joachim, an accomplished violinist and the director of the Berlin State Conservatory, recommended Komitas to Professor Richard Schmidt, who ran a private conservatory in Berlin. Komitas immediately returned there to meet with Schmidt. "After accepting me into his conservatory and examining me for the longest time, [Schmidt] took on the responsibility of giving me private lessons," he would note.[2] A few months later, Komitas also began studying philosophy at the *Königlichen Friedrich Wilhelms Universität zu Berlin* (Royal Berlin University).

The university was founded in 1810, and the foundation concept of Wilhelm von Humboldt gave it the title "mother of all modern universities." This concept envisaged a "Universitas Litterarum" which would achieve a unity of teaching and research and provide students with an all-round humanist education. From the outset, the university in Berlin had four classical faculties of law, medicine, philosophy and theology. The Prussian king, Friedrich Wilhelm III, donated the first building. It was built from 1748–1766 on the splendid boulevard Unter den Linden. From 1828 the university bore the name of "Friedrich-Wilhelms-Universitat." From 1949, the university was renamed after the brothers Alexander and Wilhelm von Humboldt. The early decades of the 20th century were characterized by great academic achievements and international recognition for the university. Twenty-nine Nobel Prizes were awarded to academics who worked at the university in Berlin.

Komitas fell in love with this university. It was a power house and he was ready to take in as much as he could. He was never scared of working hard and he felt his hard work would be rewarded. As one of his letters to Gosdanian shows, he was impressed with the rigor of this varied program. "Here, if you show ability and skill," he wrote, "they push you (or pull you) forward."[3]

His living conditions during this period were miserable. Mantashian's scholarship covered only the cost of his educational expenses and after paying for tuition, supplies, and rent, very little

Royal Berlin University then, Humboldt University today

of it was left. On some days he could afford only one meal; on others he ate nothing. The letters he wrote at this time describe his poor health, his constant need to borrow money and his feelings of homesickness.[4]

Manoog Apeghian, an old friend from the Seminary who would one day teach alongside Komitas in Etchmiadzin, was in Berlin at the time, and saw first-hand the quality of his daily life:

> His friends had rented an apartment for him on Koch Street . . . quite far from the center . . . He lived in that room for three years. Whenever you visited him he was at the piano . . . He only left the apartment to go to his classes or to attend rehearsals at the theater or opera.[5]

Nevertheless, as Apeghian's description makes clear, Komitas was able to indulge in certain aesthetic pleasures that would have been impossible in Etchmiadzin; for participating in any form of theater, including opera was traditionally off-limits to members of the Armenian clergy. In his letters from Berlin Komitas confided in only a select few about his new interest in its sumptuous concert halls. Indeed, his fear of reproach from conservative segments of the Armenian community compelled him to refuse an offer of

Komitas as a student in Berlin, 1896–1899

part-time work singing in one of the opera choruses. Nevertheless attending the Berlin operas and immersing himself in the ambitious and innovative musical ideas they presented, opened new fields of artistic knowledge and experience for him.

His academic experiences were equally lively, for his rapidly expanding interests soon connected him to a network of vigorous and exciting minds. His search for ancient manuscripts on music led him to correspond with such Armenian luminaries as Father Gabriel Menevishian, the editor of *Hantes Amsorya*, a monthly magazine published in Vienna by the Mkhitarist Congregation. Meanwhile, he was absorbing the erudition of his highly accomplished German teachers.

Richard Schmidt had an especially strong presence. Without relying on dogma, Schmidt had built a reputation as a skilled teacher of piano, choir, and operatic performance. He and Komitas often had heated discussions on theoretical matters.

Margaret Babaian (1903), one of Komitas's closest friends

Indeed, one account has it that Schmidt, after a particularly spirited episode in which he had attempted (unsuccessfully) to impose German rules of harmony on Komitas's eastern-influenced music, surrendered with the statement: "If you think that your way is more beautiful, let it be your way."[6]

Komitas also met with influential teachers in his classes at the Royal Berlin University. His knowledge of harmony and folk music grew steadily under the guidance of the medievalist Henrick Bellermann and the eighteenth and nineteenth century folk music specialist Max Friedlander. Perhaps the greatest teacher who influenced him was Osgar Fleischer, an expert on medieval neumes and Christian chant. Fleischer's vast knowledge of the subject was to be a key element in Komitas's own investigations of the Armenian *khaz* system of musical notation.[7]

As Komitas's abilities flourished, his devotion to music became still more feverish and single-minded. By the time he graduated, Professor Schmidt had become fully convinced of his intense commitment and great potential:

> Herr . . . Kevorkian Komitas was my pupil from July 1896 to July 1899. Nature gave him an extraordinary and acute feeling for tonality . . . Herr Kevorkian Komitas has, through his work, excelled in theory, composition and singing to achieve the very best results as a musician. [He] was an excellent student of harmony and instrumentation and so well trained as to teach music or even undertake the position of conductor of a choir or an orchestra. Since he possesses a well-developed baritone voice, he is at a great advantage when conducting a choir.[8]

In May 1899, Oscar Fleischer established the Berlin chapter of the International Musical Society, inviting Komitas to become a founding member and to speak on the subject of Armenian music at the chapter's inaugural meeting. The lecture argued that the roots of Armenian sacred music could be traced back to music played in pagan temples in pre-Christian times, and from there still farther back to ancient folk forms. While the music of the Armenian Apostolic Church had become increasingly ornate over the centuries, Komitas said, its foundations survived, making it a model for the study of other ancient traditions of sacred music. These ideas met with such acclaim that he was asked to present them again to the society weeks later.

* * * * *

In September 1899, only months after completing his university studies, Komitas returned to Armenia, and immediately made his way to a summer residence in Puragan, near

Etchmiadzin, where he was awaited by Khrimian Hayrig. The Catholicos was delighted to see him again, and remarked, in the half-joking manner of a concerned father, that Komitas had lost some weight in Berlin: had he not had enough to eat, or had he fallen in love with some blonde German girl? Over the following week a steady stream of guests arrived to give their regards to Khrimian's favorite "son," newly returned from a distant sojourn. Dinners were held, and Komitas readily sang and danced with his well wishers.

Komitas in Etchmiadzin (1900) with his new Royal piano donated to him by Mantashian, the benefactor who paid for his studies in Berlin

Komitas had returned home. Etchmiadzin was not merely his *alma mater*, but the source of nearly all that he possessed intellectually, emotionally, and spiritually. One indication of just how firmly his identity was rooted in the Seminary is that those around him at this time called him not by his parental surname "Soghomonian," but by the name "Kevorkian." Komitas himself continued this practice as late as 1908, often signing his name "Soghomon S. Kevorkian."[9]

Komitas had also been drawn back to Etchmiadzin by a sense of obligation. It had always been understood that he would return to teach at the Kevorkian Seminary as a means of repaying all that he had received from the church since his childhood.[10] And he soon showed his patrons that their efforts on his behalf had been worthwhile. In addition to teaching courses in music theory and

Komitas in Yerevan, 1901

performance at the Seminary, he took on the responsibility of assembling a large polyphonic choir based on the principles he had learned during his years in Tbilisi and Berlin. In recognition of these efforts, the Catholicos awarded him an elegant floral habit.[11]

The years that followed in Etchmiadzin—from 1899 to 1906—were difficult. The routine duties of teaching, along with the exhausting work of directing the choirs of the Seminary and the church, consumed most of his energy and soon felt burdensome. Students came and went, as the beginning of each school year presented him with the melancholy prospect of starting from scratch. Above all, he was bored: after Berlin, with its array of music, art, and energetic cosmopolitan culture, all of which he had been free to sample as he wished—Etchmiadzin seemed hopelessly provincial, narrow and suffocating.

It was during this period, however, that he wrote most of the theoretical and research papers that earned him his place among the pioneers of ethnomusicology.[12] He spent the summer months with the villagers in the Armenian countryside, joining them in their work, and observing the unique relationship that existed between their daily routines and the music they created as if by instinct. The power of the scholarship produced by Komitas during these extended field trips was largely due to the intensely personal nature of the work, for on many occasions the songs he overheard in the villages struck him as uncanny reflections of the pain he had endured in his own life. Once, for example, he came across an orphaned girl at work on a rooftop, and hurriedly set about transcribing the words and melody she improvised to express her feelings of melancholy:

> Oh mother dear, what can your helpless child do?
> Oh mother dear, come and care for me, where are you?
> Oh mother dear, mother dear, I do not know what to do.
> You left me an orphan; you left me an orphan . . .
> *Vay-vuy, vay-vuy, vay-vuy . . .*[13]

These words and the concluding cry of lamentation spoke directly to the anguish that Komitas had experienced in his own childhood, leading him to remark on the internal process that links grief and music-making, a process that was vital to his own art:

> [The orphaned girl] remembered her mother, of whom . . . she had been deprived since childhood, and she felt the bitterness of her orphanhood, and naturally

> expressed her pain by singing bits and pieces of a song reflecting her inner world.[14]

Often the scholarly tasks of transcription and preservation seemed to be at odds with the villagers' own attitudes about music. As Komitas soon realized, Armenian peasants rarely concerned themselves with the question of who had created a particular song; they put no stock in authorship. Indeed, he remarked, "they were even surprised that a 'singer vartabed' [like himself] would be after silly things like that . . . [in their view] the song is sung and that's it—who cares about when, where or by whom the song was created."[15] Rural Armenian folk created songs as circumstances

Komitas with his students in Tbilisi, 1905

dictated, and modified them as others came about. Work songs, for example, would be composed and sung only during the performance of specific tasks.[16] Certain songs were extemporized for funerals, others for weddings. Indeed, according to Komitas, even local geography exerted its influence, generating the musical equivalent of linguistic dialects:[17] songs from the mountains were rugged, tough, and passionate, reflecting the harsh climate and natural disasters of the region; songs from the gentle environment of the plains, on the other hand, were soft and mild.[18] But whether a particular song arose from the pains of work, from grief or joy, from the mountains or the plains, its life span was typically very short; often it was discarded as soon as it had been performed.[19] Komitas devoted years of his life to ensuring that this beautiful, ephemeral legacy would not simply disappear.

In the autumn of 1903, after three years of meticulous collecting and transcribing, Komitas published a book of folk songs entitled *Hazar u mi Khagh* [One Thousand and One Songs]. It was exacting work, carried out by collaborating with his old friend and lyricist Manoog Apeghian and with scores of his students. As Apeghian remembers:

> [Komitas] distributed thousands of small pieces of paper to the pupils who were going home for summer vacations. He asked them to transcribe the songs they heard . . . We did this for several years. As a result we collected thousands of ballads . . .[20]

The final work, however, contained only fifty carefully chosen pieces. Its popularity led to a reprinted edition the following year and to the publication in 1905 of a further fifty songs. Many of these folk stanzas became the lyrics to songs, musical suites, and choral pieces that Komitas created over the years.[21] Like a quilt-maker using taste, skill, and imagination to assemble unique works from materials indigenous to different regions, he gathered pieces of music that were rooted in tradition and synthesized them in new and surprising ways. This resulted in radical innovations that retained the textures of their ancient ingredients.

At the same time, Komitas was making significant advances in his research on the secrets of the *khaz*, drawing ever closer to a complete reconstruction of the way in which the canticles of the Armenian Apostolic Church had been sung in medieval times, before they were distorted by Turkish influence.[22] By applying the knowledge he had gained in Berlin to the vast collection of manuscripts stored in the archives of the Holy See, he was able to compile a large number of clues to the lost meaning of the neumes. He also investigated other choral traditions (particularly the Jewish *neginot*), and familiarized himself with virtually every form of Christian chant.

But the true high points of Komitas's life in Etchmiadzin were, ironically, his trips away from the town, especially his travels in Europe. He was elated when, in 1901, Khrimian Hayrig gave him

Komitas with Archag Tchobanian,
Paris, 1907

permission to return to Berlin, where he was to lecture at a meeting of the International Musical Society. Once again his work received accolades in various European music periodicals.[23] Returning home by way of Paris, he was introduced to one of the city's most distinguished Armenian residents: Archag

Tchobanian, the outspoken publisher of the Armenian monthly, *Anahid.*[24] Tchobanian had fled the pogroms of Sultan Abdul Hamid II in 1895, and had established himself in Paris as a prominent and respected writer, editor, literary critic, social commentator, and translator of numerous Armenian works into French. By the time Komitas departed for Etchmiadzin, a bond of mutual understanding and admiration had been formed between the two men, with Komitas seeking out Tchobanian's opinions and criticisms,[25] and Tchobanian writing articles hailing Komitas as the saviour of Armenian music.[26]

Archag Tchobanian

Upon returning to his work at the Kevorkian Seminary, Komitas began conducting a series of large, elaborate choral concerts, some of which involved choirs of more than sixty students.[27] The reaction of the public to his new harmonization of traditional pieces was, in these early stages, often mixed. The changes he had made, many of which reflected his admiration for

German classical music and especially for the work of Richard Wagner, sounded radical at first.

Wagner fascinated Komitas at this time—not just by the German composer's *oeuvre,* but by the tragedies of his life. Wagner, too, had been orphaned while still very young: his father died when he was just six months old, and his step-father followed a few years later. Yet, as Komitas declared in an article he wrote in 1904, " . . . with an unbreakable and powerful will, a fighting spirit, [Wagner] managed to show unprecedented creative energy and productivity, which persisted throughout his life."[28]

It was as if Komitas was describing himself in the years before illness struck him down. In identifying with the pain of Wagner's personal life, Komitas sought to emulate him artistically, and modeled the greatest of his ambitions on the German composer's achievement. "Wagner," he wrote, "gave a national music to Germany, and a lesson to foreigners"[29]—something he deeply wished to do for his own country.[30] Yet, Komitas later tried to rid himself of Wagner's influence, on the grounds that it had little to do with the distinctly Armenian forms he was attempting to resurrect.[31]

Despite the initial shock to audiences, the reputation of Komitas's Kevorkian Seminary Choir began to spread rapidly. The series of concerts held in April 1905 at the "Artisdagan Engerutyune [The Hall of the Society of Artists]" in Tbilisi were completely sold out. Because the program included sacred pieces that had previously been performed only in churches, Komitas had been forced to request the special permission of Catholicos Khrimian. This obstacle was worth overcoming, however, for it was these concerts that established Komitas's fame as a musical artist. His immense powers as a conductor were nearing their peak, with the movements of his baton commanding silence and then drawing forth waves of awe-inspiring sound from his singers. Each of the songs concluded in thunderous rounds of applause and standing ovations.

Komitas had emerged from controversy with his reputation for musical brilliance strengthened. The press in Tbilisi, which at one time had debated whether or not he should even be invited to perform his "European" music, was now singing his praises.[32]

Notes to Chapter Three: Repaying the Debt, 1896–1905

1. Komitas, Letter to Garabed Gosdanian, doc. 19, Komitas Archives, Charents Museum of Literature and Art, Yerevan: 1.
2. Komitas, Autobiographical Papers, June 1908, Komitas Archives, doc. 71, Charents Museum of Literature and Art, Yerevan: 14–15.
3. Komitas, Letter to Garabed Gosdanian, doc. 19, Komitas Archives, Charents Museum of Literature and Art, Yerevan: 3.
4. Isabela Yolian, *Komitas* (Yerevan: ARMSSR Academy of Sciences, 1969): 22; Komitas, Letter to Gabriel Menevishian, 16 April 1898, Komitas Archives, Mkhitarist Book Depository, Vienna.
5. Manoog Apeghian, "Hishoghutyunner Komitasi Masin" [Memories of Komitas], in *Zhamanagagitsnere Komitasi Masin* [Contemporaries on Komitas], edited by K.N. Kasbarian (Yerevan: Haybedhrad, 1960): 65.
6. K.N. Kasbarian, "Komitas: Gensakragan Agnarg" [Komitas: Biographical Sketch], in *Zhamanagagitsnere Komitasi Masin* [Contemporaries on Komitas], edited by K.N. Kasbarian (Yerevan: Haybedhrad, 1960): 11.
7. R. Sheskous, "Komitas Berlinum" [Komitas in Berlin], in *Komitasagan* 2, edited by Robert Atayan, (Yerevan: ARMSSR Academy of Sciences Publication, 1981): 25–38.
8. Richard Schmidt, doc. 65, Komitas Archives, Charents Museum of Literature and Art, Yerevan.
9. Komitas, Autobiographical Papers, June 1908, Komitas Archives, doc. 71, Charents Museum of Literature and Art, Yerevan. As we have already seen in Komitas Archives, doc. no. 65 (see previous footnote), even Professor Schmidt used "Kevorkian" when referring to Komitas.
10. Besides enlisting the oil explorer Mantashian to help fund Komitas's education, Khrimian Hayrig had also ordered the Seminary's principal, Gosdanian, to send Komitas four hundred rubles in the summer of 1897. See: A. Oghlukian, ed., *Kragan Nêshkhark Komitas Vartabedi Peghun Kêrchen* [Literary Fragments from Komitas Vartabed's Prolific Pen] (Montreal: Canadian Diocese of the Armenian Church, 1994): 13.
11. The habit is presently displayed at the Komitas Museum in Yerevan. A beautiful letter of appreciation from the Catholicos accompanied this gift. See: M.

Khrimian, Letter, 14 January 1902, Doc. 67, Komitas Archives, Charents Museum of Literature and Art, Yerevan.

12. Sirvat Poladian, "Komitas Vartabed and his Contribution to Ethnomusicology, Komitas the Pioneer," in *Essays on Armenian Music*, edited by V. Nersessian (London: Kahn & Averill, 1978): 14.
13. Komitas, "Hay Keghchug Yerazheshdutyun" [Armenian Peasant Music], in *Hotvadzner yev Usumnasirutyunner* [Articles and Studies] (Yerevan: Haybedhrad, 1941): 25–26.
14. *Ibid.*, 25–6.
15. *Ibid.*, 25.
16. *Ibid.*, 30.
17. *Ibid.*, 26.
18. Komitas, "Hay Zhoghovertagan yev Yegeghetsagan Yerkere" [Armenian Folk and Ecclesiastical Songs], in *Hotvadzner yev Usumnasirutyunner* [Articles and Studies] (Yerevan: Haybedhrad, 1941): 9–14.
19. Komitas, "Hay Keghchug Yerazheshdutyun," 28.
20. Apeghian, 68.
21. Robert Atayan, ed., *Komitas, Yergeri Zhoghovatzu, Arachin Hador: Menerker* [Komitas's Collected Works, volume 1: Solo Songs] (Yerevan: Haybedhrad, 1960): 12.
22. When Komitas was arrested in 1915, the manuscript of an article he had written on *khaz* notation was in the hands of Taniel Varuzhan, an Armenian writer and journal editor. Because Varuzhan was also arrested and exiled in Chankiri, and was later killed, the manuscript was lost. See: H.J. Siruni, "Komitasi Hed" [With Komitas], *Etchmiadzin* (Etchmiadzin) (May 1967): 41.
23. K.N. Kasbarian (1960) refers to this 1901 conference as the International Church Music conference. See also: A. Oghlukian, ed., *Kragan Nêshkhark Komitas Vartabedi Peghun Kêrchen* [Literary Fragments from Komitas Vartabed's Prolific Pen] (Montreal: Canadian Diocese of the Armenian Church, 1994): 16.
24. *Anahid* was an Armenian literary magazine published in Paris from 1898 to 1949. The editor and publisher was Archag Tchobanian. The magazine had a progressive patriotic mandate.
25. Matevos Muratian, ed., "Komitasi Andib Namagnere" [Unpublished Letters of Komitas], *Badmapanasiragan Hantes* 17 (Yerevan), no. 1 (1958): 251.
26. Archag Tchobanian, "Komitas Vartabed," *Anahid* (Paris) (June-July 1901): 141–144.
27. A. Oghlukian, ed., *Kragan Nêshkhark Komitas Vartabedi Peghun Kêrchen* [Literary Fragments from Komitas Vartabed's Prolific Pen] (Montreal: Canadian Diocese of the Armenian Church, 1994): 16–18.
28. Komitas, "Wagner," *Hotvatzner yev Usumnasirutyunner* [Articles and Studies] (Yerevan: Haybedhrad, 1941): 173.
29. *Ibid.*, 173.
30. Komitas also wrote in 1904 about Liszt and Verdi. It is likely that his admiration for them was based on the same conflation of music and biography that inspired his reverence for Wagner. Liszt was a composer who had enjoyed immense

popularity during his own lifetime and (after being ordained a priest) had devoted himself to ecclesiastical music. Verdi had endured the deaths of his wife and two children to compose works that became recognized as distinctly Italian. See: Komitas, "Franz Liszt," *Daraz* (Tbilisi), no. 19 (1904): 173–174; Komitas, "Giuseppe Verdi," *Daraz* (Tbilisi), no. 23 (1904): 208–209.

31. Rupen Terlemezian, "Komitasi Arvesde: Desagan, Kênnatadagan Verludzutyun" [Komitas's Art: Theoretical and Critical Review], in *Zhamanagagitsnere Komitasi Masin* [Contemporaries on Komitas], edited by K.N. Kasbarian (Yerevan: Haybedhrad, 1960): 165.
32. "Bedk e Kachalerel, te Voch" [Should We Encourage Him or Not?], *Daraz* (Tbilisi), no. 32 (1904): 294–295; "Mer Aracharge: Komitasin Hravirel Tiflis, ir Khêmpov Hamerkner Dalu [Our Proposal: to Invite Komitas and His Choir to Tbilisi for a Concert]." *Daraz* (Tbilisi), no. 34 (1904): 327–328; "Komitas Vartabedi Hokevor-Joghovertagan Hamerke [The Ecclesiastical-Folk Concert of Komitas Vartabed]." *Mshag* (Tbilisi), no. 62 (1905): 1–2.

# 4

# Attempting Independence 1906–1909

By 1905 Komitas felt as though Etchmiadzin had become a trap. Not only was he entirely dependent on the meager salary paid to teachers at the Seminary, but he felt surrounded by "brethren" who, time and again, had shown their propensity to attack him with rumor and innuendo about the alleged impropriety of his work and life. At thirty-seven, convinced that he was being treated unfairly and that his mental health was at stake, Komitas decided to set out on his own. He requested a yearlong sabbatical and was granted a ten-month leave of absence.[1]

The letters he wrote during this period to his confidante Margaret Babaian, an Armenian singer living in Paris, are filled with frustration about his growing discontent with life in Etchmiadzin, his resentment of those who were criticizing and slighting him, and his yearning to find a greater audience for his work. In March 1906 he decided "to resign from teaching and to fend for myself" by returning to Berlin.[2]

If Komitas felt that he had not been appreciated in Etchmiadzin—that he had worked "seven years for nothing," had "wasted my lungs, and destroyed my health" for the sake of being called "parasite" and "glutton" by colleagues[3]—he must have been encouraged by his reception in Europe. In October, after enjoying months of serene anonymity in Berlin, he traveled to Paris, where

Margaret Babaian helped him establish his first European choir, a group of thirty French and Armenian opera singers. In Paris, on December 1, 1906, the choir performed a repertoire of Komitas's solo and choral songs to great acclaim in the French and Armenian press. Here as on many other occasions, his audience was taken by

Margaret Babaian

surprise. Komitas was transforming simple folk melodies into waxing and waning tides of sound, using powerful male voices that rose suddenly over a receding background of female altos to produce virtual eruptions of music in which the whole choir joined together in song. Over the years that followed, transcripts of the fourteen pieces sung that evening became standards by which Armenian singers would measure their performances.

Soon after the concert, a group of Armenian students from Switzerland asked Komitas to organize a choir for a benefit concert in Geneva. By May 1907 he had auditioned an entirely new choral group comprised of mostly Armenian and Russian students, taught them the rudiments of Armenian musical structures, and conducted them in concert at the hall of the Geneva Conservatory. Afterwards, he embarked on a lecture tour with Archag Tchobanian, first to Bern and Lausanne, and then to Venice.

Margaret Babaian

For nearly two centuries, Venice had harbored one of the Armenian diaspora's richest enclaves of culture. The Armenian monastery, founded in 1715 on the city's abandoned "Isle of Lepers," San Lazarro, housed many of the spiritual and artistic treasures of the scattered Armenian people and served as the focal point of a community known as "Pokrig Hayasdan [Little Armenia]." Komitas arrived there in July 1907, and began lecturing on the traditions of folk and sacred music in Armenia, often performing the songs himself in order to demonstrate his theories. In the monastery's library he also continued his research on *khaz* notation.

The frantic pace at which he worked during this period did not prevent him from completing a project that had occupied him for many months. Before he left Etchmiadzin in 1906, he had been laboring over an ambitious set of harmonizations based on folk songs. These manuscripts had formed an integral part of his plan to free himself from the abbey, for he had always aspired to publish them in Europe. Unfortunately, on the voyage to Berlin they had suffered a disheartening fate: the bag in which they were packed was stolen in the train station at Rostov. Along with a hundred and fifty rubles, Komitas had been robbed of his most cherished creations, and all would have been lost if he had not also brought with him a set of draft copies.

Komitas in Berlin, 1907. He appears in the civilian clothing in which he was often seen during his travels in Europe

The process of restoring the songs was arduous and time-consuming; at one point Komitas wrote to Tchobanian that "the copying of my songs is killing my hours."[4] The finished work, entitled *Hay Knar* [Armenian Lyre], was released in Paris in 1907. It contained twelve exquisite songs and was Komitas's first major publication. The title page bore an illustration by his friend, the artist Eghishe Tatevosiants. It showed a woman dressed in the traditional attire of the Armenian peasantry carrying a water jar to a fountain upon which was written "*Keghchug Yerker: Havakets,*

*Tashnagets Komitas Vartabed* [Rustic Songs: Transcribed, Harmonized by Komitas Vartabed]." Was this depiction of flowing spring-water and a melancholy-looking woman intended to imply the sources of Komitas's creative life—the Armenian countryside and his pensive, musical, long-lost mother?

The theme of secular love recurs throughout *Hay Knar*, a feature of Komitas's work that would soon incite denouncements by conservative clergymen of the Armenian Church. Typical of the songs produced by Komitas, the tensions and pains of love are often expressed through images of the natural world. The solo song "Hov Arek," for example, features a lover who invokes mountain breezes to extinguish the burning in his soul, and rain to darken the days of those with vicious hearts. The overcast sky appears again in the stanzas of "Yerginken Ambel a," where it forms a backdrop for the rural scene in which the singer pours out his emotions. In the doleful melodies of "Anduni," a heartbroken man compares his anguish to the ruins of a house where wild animals now take refuge. And in "Karun a," a rejected lover sings of disappointments that are as bitter as a snowfall in spring.[5]

Aside from the comical duet "Haberban," in which a soprano and a tenor play characters attempting to seduce each other, the remaining songs in *Hay Knar* are choral pieces. "Im Chinari Yare" tells of a young girl who disobeys her family by marrying her lover, whom she compares to a tall and beautiful plane tree.[6] The forceful "Kutanerk," also known as "Tsik du, Kashi," is a plowing song about the farmer's concern for his livestock and crops. "Antsrevn Yegav," a song, which quickly became a favorite of Komitas's audiences, sings of falling rain. Whether they are about love or work, joy or sadness, the songs of *Hay Knar* are instilled with the vitality of their birthplace, rural Armenia.

* * * * *

After eighteen months of successfully publishing songs, organizing choirs, and delivering lectures in Germany, France, Switzerland, and Italy, Komitas was eager to settle in Europe permanently. His fame as a specialist in the sacred and folk music of the East had grown steadily, and his choirs were attracting large audiences wherever they performed. Above all, his work had become a source of pride for the Armenian communities scattered throughout Europe and the Caucasus. He had become a living symbol of cultural revival, frequently quoted in the Armenian press,[7] and widely considered by European musicologists to be making some of the most valuable contributions in the field. But he had struggled without success to find employment or financial support, a setback that inflicted deep emotional wounds.

Jean-Baptiste church, Paris

An intense sadness, a feeling of having been defeated, settled over Komitas when he was forced to return to Etchmiadzin in 1907. "The ideal solution for all the difficulties that Komitas was experiencing," writes Tchobanian, "was staying in Paris."[8] Yet when he had turned for help to Paris's small Armenian community, the board of the recently built church decided that it could not afford to offer him work as a choirmaster. Whether or not Komitas's request was a reasonable one is difficult to discern, but certainly his feelings of being unappreciated by church authorities were reinforced by this rejection.

Louis Laloy (1874–1944). French musicologist, critic and professor of Music at the Sorbonne University. He was married to Margaret Babaian's sister, Shushanig. He played a great role in promoting Komitas in Paris

Angry and disappointed, he returned to Etchmiadzin that September and settled in a small house on the grounds of the abbey. He fought despair by immersing himself in his work—in what he called in a letter to Margaret the "pure and pristine lake" of his "inner self," into which "bad people throw stones."[9]

This self-made sanctuary was soon disturbed by the arrival of new sorrows. On October 29, Khrimian Hayrig, the adoptive "father" who had given him years of unwavering love and support, died suddenly at the age of eighty-seven. It was as if the old Catholicos had been holding death at bay until the "favorite son" had finally returned.

Komitas had little time to mourn. He was responsible for preparing the Kevorkian Seminary Choir for the funeral processions, a task that required him to put in fourteen-hour days for the sake of maintaining "my honor and the honor of the church high."[10] But his grief was merely postponed: for many weeks after the hurried and painful farewell to yet another "father," he found that he could not "put myself and my thoughts together."[11]

This grief-induced restlessness was a harbinger of the profound uneasiness Komitas soon began to feel with the routines of Etchmiadzin and the insular tightly politicized community it housed. With Khrimian's death he had lost the one redeeming presence in his life at the abbey. As he wrote to Margaret, it was as if Etchmiadzin were once again filling him with a dreaded sense that he had

> neither any mind nor brains left. I am restless and I don't know what to do. Imagine that I am surrounded with thick clouds, I want light, bright light, I want to soar up, go up and live with the burning sun, but I can't find the way, and I suffocate in this stifled air.[12]

Etchmiadzin was a place where you could sit at your desk writing "from morning to night," he said, only to discover that there was "nobody with whom you [could] share and sing what you have written."[13] Indeed, his sense of spiritual and artistic isolation, his realization that there was no one "to whom I can open my heart, from whom I can learn something"—was so complete that he had begun to fear for his sanity: "I am surprised that I have not yet gone mad in this environment full of deception."[14]

Clearly, Komitas was suffering from feelings of depression and emptiness—a state of anhedonia, to use the clinical term. So deeply felt were his afflictions that he desired to "fly far away and be left alone" to escape into a state of dissociation. At this point his troubles were not so great as to be crippling "I am not hopeless," he declared to Margaret. "I am working hard, I have written many things."[15] Indeed, he was working with as much intensity as ever. Full-blown, debilitating mental illness was still many years in the future.

Komitas's life in Etchmiadzin, it seems, was always one of extreme highs and lows. Not long after Khrimian's death, for example, he wrote Margaret to tell her that a donation of a thousand rubles from Bishop Hovannes Shiraguni, an older monk at the monastery who had always supported his work, had finally

Komitas Vartabed, Etchmiadzin, 1909

allowed him to purchase a grand piano, an instrument he had wanted desperately for many years and to which he felt entitled. The event brought him to the point of tears: finally he could compose to his heart's content.

Komitas's hopes were also revived by the election of a new Catholicos, Mateos II, in July 1909, a choice that ended more than a year and a half of chaos at the abbey. Under the misrule of Archbishop Sourenian, who had served as interim head of the church after the death of Khrimian (and who was himself destined to be elected Catholicos Kevork V), the community of

Etchmiadzin had been torn apart by internal conflicts: disputes between students and teachers, and quarrels between factions supporting one or another candidate for Catholicos.[16] With the long-awaited ascension of Mateos to the church's highest office, Komitas looked forward to the leadership of an energetic, spirited man, one who might share the passion that Kevork IV and Khrimian Hayrig had felt for music and musical education.

Komitas now saw an opportunity to realize his dream of founding a conservatory of music in Armenia. Encouraged by a long and cordial meeting with the new Catholicos, he prepared a proposal for the school. The letter he wrote to accompany it ended in a torrent of devotion and enthusiasm:

> . . . I am ready as of today to dedicate all my efforts to a task as sacred as this one is. This sacred work has inspired me since my childhood years, it has bound me to the mother church of Etchmiadzin, this sacred work gave me hope over the last 20 years, swayed me with silver hopes, and has grown in me without being realized . . .
>
> I set my foot upon the second stage of my life [i.e. 39 years old] but I am still full of undiminished, unrelinquished hopes. Although the excitement of my youth has become more serious and the vigor of my adulthood has become more refined, my masculine strength is exploding with fire and with unyielding hope.[17]

The response was disheartening. After remarking that the establishment of a music school was "important and mandatory, but requires a large amount of capital, which needs to be found," the new Catholicos simply returned the letter.[18] This was the first of many frustrations that Komitas would experience during the rule of Mateos II, many of which probably arose from the fact that the new leader learned through the abbey's network of gossip that Komitas had opposed his candidacy for Catholicos.

In an article published in 1931,[19] Archag Tchobanian described how little support Komitas's plans received from church officials after the death of Khrimian Hayrig. Tchobanian wrote that on one occasion Komitas asked church leaders to help him organize a second series of concerts in Tbilisi, and was promptly told that they could do no more than help him sell tickets, hardly a generous offer in light of the fact that Komitas's concerts were nearly always sold out. Tchobanian, who had been Komitas's guest in Etchmiadzin at the time of the election of Mateos II, saw clearly that the atmosphere at the ancient monastery

> was suffocating and stifling for [Komitas] . . . It was bizarre that the Holy See . . . did not even sponsor the publication of his Divine Liturgy. . . . The indifference and the difficulties that he experienced in the Caucasus clipped his wings and affected him badly . . . people were amazed by his talent, and applauded his achievements, but nobody could really support him. Catholicos Izmirlian [Mateos II] did not have the vision that his predecessors had. He was influenced by the backward clergy, who were plotting against [Komitas], to drive him to desperation and to destroy his ambition . . . Komitas experienced sleepless nights and moments of desperation . . . [20]

Komitas's fortunes in Etchmiadzin worsened steadily. His salary was reduced by half; the stipend he was paid for conducting the Seminary choir was eliminated entirely.[21] He was now living on roughly one tenth of what a member of the laity was paid to teach music. The cuts devastated him both financially and psychologically, and he could not help but perceive them as unequivocal signs of disrespect for his work and for himself. On September 5, 1909, he wrote a despairing letter to the Catholicos in which he hinted that a nervous breakdown was imminent:

> I have been a monk of this monastery for twenty years. I entered it with the intention of serving it. During these past twenty years I have seen only traps and injustice. My nerves are exhausted; I cannot endure any longer. I am looking for peace but I don't seem to find it. I am thirsty for honest work but I am disturbed. I would like to run away so I will not hear. I would like to close my eyes so as not to see. I would like to tie my legs so as not to drift. I would like to restrain my feelings so I won't be perturbed,

> but I am just a human being. . . . If it pleases your Holiness to find me and not to lose me, I beg you with tears to free me from the Etchmiadzin order and to assign me to the distant Sevan monastery as a hermit-monk where I can finish the research that I have started as an important work for the Armenian Church and for science.[22]

This compendium of grievances that Komitas felt he had endured over the course of decades serves as a portrait of his complex inner world, in which he simultaneously feared and defied the "parental" authority of the church. Using language that is almost biblical in its cadence, e.g. "I would like to close my eyes so as not to see, I would like to tie my legs so as not to drift . . . , he pleads for recognition of the pernicious effects that the salary cut has had on his psychological integrity, his sense of inner peace and harmony. Out of respect for his vows, he accepts his "punishment" obediently, but he does so with an ambivalence that hardly disguises an undercurrent of tremendous anger and agitation. His request for solitude—a quasi-romantic concept in Komitas's mind, incorporating both suffering and freedom—is partly a cry of pain and disappointment, calling the Catholicos to account for the actions of church administrators. Komitas is not asking to be left alone in order to atone for his supposed "sins," but to be released from Etchmiadzin and the routine injustices of its petty internal politics.

The religious assignment for which Komitas pleads in this statement is that of *menagyats*, translated here as "hermit-monk." The term is a variant of the adjective *menavor,* a word which appears repeatedly in Komitas's poems and letters. *Menavor* and its variants, all of them resonating with a sense of deep solitude, of having been abandoned, seem to express a complex range of notions for Komitas, and appear in his writings whenever he falls prey to self-pity. Here the variant has religious connotations, expressing the kind of Christian self-sacrifice made by ascetic scholar-monks throughout the centuries. As in the poem dedicated to his dead mother "leaving me alone and lonely," it articulates the grief of having been "left behind" by a deceased parent. In still other works, *menavor* expresses romantic-sexual yearning. His poem "In Your Dream," for example, describes the birth of the alienated romantic lover from the forms of nature:

> . . . we recognized each other in the sea of love
> And your love has turned into a mountain
> Encircled by clouds;
> From that mountain and those clouds
> The spirit of the loner was born.[23]

In another poem, Komitas portrays himself as a hermit who is drawn from his cell, his *menavori khetsigen*, by the world and its promise of romantic love:

> From the cell of the hermit
> I came to the world
> I followed the scent of your rose
> And I found you.[24]

The last two examples lead us into a realm that Komitas, as a clergyman sworn to celibacy, kept private. In what follows we will be exploring this area of his life, in which Komitas, like any other artist and bachelor of his age, experienced the joys and pain of love.

Notes to Chapter Four: Attempting Independence, 1906–1909

1. Matevos Muratian, ed., "Komitasi Andib Mamagnere" [Unpublished Letters of Komitas], *Badmapanasiragan Hantes* 17 (Yerevan), no. 1 (1958): 252.
2. Margaret Babaian, "Komitas Vartabed ir Namagneri Michov" [Komitas Vartabed Through his Letters], in *Zhamanagagitsnere Komitasi Masin* [Contemporaries on Komitas], edited by K.N. Kasbarian (Yerevan: Haybedhrad, 1960): 116–117.
3. *Ibid.*

4. Matevos Muratian, ed., "Komitasi Andib Namagnere" [Unpublished Letters of Komitas], *Badmapanasiragan Hantes* 17 (Yerevan), no. 1 (1958): 251–252.
5. Komitas first transcribed this song in 1891, when he was only twenty-two. *Hay Knar* contains two versions of the piece: one for choir and one for solo voice.
6. This song contains a segment Komitas wrote for piano and solo voice, which Margaret Babaian performed during the concert in Paris on December 1, 1906.
7. "Haygagan Nvakahantes i Paris" [Armenian Concert in Paris], *Anahid* (Paris), no. 10–12 (1906): 240; A. Ohanian, "Letter from France: Komitas's Armenian Concert in Paris," *Mshag* (Tbilisi), no. 265 (1906): 3–4; "Komitas Vartabedi Nvakahantese Parisum" [Komitas Vartabed's Concert in Paris], Husharar (Tbilisi), no. 4 (1906): 59.
8. Archag Tchobanian, "Komitase yev Hay Yerazheshdutyune" [Komitas and Armenian Music], *Anahid* (Paris), no.1–2 (1931): 119.
9. Babaian, *Ibid.*, 118.
10. *Ibid.*, 124.
11. *Ibid.*, 125.
12. *Ibid.*
13. *Ibid.*
14. *Ibid.*
15. *Ibid.*
16. Matevos Muratian, ed., "Komitasi Andib Namagnere" [Unpublished Letters of Komitas], *Badmapanasiragan Hantes* 17 (Yerevan), no. 1 (1958): 258.
17. Matevos Muratian, ed., *Haygagan Yerazheshdagan Mshaguyti Badmutiun* [History of Armenian Musical Culture] (Yerevan: ARMSSR Academy of Sciences, 1970): 418–419.
18. *Ibid.*, 420.
19. Archag Tchobanian, "Komitase yev Hay Yerazheshdutyune" [Komitas and Armenian Music], *Anahid* (Paris), no.1–2 (1931): 103–127.
20. *Ibid.*, 120.
21. Nimant, "Etchmiadzni Mêtnolordits" [From Circles of Etchmiadzin], *Mshag* (Tbilisi), no. 40 (1909): 2.
22. Toros Azadian, *Komitas Vartabed* (Constantinople: Gutenberg, 1931): 98.
23. Komitas, *Knarerkutyunner* [Poetry], edited by Toros Azadian (Istanbul: Mshaguit, 1939): 39
24. *Ibid.*, 43.

# 5

# Fame and Sanctuary 1910–1915

Catholicos Mateos II did not grant Komitas's desperate request to be transferred to the seclusion of Sevan Monastery. It was clear now that he could rely no longer on the understanding and support of the church's highest office. He was now more determined than ever to leave Etchmiadzin. He was ambivalent about leaving the order but leaving Etchmiadzin meant that by default.[1]

Word of his intentions spread quickly. The Nersessian College in Tbilisi, where his old master Yegmalian had once taught, offered him the position of principal and music teacher. An invitation also arrived from Constantinople, where a friend from his student days at the Kevorkian Seminary, Garabed Bardizbanian, required a choirmaster for the Church of St. Gregory the Illuminator.

Komitas accepted Bardizbanian's offer, but with some apprehension. The internal conflicts of Etchmiadzin distressed him to the point that moving as far away as possible—to Constantinople in Western Turkey, rather than to Tbilisi, which was only a one-day journey by train from Etchmiadzin—may have seemed vital. But a return to Turkey had its perils. Komitas had grown up there, in an environment tainted by political oppression, and he could not ignore the truth that in Turkey his Armenian parents had not been free to speak their own language. Moreover, it had only been slightly more than a year since the massacre of 30,000 Armenians in Adana.[2] For these reasons, Komitas found it difficult to trust the Turkish government and the democratic and constitutional reforms that it was promising to make.[3] It is a sign of his sense of caution—of his hyper vigilance—that upon his departure for Turkey he left most of his personal belongings behind, to be collected at a later date if he decided to stay on permanently.

Arriving in Constantinople in September 1910, he rented an apartment at 83 Pangalti Street in Pera, a neighborhood at the city center. The house belonged to a wealthy Armenian family named Karageozian. His new roommate was the painter Panos Terlemezian, whose works covered the walls of the house. Komitas and Terlemezian discovered that they shared many opinions about art and creativity, and they quickly became close friends. Komitas also enjoyed the companionship of the old cook from Mush, who cared for him. Now that he was no longer dependent on Etchmiadzin for shelter or sustenance, it was as if he were gathering a new family around himself, creating a new sense of belonging.

He set to work immediately, organizing a large, mixed choir of three hundred members, which he dubbed *Kusan,* after the wandering minstrels of Armenia. He selected the choir's female singers from Yesayan College, the local girls' school, and recruited the male voices from the Galata church choir. As Kusan took shape and began performing, interest in Komitas and his work burgeoned among the Armenians of Constantinople, and his activities were given extensive coverage in the Armenian press.[4] Soon his name was known in virtually every Armenian household, and his apartment became a meeting place for intellectuals of all cultural backgrounds.

But church politics, which he thought he had left behind in Etchmiadzin, returned to haunt him. The synthesis of ecclesiastical and folk elements in his concert repertoire, a synthesis that formed the very core of his identity as an artist, again provoked objections from powerful and deeply conservative

*(Left to right)* Musicologist Spiriton Melikian, Komitas Vartabed, and tenor Armenag Shahmuratian, Etchmiadzin, 1909. Both Melikian and Shahmuratian had been Komitas's pupils at the Kevorkian Seminary

members of the clergy, who considered it their duty to warn him that performances of ecclesiastical music in public theaters or music halls ran against the traditional beliefs and practices of the church. Merely attending such a concert was considered unethical conduct for a clergyman; organizing, conducting, and performing in one was, according to the Patriarchate of Constantinople, tantamount to blasphemy. On December 4, 1910, just before Komitas was to lead his choir in a concert at the "Petit-Champ" theater in Constantinople, he was presented with a decree from the deputy patriarch of Constantinople, Ghevont Turian, forbidding the performance of sacred canticles in the public hall. "We regret to inform your Reverend Highness," it read,

> that it is contrary to the rules and the regulations of the Armenian Church to perform the canticles of the Holy Mass on a secular stage such as the stage of the "Petit-Champ" theater. Therefore we forbid you from performing the first part of your concert . . .[5]

In an attempt to ensure the success of this challenge, Komitas's opponents in the clergy also contacted the Turkish secret police and falsely accused him of including politically subversive songs in the concert program.[6] In this way, they made it clear that they were concerned not so much with protecting their church from sacrilege as with obstructing the work of their headstrong colleague by all available means.[7]

Komitas simply ignored the decree and performed the concert according to plan. He was, after all, no longer an active member of any specific order within the church, and thus did not owe allegiance to any of the local church authorities. Moreover, he had given a similar concert in Tbilisi in 1905 with the written permission of Khrimian Hayrig, a fact that Komitas now pointed out defiantly to Turian's messenger. "I recognize no Patriarch," he declared. "I have the permission of His Holiness in my pocket."[8]

The concert turned out to be one of the most brilliantly performed and enthusiastically received of Komitas's career, spreading his reputation to Armenian communities everywhere and vindicating his daring act of disobedience.[9] Once it was brought to the attention of the Armenian public, the deputy patriarch's decree provoked outrage, fanned by editorials in the Armenian-language newspapers of Constantinople and the

Caucasus that fiercely defended Komitas and his work. "Whether ecclesiastical or folkloric," wrote one Armenian journalist, "the music of the artist Vartabed brings turbulence to our hearts . . . we feel [the music] is ours, it is our music." [10]

What lay behind these ruthless attacks by Komitas's fellow clergymen? Why did the quality of their disapproval make Komitas feel as though he had been dragged before a "medieval court of the Inquisition" bent on "killing the person and then [defaming] him"?[11] Komitas was, without a doubt, unique among members of the Armenian clergy. His personality contained a number of paradoxes that baffled colleagues who were less imaginative, less creative, and therefore more dependent on regulation and precedent. He was a hybrid who could not settle comfortably into the mold of "propriety" that the Armenian clergy had cast for itself over the course of centuries. While he maintained a modest diet, never drank or smoked, and slept on bare floors, without mattress or pillow, he always took care to furnish his rooms with sumptuous rugs and works of art.[12] He enjoyed attending family gatherings and social events where he could play the comedian and entertain friends with light-hearted conversation. Clearly, he never felt compelled to suppress the "secular" side of his nature. As Gosdanian observed, Komitas "was a monk, but completely removed from the abbey's specific [religious] atmosphere."[13] Karekin Levonian added that he "was a clergyman only in the realm of art."[14] The reputation for worldliness that he later gained in the more conservative circles of the clergy merely enraged him, to the point that he could no longer place any trust in the network of ecclesiastical power that fanned out from Etchmiadzin.

At the very core of this struggle over "propriety"—a struggle, which constantly undermined Komitas's psychological integrity—was the issue of music. His publication of peasant love songs roused the conservative clergy's anxiety and anger to such an extent that they were prepared to accuse him of a peculiarly aesthetic form of misconduct: his dedication to collecting, publishing, and conducting performances of these songs was, in their eyes, proof of his troubling preoccupation with romantic love and its worldly trappings. Their wayward brother was tampering with the centuries-old traditional role of the Armenian clergyman. By performing sacred music in secular settings, he was flouting the church's hierarchical order; by involving himself with the love songs of the folk, he risked corrupting his pupils.[15] Even the practice of including female performers in his choirs was a contravention of both tradition and propriety. For these reasons, whenever and however they could, they expressed their displeasure. Their opposition to Komitas's efforts to polyphonize the Divine Liturgy, for example, was ostensibly based on the theological notion that "because God is one, the mass should be sung in unison."[16]

Komitas, an artistic revolutionary, one who wanted both to modernize and to safeguard the ancient music of Armenia confronted the conservative clergy. Public admiration for his unorthodox artistic pursuits was only grist to their condemnation mill: Komitas was a sinner in artistic creation and, quite possibly, in physical act. Accusations like these were to pursue him throughout his life: even the mental illness that struck him down in his later years would be attributed by some as the outcome of neurosyphilis.[17]

These accusations were weapons in what was nothing less than a battle over the musical heritage of the Armenian Apostolic Church. Who was responsible for its corruption, and who could claim to be the rightful guardian of its purity? Many of the church's high officials came to view Komitas's reworking of the Divine Liturgy as a senseless attempt to Europeanize an essential part of the national identity, one which they and their predecessors had carefully preserved for centuries. History showed how incursions by missionaries of the Greek and Roman churches had been warded off, how one foreign power after another had tried unsuccessfully to force the Armenian nation to renounce its ancient traditions. Now here was one of their own, tainting the music of the nation's oldest institution with elements that "smacked" of the Lutheran Church.[18] Not only was Komitas disfiguring an invaluable element of Armenia's cultural legacy, they maintained, but he was doing so for personal aggrandizement and profit, performing his hymns in common theaters and then recording them for sale!

Never meek or reserved when musical matters were being discussed, Komitas responded to these charges in kind, openly criticizing the manner in which Armenian clerics had learned to sing the mass. In his public lectures he often referred disparagingly to the custom of singing church canticles at social gatherings held in the houses of the wealthy. "In Turkey," he explained,

> Armenian priests started to sing the Armenian canticles with the intonation of Turkish songs, which was more pleasing to the ears of the party crowds, the rich. Many had adapted themselves to the local Turkish culture, and, influenced by it, had no liking for . . . Armenian canticles sung in the original, austere way. Soon this way of singing was used in the churches as well, and everywhere the Armenian canticles began to be sung nasally and from the throat.[19]

Komitas was implying that it was the clergy itself who had allowed the liturgy to fall prey to worldly influence. His critics in the church now found their own accusations turned against them—and with considerable force—for they had based their claims on a hollow appeal to convention. Komitas's response, on the other hand, was steeped in years of painstaking research.

The controversy deepened. Komitas soon found that he had opponents not only in the church but also among Constantinople's Armenian musicians, many of whom found his stance arrogant and difficult to accept.[20] In defending his own musicological conclusions, he appeared to be dismissing their work as corrupt and distorted, and claiming that he alone had access to the genuine spirit of Armenian music. This ambivalence about his work reflected divisions in Constantinople's Armenian community as a whole: some agreed with the attacks on Komitas launched in the daily newspaper *Zhamanak,* and others with his

An advertisement for a benefit concert for an Armenian conservatory, of the "Kusan" choir, May 26, 1912

praises in other publications, such as *Puzantion, Azadamard,* and *Arevelk.*[21] Humbled by the accusations of haughtiness, Komitas published a statement in *Zhamanak* on October 10, 1910 in which he attempted both to justify and to play down his theories and observations by emphasizing the role of good fortune in his life: "If I hadn't the luck first to go to Etchmiadzin in my homeland, and later to go to Germany, then probably I would have stayed in Gudina [Kütahya] and ended up being a cobbler like my uncle, who cared for me as an orphan . . . ."[22]

Komitas's fame was spreading quickly, fueled by the vociferous debates over his work that were being carried in the press. He received a stream of invitations, more than he was able to accept, to lecture, perform, and conduct in the various Armenian communities of the Ottoman Empire. Before his arrival in a given city, its newspapers would carry articles about him and his work directed to the local Armenian public.

In the early spring of 1911, he accepted an invitation from the Armenian community of Egypt. Traveling alone, he went first to Alexandria, where in a matter of six arduous weeks he completed the formidable task of assembling yet another large Armenian choir, this one of a hundred and ninety members. After performing with them in Alexandria, he took them to Cairo. The reviews were glowing: "Last night," exclaimed Dikran Gamsaragan, a prominent Armenian writer,

> by singing, jesting, and using national dialect and playing with words [he] took us on a pilgrimage to Armenia, or . . . brought a bit of Armenia to the Armenians of Egypt . . . [He] brought Mount Masis . . . to us; who said that mountains cannot walk . . . [23]

Komitas's popularity continued to rise in the Armenian communities of Turkey, Europe, and the Middle East. According to some that attended his concerts, Komitas's work had a hypnotic power over audiences, holding them spellbound long after the music ended.

By this point, the months of grueling work and travel had taken their toll. Exhausted, Komitas made his way to Paris, where he sought peace in the company of his closest friend, Margaret Babaian, who played a central role in his life and art.

### Margaret Babaian and Komitas

And his heart, His heart . . .
And the heart of the person
Awakened by love . . .
Desires someone
Someone to say, "You're my desired" . . .
He wants to cross his face
But his arm is frozen
He wants to cry "*Megha*" ["God have mercy"] . . . [24]

—Baruyr Sevag, *The Ever-Ringing Belfry*

* * *

Not to love you?
—It's in hell to be cast
And with fire your soul to blast
But to love you,
—O, it's to heaven a trip,
And in roses to sleep.

—Komitas, *Knarerkutyunner [Poetry]*[25]

Much of Komitas's inner life, particularly his deepest feelings about women, necessarily remains hidden from the biographer. Unlike many of the prominent musical artists of the nineteenth century (Schumann, for example),[26] he did not keep a diary or journal. The notebook he filled with poems has given us a few fragmentary insights, but for the most part we are left with his letters, the majority of which are concerned with the details of his daily business: his various musical projects, tours, concerts, and publications.

Fortunately, the many letters Komitas wrote to Margaret Babaian offer us glimpses of his emotional life, particularly of his relationship with Margaret herself, a young Armenian singer and teacher of music who lived most of her life in Paris.

Born in 1874 to an Armenian couple living in Germany, Margaret Babaian was five years Komitas's junior. Her father,

Avedik, was a physician, and her mother, Sofia, had come to Germany in order to take courses in pre-school education at a seminary in Gotha. Given the social standards of the time, Sofia's long-ranging pursuit of an independent education was bold and ambitious for a woman, especially one who was only nineteen when Margaret was born. In 1876, when Margaret was a child of

Margaret's father, Avedik Babaian

two, the family moved to Vienna, where Sofia continued her studies. Here, Margaret's younger sister Armine was born in 1877. A third girl, Shushanig, was born in 1879, after the family had moved back to Tbilisi. Three years later, with the help of her husband, Sofia founded Tbilisi's first public kindergarten, and ran it according to her firm convictions about the role of the family in the formation of social values in young children.

This intrepid, self-reliant woman had a powerful influence on the lives of her three daughters. Armine went on to distinguish herself as an important painter whose works now hang in the Armenian National Gallery. Shushanig became an accomplished pianist who devoted much of her career to Armenian music, eventually performing many of Komitas's works on the stages of Paris. Margaret responded to the progressive, culturally rich environment of her childhood by becoming a celebrated singer and musicologist.

Mixed choir, Alexandria, 1911

When she first met Komitas in Tbilisi in 1895, Margaret was only twenty-one, but her diverse career in music was already firmly established. She had begun as a pianist, touring throughout the Caucasus. She had also used her fluency in several languages to translate a German book on Beethoven into Armenian. Dissatisfied with vocal training she was receiving in Tbilisi, and following her mother's example, she moved to Paris to study with the renowned teachers Polin Viarto and Arto de Badilla. After returning to Tbilisi she was hired as a vocal teacher at a local music college, where she taught until she departed for Paris again in 1904: the Babaian family had decided to leave the Caucasus for good, finding it too provincial for their artistic interests. Margaret continued her singing career in Paris and gave concerts in several European cities. Her rich mezzo-soprano voice, combined with her easy rapport with different cultures, made her a uniquely flexible artist. She was accomplished at performing the works of European, Russian, and Armenian composers, including Komitas.

Throughout her long life, Margaret would continue to widen her musical horizons. Along with establishing her own vocal school in Paris in 1911, she joined "The Vocal Masters of France" society and the French musicological union, and continued to perform as a soloist in the Colonn-Lamureau concert ensemble. In 1951, after many years as a music critic on French radio, she was recognized with a national prize. She was also asked to write an entry on Armenian music for the Larousse Encyclopedia.[27]

The title of *Hay Knar,* 1907

She never married, and died in Paris on October 18, 1968 at the age of ninety-four.[28] From the fragments of correspondence that survive, we can see that Margaret's relationship with Komitas was deep and intricate. It was comprised of two distinct facets: a public, professional relationship between a singer and a composer/conductor; and a private, clandestine relationship between two creative and mature individuals. As we shall see, it seems likely that, before allowing excerpts of Komitas's letters to her to be published shortly after his death in 1935, Margaret attempted to protect Komitas by withholding passages where Komitas showed suspiciousness and anger towards others.

We do, however, have Margaret's writings about Komitas, including the journalistic pieces she composed after his concerts in Paris, as well as a short memoir that she published after his death.[29] Nowhere here does she attempt to conceal her adoration of him. Apparently the fact that she was a single woman and he a celibate priest did not concern her much. Curiously, she never makes any reference to the unorthodox nature of their relationship, and to the social barriers that stood in its way. This hardly meant that such obstacles did not exist. Their relationship would become the subject of damaging gossip in Paris, a fact that disturbed Komitas greatly.

In any case, it is still difficult for us to discern what Margaret truly felt for Komitas—whether she loved him as more than a friend, or suffered while awaiting his returns to Paris, or felt guilty for loving the "wonderful soul" of this artist-monk.

When she and Komitas first met in Tbilisi in 1895, Margaret was a young woman of twenty-one and he a bachelor of twenty-six.[30] Precisely how the introduction came about is not clear, but it is likely that she was a soloist in the Armenian Church choir directed by Magar Yegmalian. As we have noted, Komitas was himself a student of Yegmalian's at this time, having come to Tbilisi in the company of Khrimian Hayrig. In her memoirs Margaret recalls her first meeting with Komitas in tender and affectionate terms, describing him as a young, slender, good-humored monk, full of hopes for a bright future.[31]

Another six years passed before they saw each other again, in 1901.[32] At that time Margaret was continuing her vocal training in Paris, and Komitas stopped off in the city while traveling home to Etchmiadzin from Berlin, where he had attended another meeting of the International Music Society.

When they met in Tbilisi in 1902, Margaret was teaching classes in singing at the local music school, and her recollection of their reunion gives the impression of an infatuated young woman:

> . . . one spring day, Dirair Vartabed [a member of the Armenian clergy in Tbilisi] wanted to introduce us to Komitas, who had just arrived from Etchmiadzin. He informed us that Komitas would be happy to sing for us, but that he would prefer to sing in a large hall for a few selected people rather than for the public. I rushed with great pleasure to get permission from the management for the newly built conservatory hall, and the same night we got together with a group of friends. We were waiting for Komitas with our hearts pounding. The servant lit a dim light in the corner; we were sitting in near-darkness. And behold, a thin, young man in black entered the stage and sat at the piano. In that impressive silence I heard for the first time his voice, which seemed to come forth from deep down in his burning soul, vibrant with ardor and sorrow. . . . The tears were running down my cheeks. Finally, Dirair Vartabed intervened after noticing my great emotion: "This is enough, this is enough, Komitas, you killed the girl."[33]

Over the following two years, from 1902 to 1904, Margaret and Komitas lived in relative proximity to each other, she in Tbilisi and he in Etchmiadzin, but it is not known whether they met during this time. It is certain, however, that Margaret was able to follow the progress of her friend's career, for Komitas and the controversies that his musical interpretations caused in Armenian intellectual circles were often discussed in Tbilisi's Armenian press.

Their correspondence began in 1904 or 1905. One of the excerpts that Margaret eventually published in 1935 is characteristic of his early letters to her. Written in Etchmiadzin on June 25, 1905, when he was sick in bed with a fever, it is rather formal in tone, and notes the state of his health, his work, and his mood:

> I received your letter with great pleasure . . . . I am exhausted this summer and can't work. The doctors forbade me from working until the end of September. I am planning to go to Harij and stay there all summer. I hope you are all well. Of course, in a musical sea like Paris you

> do not have a single moment of boredom. Whereas I, in this backward dump, am getting nourished with silence. Poor us. The illness really exhausted me, and my pen does not seem to move forward . . . [34]

The bond between them grew stronger when, in 1906, Komitas decided to leave the stifling, oppressive atmosphere of Etchmiadzin and settle in Europe, where he planned to earn his living through music. By this time Margaret had moved back to Paris with her family. Now that the barrier of distance between them had been removed and Komitas was free to be himself, far from the curious eyes and ears of his colleagues in Etchmiadzin, he wrote to her frequently. He was not, however, in the habit of dating his letters; often he would specify only the city and the year in which he was writing. This fact, combined with Margaret's insistence later on offering only fragments of the correspondence "Let me give you some excerpts of two letters from that period . . . "[35] makes it especially difficult to reconstruct the chronology of their relationship.

Arriving in Berlin in March 1906, Komitas informed Margaret that he intended the move to mark a permanent change in his life: "I have decided to leave teaching, and to provide for myself."[36] He poured out his heart about the troubles he had faced in Etchmiadzin, and then concluded with apologies for "disturbing you with my personal issues"[37]—an indication that he still thought their relationship required a certain degree of formality and reticence. Because he was addressing Margaret, however, he dared to be far more open about his intentions than he was with any of his other correspondents. For example, in a letter he wrote to Archag Tchobanian a month after arriving in Berlin he discussed the move from Etchmiadzin as being based on his "right to be away for ten months,"[38] as if he was merely on sabbatical and had plans to return.

After six months in Berlin, during which he oversaw the publication of a collection of his works, Komitas traveled to Paris, where he was being awaited eagerly by Margaret. It was a happy and productive time. They were in their thirties now and enjoying increasing professional success. Margaret introduced Komitas to Paris's musicological society, and together they organized a choir of thirty Armenian and French opera-singers. Komitas conducted this ensemble, Margaret performed as a soloist, and her sister Shushanig played the piano accompaniments. As we saw earlier, the concert they gave in Paris on December 1 was an enormous success.

Komitas in Paris, 1907

Living in the same city and exhilarated by the praise of their first joint effort, Komitas and Margaret were in daily contact. As their careers exposed them to the public eye, the closeness of their relationship did not go unnoticed, and gossip soon began to circulate through Paris's Armenian community. The heartfelt letter Komitas wrote Margaret on December 6, only days after their concert, was in part a long and bitter complaint about the "bad people" who were spreading rumors about them. It is interesting that Komitas declared that he wished he "had done something wrong then that would have been shameful to my calling [and] I would have said to myself, you asked for it." Discussing the gossip almost seems to have moved him toward a guilty, half-conscious recognition of hidden desire. Overcome by his feelings for Margaret, he turned to metaphor:

> My kind, trustworthy instrument, which is a simple music box with metallic strings, understands me, and I open my heart to it. It makes me as drunk, as I desire, it understands and consoles me with empathy and echoes my weeping.[39]

He ended the letter by telling her of the emotional relief he found by confiding in her: "The pain is gone, nothing left. God forgive them [i.e. those spreading gossip]. I will see you tomorrow . . . ."

During Komitas's stay in Paris, the two friends simply tried to ignore the gossip and spent many happy hours together, attending operas and concerts. The letter he wrote to Margaret after they had seen Debussy's *Pelléas et Mélisande* is jubilant: "Many-many thanks to jewel Margaret for Pelléas et Mélisande. Every time I play it, it reminds me of you."[40] The strength of his feelings for her was revealed when he mentioned a couple who had sat next to them at the performance, for he seemed to be implying that he thought of her as something more than friend and companion: "They achieved their life's dream [*muraz*]. Let us achieve ours too. Amen."[41] Romantic feelings for Margaret may also have served as the inspiration for a short (and undated) poem he wrote, entitled "In My Dream":

> Tonight, in my dream, we danced together,
> The love-spirits set wax candles on the altar,
> They made red and green love shirts for us
> Of delicate veil cut from a cloud of gold and silver.[42]

Komitas must have known that this dream was unattainable, his vow of celibacy was not enough to prevent him from loving Margaret and wanting to be with her constantly. And so once again he was pitted against himself: Komitas the clergyman against

Komitas the secular artist. Even in the rare moments when the absence of onlookers meant that he was free to express his feelings he was compelled to avoid making direct statements.

Komitas, 1907

This reticence, though tempered by feelings of increasing intimacy and ease, is particularly apparent in one of the letters to Margaret, which also illuminates his sense of humor. His wit was familiar to virtually everyone who worked or studied with him, and when it was addressed to Margaret it took on an especially playful air, as if Komitas, like someone in love, was not afraid to show her the silly side of his personality. Throughout this letter he replaces the "r" sounds of his words with "l" sounds, and the Armenian letter pronounced "sh" with the one pronounced "s": "Dear Miss Malgalit, filst of all I ask about youl health. If you ask us, thanks to God we ale vely well and happy . . . I miss you a lot and I gleet you . . . ."In another letter an unsettling drawing appears to reinforce the words to express the conflict inside him. The sketch looks like an unfolded envelope, the triangles of which display human faces wearing cowls. At the center, surrounded by these faces, is the frowning image of his face, accompanied by a depiction of Margaret, looking worried or angry.

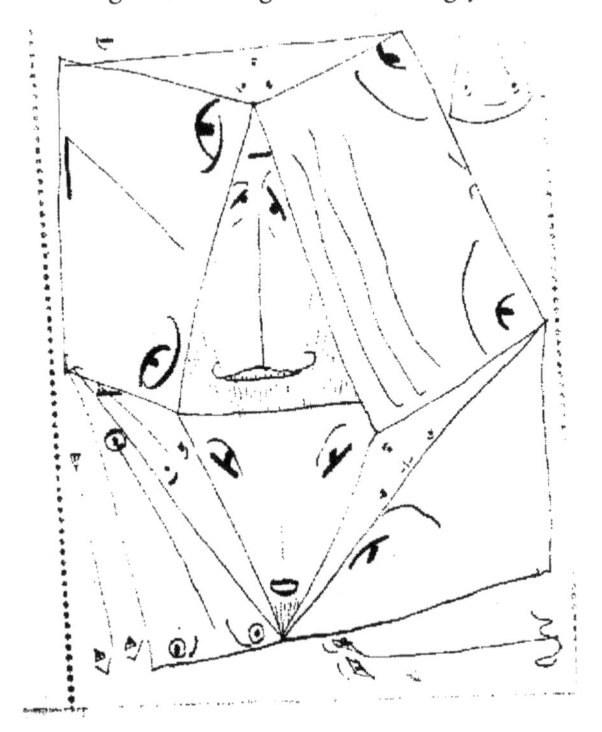

Drawing in letter to Margaret Babaian dated December 1, 1906

When Komitas left Paris to go on a hectic concert tour of Switzerland, he continued to write to his "golden pearl." In early June 1907 he sent Margaret the following news from Lausanne:

> The concert in Geneva was marvelous. I gave lectures in Geneva, Lausanne and Bern. We returned to Lausanne today, Archag [Tchobanian] will recite Armenian poetry and I will sing. I have good impressions of Switzerland. I hope that by Sunday or Monday we will return to Paris. When I come, I will tell you in detail of everything that happened.
>
> My best greetings to you all, to the young and old, to the light and the fire, to the golden pearl . . . and to your mother and father.[43]

The next month he took his leave of Margaret and her family and returned to Berlin, where he continued to oversee the publication of his work. His letters from this period—or, more precisely, the excerpts that Margaret later allowed to be published—show him completely preoccupied with his work. Nowhere does he mention any emotional suffering that he might have been experiencing at the time. By this time, Komitas knew that his inability to find permanent employment in Paris or Berlin meant that his sojourn in Europe was finished—that a lack of funds would soon force him to leave behind a fulfilling and independent life, an intimate friend, and a surrogate family, in order to return to Etchmiadzin. It seems likely that by focusing on his work he was attempting to lessen the impact these losses would have on him.

Komitas's return to Etchmiadzin in September 1907 did nothing to diminish his deep attachment to Margaret, even though they were again thousands of miles apart. Soon after Khrimian Hayrig's death in October, he fought through his grief and fatigue to write her a long letter in which he implied just how closely entwined their emotional lives had become:

> Three weeks after the funeral, I still feel weak and shaky, yet, though I am writing with difficulty, I want to give you a report and tell you about the things I have done and the things I plan to do. I know that you have been waiting for and are interested in my news.[44]

The letter ends with his yearning for the intimate domestic comforts he experienced with Margaret and her family: "To have supper together one more time in that small, cozy dining room. Keep a place setting ready for me; you never know, suddenly perhaps, in that moment I will be there."[45] Once more, the act of writing to her seems to have lifted his spirits: "I am not hopeless. I am working. I've written many things, and I have done many things, and I have not forgotten you."[46]

* * * * *

Much of the elation Komitas felt when he finally gathered the courage to abandon Etchmiadzin in 1910 arose from newly awakened hopes that, with the pressures of life in the monastery behind him again, and with a renewed freedom to go wherever he pleased, his relationship with Margaret would blossom again, as it had three years earlier. "I miss you so much," he wrote her a letter from Smyrna. "I feel so happy when I think that soon we will see each other again."[47] As his delight in his rediscovered freedom grew with the move to Constantinople in September 1910, the frequency of his letters to Margaret increased. His concerts were consistently drawing large crowds; for the first time in many years he did not have to worry about money. But, as ever Margaret was foremost in his thoughts.

> People relate to my work with great love, which is very pleasing and encouraging to me. You cannot imagine how much I wish you were here with me at this moment, to share all these with me, so that I could tell you all the interesting things that are happening to me.[48]

The 1911 invitation to organize a choir for the Armenian community in Egypt delayed Komitas's hurriedly made plans to visit her in Paris. He toured triumphantly through Egypt with the choir; the reviews in Cairo's foreign press and in the local Arabic and Armenian papers were glowing, and the Armenian community honored him with gifts. He was utterly exhausted at the end of this three-month trip, but it was with an immense feeling of accomplishment that he finally set out to see Margaret.

It was at this point that the relationship between them was at its closest. In late June 1911, when Margaret had just completed the work of establishing her own voice school, Komitas arrived in Paris unannounced. We can only imagine Margaret's great surprise and happiness when she opened her door and found herself face to face with the man she had not seen in four years. She was in the midst of preparing for a two-week break from her work, and was planning a vacation in a small inn in the town of Shenklin on Britain's remote Isle of Wight. With her characteristic courage, she asked Komitas to accompany her. Silencing the guilty inner voice that warned him against such a daring act, he agreed.

Margaret Babaian

Komitas used the time to compose the songs "Es Arun" (also known as "Sirerk [Serenade]") and "Hoy Nazan," and Margaret helped him make clean drafts of the manuscripts he had brought with him.[49] But it was a highly unorthodox arrangement for a celibate priest, as both of them were well aware. At this point he was relatively free of the official strictures of his church: he was no longer a member of an order; the superior to whom he had been accountable, Khrimian Hayrig, was dead; and the opinions of the new Catholicos, Mateos II, by whom he had been so deeply disappointed, mattered little to him.

Still in a state of great creative agitation, driven to write down the music that coursed through his mind and kept him from sleep, Komitas found solace in evening walks with Margaret along the island's beaches. Enchanted, alight with love and ignoring all feelings of guilt, Margaret wrote:

> As we listened long to the sounds of the waves, at times so tender and at others so violent, Komitas would liken them to the sounds of the Armenian language. Sitting on the sand, he would sing new songs, while a cold British moon overhead would look down in bewilderment, unable to understand which land such ardent melodies could come from. And I was his sole audience, along with the frowning silhouette of the rocks and the rippling waves.[50]

This passage seems laden with unconscious symbols, images conveying not only Margaret's inarticulated feelings for Komitas, but also the social reactions that she expects will be caused by this complex and highly charged relationship between male priest and female singer. Was Margaret, like the moon she describes, "bewildered" by what was happening? According to the norms of Armenian society, a man dressed in black should not be singing such "ardent melodies" of love. Were the "frowning rocks" the representatives of the Armenian clergy, silently disapproving of the "rippling waves" sent forth by Komitas's songs, waiting to exact punishment? Soon after returning to Constantinople, Komitas saw an opportunity for luring Margaret away from Paris. By 1912, he had begun preparations for the realization of his greatest dream, to establish a conservatory of Armenian music in Constantinople. Writing to Margaret, he refers to this project as if it were another shared ambition:

> . . . I have high hopes, I am confidant I will make this come through, and I will drag you here. It is my greatest wish, that our conservatory would open and you would come here and we would work together to promote music in our community.[51]

This is the last of Komitas's letters that Margaret published.[52] Why? Did she receive more letters from him which she decided not to publish? Or did their correspondence begin to wane, so that this letter was one of the last she received? It is possible that their relationship had reached a level of intimacy that frightened them both, or that Komitas had begun to feel a certain ambivalence about associating himself so closely with a woman and started to withdraw. In any case, after his next tour of Europe, which took place in the summer of 1912, Komitas recuperated by traveling to a mountain resort near his native town of Kütahya, in the company of his roommate, the painter Panos Terlemezian—not by spending time with Margaret, as he had done the year before.[53]

Komitas and Margaret did not see each other again until 1914, when he returned to Paris to speak at a conference of the International Musical Society. After the conference, he organized a concert of Armenian music at Paris's Jean-Baptist Armenian Church, in which Margaret performed. She offers us no information about these events. We can only conclude that, if the "romantic" period of their relationship was over, they were still close friends.

### Notes to Chapter Five: Fame and Sanctuary

1. On December 26, 1911, Komitas could not come personally to say goodbye, instead he wrote officially to the catholicos informing him that he will not return to Etchmiadzin. On February 5, 1912 in "Hovid" news appeared " . . . Komitas Vartabed abandons his religious vows . . . " Later Komitas wrote to this paper and denied this allegation.
2. Vahakn Dadrian, *History of the Armenian Genocide* (Oxford: Berghahn Books, 1995): 386.
3. See: Richard Hovannisian, "The Historical Dimensions of the Armenian Question, 1878–1923," ed. Richard Hovannisian *The Armenian Genocide in Perspective.* (Oxford: Transaction, 1986): 26.
4. "Komitasi Hamerke Masnagtsutyamp Yergser Khêmpi, Paghgatsatz 300 Yerkichnerits" [The Concert of Komitas, with the Participation of 300 Male and Female Choir Members], *Dajar* (Constantinople), no. 33 (1910): 746; "Komitas Vartabedi Arachin Adenapanutyune" [First Public Lecture of Komitas Vartabed], *Dajar* (Constantinople), no. 34 (1910): 698; "Komitas Vartabedi Hamerke" [The Concert of Komitas Vartabed], *Puzantion* (Constantinople), no. 4290 (1910): 4.
5. Toros Azadian, *Komitas Vartabed* (Constantinople: Gutenberg, 1931): 107.
6. *Ibid.*, 107.
7. It can be argued that these groundless accusations contributed to Komitas's arrest by the Turks in 1915.

8. K.N. Kasbarian, "Komitas: Gensakragan Agnarg" [Komitas: Biographical Sketch], in *Zhamanagagitsnere Komitasi Masin* [Contemporaries on Komitas], edited by K.N. Kasbarian (Yerevan: Haybedhrad, 1960): 22.

9. Anais, "Kegharvesdagan Dbavorutyunner" [Artistic Impressions], *Puzantion* (Constantinople), no. 4305 (1910): 1.

10. "Komitas Vartabedi Hamerke Bolsum" [The Concert of Komitas Vartabed in Constantinople], *Luys* (Nor-Nakhichevan), no. 44 (1910): 12–13; "Komitas Vartabed yev Hay Yegeghetsagan Yerazheshdutyun" [Komitas Vartabed and Armenian Church Music], *Puzantion* (Constantinople), no. 4156 (1910): 1, and no. 4157 (1910): 1; Puzant Kechian, "Khêmpakragan Bahbanoghaganutyun, te Khavaramêdutyun. Komitas Vartabedi Hamerkin Tem Gêgheramid Arkelknere. Yergu Khosk Badriarkagan Pokhanortin Hastseyin" [Editorial: Conservatism or Obscurantism? The Clerical Obstacles to Komitas Vartabed's Concert. Two Words Addressed to the Deputy Patriarch], *Puzantion* (Constantinople), no. 4293 (1910): 1; Shahen, "Bolsagan Namagner Gosdandinoubolis 23e Noyemperi" [Letters from Constantinople, 23rd of November], *Mshag* (Tbilisi), no. 272 (1910): 2.

11. Komitas, Letter to Garabed Gosdanian, doc. 15, Komitas Archives, Charents Museum of Literature and Art, Yerevan: 1.

12. Karekin Levonian, "Mer Komitase" [Our Komitas], in *Zhamanagagitsnere Komitasi Masin* [Contemporaries on Komitas], edited by K.N. Kasbarian (Yerevan: Haybedhrad, 1960): 150.

13. D. Gosdanian, "Im Hishoghutyune Komitas Vartabedi Masin" [My Reminiscences of Komitas Vartabed], doc. 81, Komitas Archives, Charents Museum of Literature and Art, Yerevan.

14. Karekin Levonian, *Husher* [Memoirs] (Yerevan: Haybedhrad, 1959): 120.

15. See "Letter to the Editor," *Nor-tar* (Tbilisi), no. 110 (1903): 2–3. This is a request for an authoritative opinion on the morality of Komitas's apparent preoccupation with peasant love-songs.

16. This was the official complaint lodged by a delegation of Etchmiadzin clerics. Khrimian Hayrig dismissed it. See: H.J. Siruni, "Komitasi Hed" [With Komitas], *Etchmiadzin* (Etchmiadzin) (Aug-Sept 1965): 74.

17. This rumor was whispered to me when I first started asking questions about Komitas's illness. I have been unable to track down an article that allegedly was published during the mid-thirties in a Parisian medical journal, in which a doctor discusses the possibility of neurosyphilis in regard to Komitas's case. I would be grateful to any reader who can inform me of the whereabouts of this article.

18. H.J. Siruni, "Komitasi Hed" [With Komitas], *Etchmiadzin* (Etchmiadzin) (Aug-Sept 1965): 77.

19. Komitas, "Hay Keghchug Yerazheshdutyun" [Armenian Rustic Music], *Anahid* (Paris) (Jan-Mar 1937): 29–30.

20. See, for example: Levon Tchilingerian, "Komitas Vartabed yev Haygagan Yerazheshdutyune" [Komitas Vartabed and Armenian Music], *Jamanak* (Constantinople), no. 592 (1910): 1.
21. L. Jerrakian, "Komitasi Hayatsknere Haygagan Yerazheshdutyan Vra (Ir Isg Haydararutyunnere)" [The Views of Komitas on Armenian Music (His Own Views)], *Jamanak* (Constantinople), no. 584 (1910): 1; Puzant Kechian, "Khêmpakragan Bahbanoghaganutyun, te Khavaramêdutyun. Komitas Vartabedi Hamerkin Tem Gêgheramid Arkelknere. Yergu Khosk Badriarkagan Pokhanortin Hastseyin" [Editorial conservatism or obscurantism? The Clerical Obstacles to Komitas Vartabed's Concert. Two Words Addressed to the Deputy Patriarch], *Puzantion* (Constantinople), no. 4293 (1910): 1.
22. Toros Azadian, *Komitas Vartabed* (Constantinople: Gutenberg, 1931): 106.
23. A. Oghlukian, ed., *Kragan Nêshkhark Komitas Vartabedi Peghun Kêrchen* [Literary Fragments from Komitas Vartabed's Prolific Pen] (Montreal: Canadian Diocese of the Armenian Church, 1994): 26. "Masis" is another name for Mount Ararat, the two-peaked mountain that is for many a symbol of Armenia.
24. Baruyr Sevag, *Anlreli Zankagadun* [The Ever-Ringing Belfry] (Beirut: Sevan, 1960): 33–36.
25. Komitas, *Knarerkutyunner* [Poetry], edited by Toros Azadian (Istanbul: Mshaguit, 1939) 59.
26. See, for example: Robert and Clara Schumann, *The Marriage Diaries of Robert and Clara Schumann*, edited by Gero Nauhaus, translated by Peter Ostwald (Boston: Northwestern University Press, 1993); Robert Schumann, *Tagebucher 1827–1838*, edited by George Eismann (Leipzig: Deutscher Verlag für Musik, 1971); Robert Schumann, *Tagebucher 1836–1854*, edited by Gero Nauhaus (Leipzig: Deutscher Verlag für Musik, 1987).
27. Robert Atayan, "Margaret Babaian," in *Haygagan Sovedagan Hamaynakidaran* [Soviet Armenian Encyclopedia], edited by B.A. Simonian, vol. 2 (Yerevan: ARMSSR Academy of Sciences, 1976): 187.
28. According to Mrs. Kevonian, one of Margaret's pupils in Paris in the 1940s, Margaret's funeral was well attended but the burial was poorly attended.
29. During a recent research trip in Yerevan, the present author discovered a series of postcards written by Margaret to Komitas. This discovery opens up new avenues for research in the future.
30. Margaret Babaian, "Husher Komitas Vartabeden" [Memories of Komitas], *Arevmoudk* (Paris), no. 5 (1946): 2.
31. *Ibid.*, 2.
32. Both of them were studying in Europe at different times during this six-year period. Margaret was training her voice in Paris, and Komitas was studying music in Berlin. Komitas returned to a teaching position at the Kevorkian Seminary in Etchmiadzin in 1899. See: Kristapor S. Kushnarian, Matevos H. Muratian, and Kevork Keotagian, eds., *Agnarg Hay Yerazheshdutian*

*Badmutian* [Overview of the History of Armenian Music] (Yerevan: ARMSSR Academy of Sciences, 1963): 182.

33. Margaret Babaian, "Dbavorutyunner Komitasi Antsin yev Kortzin Shurch" [Impressions of Komitas and his Work], in K. N. Kasbarian, ed., *Zhamanagagitsnere Komitasi Masin* [Contemporaries on Komitas], (Yerevan: Haybedhrad, 1960): 139.
34. Margaret Babaian, "Komitas Vartabed ir Namagneri Michov" [Komitas Vartabed Through His Letters], in K. N. Kasbarian, ed., *Zhamanagagitsnere Komitasi Masin* [Contemporaries on Komitas], edited by (Yerevan: Haybedhrad, 1960): 116. Harij was a monastery in Northern Armenia used by the Etchmiadzin monks as a summer retreat.
35. *Ibid.*, 118.
36. *Ibid.*, 117.
37. *Ibid.*, 117.
38. Matevos Muratian, ed., "Komitasi Andib Namagnere" [Unpublished Letters of Komitas], *Badmapanasiragan Hantes* 17 (Yerevan), no. 1 (1958): 252.
39. Babaian, "Komitas Vartabed ir Namagneri Michov," 119. 42. *Ibid.*, 119.
40. Komitas is probably referring to "playing" the piece on a gramophone, rather than on a piano or some other musical instrument. It is noteworthy that this opera—the only one that Debussy completed—tells a story of idealized love.
41. The Armenian term *muraz* strongly implies that the "dream" is somehow unattainable.
42. Komitas, *Knarerkutyunner* [Poetry], edited by Toros Azadian (Istanbul: Mshaguit, 1939): 32.
43. Komitas, Letter to Margaret Babaian, June 1907, doc. 1507, Komitas Archives, Museum of Literature and Art, Yerevan. "Golden pearl" is something of a pun on Komitas's part, since the name Margaret (or *Markrid*) means "pearl" in Armenian. Komitas's letters to Margaret often contain greetings to her entire family. His relationship with them was close and apparently untroubled, despite his potentially scandalous friendship with Margaret. In December of the previous year Komitas had even presided over the wedding of Margaret's sister Shushanig. Considering how often Komitas found himself the victim of malicious gossip, his acceptance into the Babaian family must have been greatly comforting to him.
44. Babaian, "Komitas Vartabed ir Namagneri Michov," 125.
45. *Ibid.*, 124.
46. *Ibid.*, 126.
47. *Ibid.*, 126.
48. Babaian, "Dbavorutyunner Komitasi Antsin yev Kortzin Shurch," [Contemporaries on Komitas]. 140–141.
49. Komitas, *Yergeri Zhoghovadzu, Arachin Hador: Menerkner* [Collected Works, First Volume: Solo Songs], R. Atayan, ed,. (Yerevan: Haybedhrad, 1960): 182. Many of the clean drafts that Margaret helped Komitas make eventually became part of her personal library, and survived as the only manuscripts of the works.

50. Babaian, "Dbavorutyunner Komitasi Antsin yev Kortzin Shurch," [Contemporaries on Komitas]. 140–141.
51. Babaian, "Komitas Vartabed ir Namagneri Michov," 127.
52. However, a letter from him to Margaret, dated February 9, 1913, is quoted in Oghlukian's book (p. 28). In it, Komitas asks her to buy him a particular musical instrument (a *flugeh*), and offers his usual reports of his daily life.
53. During this holiday, Terlemezian painted his beautiful and widely known portrait of Komitas seated and leaning against a tree.

# 6

# The Crisis Looms 1913–1914

After the trip with Margaret to the Isle of Wight and some much needed rest, Komitas was back in Constantinople with his energy renewed in November 1911. At forty-two, he spent that winter and the next spring giving a half dozen concerts to enthusiastic audiences.

Indeed, his following in the city was so great and so loyal that the Turkish authorities began to take interest in him as well, and invited him to participate in a fund-raising concert for the benefit of the Turkish military. Komitas accepted and prepared a small group of eight singers, to whom he taught a number of Turkish songs. The performance was an unqualified success. Komitas's fame began to spread into Turkish society at large.

Touring Europe the next summer, he went first to Leipzig, where he lectured and oversaw the publication of a two-volume collection of his work, *Hay Keghchug Yerker* [Armenian Rustic Songs], which extended the series of songs that had begun with *Hay Knar*. He moved on to deliver lectures in Paris, London, and Berlin and when he returned to Constantinople at the end of July, he began rehearsing with the "Kusan" choir. The Balkan War erupted in September and plunged Ottoman Turkey into war with Greece, Serbia, and Bulgaria, quickly bringing an end to this work. With many of his singers drafted into the army, he was forced to occupy himself by teaching music at a local Armenian secondary school, and by continuing his research.

In the summer of 1913, Komitas decided to return briefly to Etchmiadzin, partly for the sake of nostalgia, and partly because he had managed during his time in Constantinople to set aside his grievances and now wanted to return "home" with news of his success. If he expected to receive a spirited welcome from Mateos's newly elected successor, Catholicos Kevork V, he was disappointed. The Catholicos merely remarked sarcastically upon the amount of money Komitas was making in Constantinople and inquired about the date of his departure. Komitas had abandoned the brotherhood; now the brotherhood—in the person of the Catholicos—was abandoning him. Wounded by this rejection, he wrote defiantly to his old friend and confidante in Paris, Archag Tchobanian:

> I didn't come to stay, but to work at the ancient manuscript depository, and to collect some new folk songs. By the middle of September I'll be in Istanbul [Constantinople] . . . My friends [in Etchmiadzin] are unappreciated . . . they don't even have their own rooms . . . I just got out of that quicksand, how can I go back? Not once did they ask me to stay; they didn't even ask, "Why are you leaving, why are you not staying?"[1]

This was Komitas's last attempt at reconciliation with Etchmiadzin. Its failure hurt him deeply, for in many ways he had remained emotionally attached to the abbey in spite of all the conflict he had endured there over the years. As he often did in times of suffering, Komitas now turned to his work with feverish energy. Using the abbey as a base, he embarked on a six-week tour of neighboring Armenian provinces, collecting and transcribing folk songs as he moved.

When he returned to Constantinople in August 1913, the Armenian community was preparing to observe a momentous historical occasion: the fifteen-hundredth anniversary of the Armenian alphabet. Komitas was eager to compose a work in honor of this event, not only because creative work would again offer escape routes from the pain he was feeling after his rejection in Etchmiadzin, but because the Armenian language conjured powerful emotions in him. As an orphaned boy of twelve, he had come to Etchmiadzin knowing only the Turkish that his parents had spoken. Learning Armenian, the ancient language of his people, had been one of the rites of passage in his transformation from orphan to artist, from Soghomon to Komitas; it had marked his inclusion in a new community, a new "family." So it was that his great love for Armenian resounded throughout *Ov Medzaskanch Tu Lezu* [O Glorious My Language], the song he wrote to commemorate the anniversary.

In hindsight, it is clear that the celebrations were overshadowed by terrible portents. Turkey's interior minister Talaat Bey, the man who, two years later, would be one of the chief architects of a genocidal campaign against the Armenians, delivered a speech. The solidarity displayed by leading Armenian intellectuals, clergy, writers, poets, and artists during the celebrations served to exacerbate the Turkish government's already profound sense of fear and anger. For centuries, Turkish authorities had forbidden the use of the Armenian language in the hope that the Armenians themselves would eventually become assimilated. The anniversary celebrations were proof that these plans had failed. For these reasons, the celebration's display of pride in the survival of the Armenian language was probably interpreted by many of the Turks in power as a prelude to insurrection.

The majority of Constantinople's Armenian intellectuals, Komitas included, still believed in the government's promises of reform, and remained oblivious to the mounting threat of retaliation against Armenian culture. After the celebrations, they established a special committee of writers, artists, and historians for the purpose of combing the Armenian provinces in search of neglected cultural monuments and artifacts. Komitas's own plan was to accompany the poet Taniel Varuzhan to the historic town of Sassun, where they were to record such oral histories as "The

Dare-Devils of Sassun," an Armenian myth upon which Komitas was planning to base an epic opera. The project never came to fruition.

Komitas in Berlin

In all, it was a happy and rewarding time for Komitas. He was a favorite of the foreign dignitaries who lived in Constantinople, many of whom attended his concerts and invited him to perform at official functions. Mrs. Henry Morgenthau, the wife of the American ambassador to Turkey, was an especially devoted patron.[2] Komitas was also devoting more time to teaching than he had in many years, giving lessons in harmony and vocal performance to promising members of his choir in order to prepare them to be teachers in the conservatory he hoped to establish.[3]

In early June 1914, on the eve of the First World War, Komitas returned to Paris to lecture at a conference of the International Musical Society, and, of course, to visit Margaret. His powers as a scholar, honed by years of careful labor, were at their peak. The first lecture was on the study of Armenian musical notation (*khaz*); the second, on Armenian folk music; the third, on the distinctive features of Armenian musical structures. At the request of the conference members, Komitas, with the assistance of Margaret Babaian, then organized an evening of performances by Paris's most prominent Armenian musicians, among them Margaret herself and the singer Armenag Shahmuratian. Held in the intimate surroundings of the Saint Jean-Baptist Armenian Church, the concert quickly transcended mere scholarly interest: many members of this audience of academics later claimed to have been deeply moved by what they heard, to the point of experiencing the spirit of the Armenian people and the urgency of their plight. "When Komitas sat at the piano to sing," remarked Frédérick Mahler, a professor of music at the Sorbonne, "the audience was frozen in silence by the majestic charm that flowed from the Armenian songs." At the end of the evening, Professor Adler of Vienna felt compelled to declare to Komitas that "if God does not hear the pleas of the Armenians, whose will he hear?"[4]

With these arresting presentations, Komitas was able to convince the musicians and musicologists attending the conference that the core of Armenian Church music had proven remarkably resistant to foreign influence over the centuries, and could therefore serve as a crucial reference point for studying the ancient music of the Romans, Greeks, and Assyrians.[5] Frédérick Mahler immediately recognized the value of Komitas's contribution to musical scholarship, and recorded his reaction to the lectures in a book entitled *Music in Armenia*: "Father Komitas's work has immense credibility because of his field trips . . . [he] was able to distinguish Armenian music from other regional influences, i.e. Arabic, Persian, Turkish, and Kurdish . . . . He was able to find [its] proper harmonic structure."[6]

While he was in Paris, Komitas recorded twenty folk songs and canticles ("Hayasdan," "Bom! Porodan," "Grung," "Der Getso,"

"Mayr Araxi," "Hov Arek," among others), singing some of them himself and in others accompanying Armenag Shahmuratian on the piano.[7] Because these recordings were soon being advertised in Armenian papers in Constantinople, certain members of the Armenian National Church Assembly once again felt compelled to publish their displeasure at Komitas's "commercialization" of sacred church property:

> In view of the fact that Father Komitas has put on sale the canticles belonging to the Holy Church . . . and [that] they are being sung everywhere . . . we ask the Catholicos to reprimand him for this disgraceful behavior.[8]

This request quickly caused uproar in the Armenian intellectual circles of Constantinople, and a heated debate on the matter ensued in the Armenian press.[9] So intense was the reaction that the church finally relented: by the time Komitas returned to Constantinople in July 1914, the Council members had already publicly retracted their statement. Nevertheless, Komitas felt wounded again and compelled to defiance. His interview with Hagop Jololian Siruni, an Armenian journalist assigned to cover his activities for the Constantinople-based periodical *Azadamard*, shows just how weary and resolute he had become in the face of controversy. Siruni notes how

> [Komitas's] voice dropped, his enthusiasm vanished, you could see bitterness in his eyes, then you could see indifference slipping in when he continued: "I have a path to follow, and I will follow it. Nobody can stop me, as long as I have energy. I believe in the mission that I follow."[10]

It was not long before yet another debate erupted in the news, this time over whether or not there existed a purely Armenian musical tradition. It was provoked by the publication in Paris of an encyclopedia of music that made no reference to Armenian music. Komitas was invited to give his professional opinion, but he could only express his growing exacerbation with such quarrels:

> Most of the material of our ancient music is not researched, collected, studied, nor debated . . . an encyclopedia of music is a dictionary, that will be re-edited and published . . . but what concerns me is that I have no time for this kind of arid discussion in daily newspapers. I have better things to do. Leave me alone so I can work.[11]

But politics could not be evaded so easily in the period of upheaval. As he would soon discover, the political atmosphere of his native country was capable of producing inexorable nightmares—nightmares that would engulf him and millions of his fellows Armenians, and haunt him for the rest of his life.

In September 1914, Komitas left Constantinople for Berlin, where he spent a pleasant month. As he attended the daily performances of Wagner's work at the Berlin opera house,[12] he had no reason to think that when he returned home in October he would be walking into a death trap devised by the Turkish government to wipe out the Armenians of the Ottoman Empire.

The tension was growing. For centuries the fortunes of Armenians living in the Ottoman Empire were directly related to those of the empire itself. As long as it remained powerful and stable, its Armenian subjects were allowed to live in relative tranquillity. But as the government succumbed to reckless spending habits and corruption over the course of the eighteenth and nineteenth centuries, eventually bringing it to bankruptcy in 1874 and forcing it to accept European supervision of its finances, the treatment of the Armenians rapidly worsened. They were burdened with extortionate taxes that left many of them destitute and near starvation. Even more ominous were the many government sanctioned cases of murder, rape, vandalism, and persecution, particularly in the provinces. Government officials, soldiers, and members of the populace who had been incited by the authorities perpetrated these acts. All of this left the Armenian people terrified, demoralized, and angry.

Armenian leaders pleaded with the government for protection from corruption and violence. But to allay suspicions that they might be organizing some seditious campaign for national autonomy, they made repeated pledges of allegiance to the ruling sultans.

Komitas with his Constantinople pupils, c. 1913

For a brief time their hopes were raised by international developments. The European powers had begun to express serious concerns about the treatment of Christian peoples in both Asia Minor and the Balkans, who had been suffering under Ottoman rule. In response, Sultan Abdul-Hamid (1876–1909) made a show of support for a new constitution that had been drafted by proponents of reform. This perfunctory display of good will was short-lived when the 1877–1878 Russo-Turkish war erupted and the victorious Russian army came within fifteen miles of Constantinople, the Sultan suspended the constitution. In a desperate attempt to protect their people, leaders of the Armenian communities sought international assistance. They requested that provisions for their security be included in the forthcoming peace negotiations between the two countries. The results were encouraging: the treaty of San Stefano, signed in 1878, stipulated that the withdrawal of Russian troops was contingent on guarantees from the Turks that reforms would be carried out in the Armenian homelands.

The rivalry between Czarist Russia and Great Britain caused these provisions to be radically modified at the Berlin Conference, convened towards the end of the same year. Once again, the promised reforms remained on paper.

Eventually Sultan Hamid had decided upon a more drastic method for dealing with the "Armenian problem." In 1894, the Armenians of the district of Sassun, who had been refusing to pay taxes to local Kurdish chieftains, were massacred and the tide of violence against Ottoman Armenians began to rise again. The historian Richard Hovannisian observes:

> The slaughter of between 100,000 and 200,000 Armenians, the forced religious conversion of the population of scores of villages, the looting and burning of hundreds of other settlements, and the coerced flight into exile of countless Armenians were Abdul-Hamid's actual response to European meddling.[13]

The Ittihad Party finally overthrew Hamid's government in 1908, and the ascension of the "Young Turks" to power was heralded by slogans of equality and liberty for all the peoples of the empire. Secretly, however, the Young Turks envisioned the creation of an ethnically "pure" Turkish state, free of "foreign" peoples. This looming threat to the already besieged Armenians was compounded by the outbreak of the First World War, when Turkey chose to ally itself with Germany against Russia. With the Armenian homelands straddling the border between Turkey and Russia, Armenians were in peril no matter what the outcome.

The Turks were embittered after losing the Balkan War of 1912, and with it vast amounts of land formerly under Ottoman control. European interest in the well being of the Armenians, who had for decades been enjoying a sweeping cultural renaissance, only angered them further. The "Armenian question" was an internal issue, they declared, to be solved by their own methods. With the outbreak of the First World War, the Turks seized the opportunity to put a swift and brutal end to the matter. A state of emergency was declared: all Armenians were required to surrender their "arms," including even kitchen knives. The government justified this move by accusing Armenians of "collaboration" with Russia, which was the enemy.

If the Armenian citizens of the Ottoman Empire complied and surrendered their weapons, they were accused of having conspired against the government and, in many cases, summarily executed; if they did not comply and were caught, the results were the same. At the beginning of the persecutions hundreds of thousands of Armenian men were ordered to report to police stations under the pretext of drafting them as soldiers; most of them never returned. As the Turkish author Taner Akçam has pointed out, it was with "the pretext of searching for arms, of collecting war levies, of tracking down deserters" that the Turks established "a practice of systematically carried-out plunders, raids, and murders" against Armenians.[14]

The large Armenian communities of Constantinople and Smyrna were horrified by the reports that trickled out of the provinces and immediately resorted to diplomacy in an attempt to restore stable relations with the Turkish government. Representatives of various segments of the Armenian community pleaded with the Turkish authorities to stop the killings, declaring their loyalty to the government and pledging their commitment to the war effort.

Despite these frantic efforts, many of the Armenian intellectuals living in Constantinople believed that it was only a matter of time before they would be hunted down like their fellow Armenians in the provinces. The city was filled with rumors that agents of the police had been sent special envelopes containing lists of prominent Armenian artists and thinkers who were slated for persecution, and that these agents were merely awaiting the order to begin the mass arrests.[15] The fear was reinforced by the intense religious fervor that was sweeping the Muslim soldiers of the Turkish Army. As Komitas's friend Siruni remembers:

> In Constantinople there were demonstrations against the Christians every day. Komitas's house had a view of the street where most of the demonstrations took place, and he could hear the soldiers sing:
>
> Don't ask me where I am going
> I am going to the war
> You can't hear the Ezan any more
> There are crosses on the roofs
> The infidel Russians have their flags even on the mosques.[16]

Notes to Chapter Six: The Crisis Looms

1. Matevos Muratian, ed., "Komitasi Andib Namagnere" [Unpublished Letters of Komitas], *Badmapanasiragan Hantes* 17 (Yerevan), no. 1 (1958): 265–266.
2. Ambassador Henry Morgenthau went on to document the Armenian Genocide and later published his memoirs, in which he described the atrocities. See: Henry Morgenthau, *Ambassador Morgenthau's Story* (New York: New Age, 1975).
3. A number of these students soon distinguished themselves. Their careers were built on the foundations that Komitas had laid for them, just as his own career was based on the work of Gara-Murza and Yegmalian: Barsegh Ganachian went on to become a composer and choirmaster in Beirut, renowned for his performances of Komitas's songs. Vartan Sarxian traveled to

Paris and took up the responsibility of editing and publishing Komitas's work. And Mihran Toumajan, perhaps the most faithful in following the example of his master, moved to the United States and became an ethnomusicologist, collecting and transcribing the folk songs remembered by the Armenian refugees who had fled there after the Genocide. See: Matevos Muratian, "Azkayin Yerazheshdagan Uzheri Badrasdman Komitasian Tsêrakrere" [Komitas's Plans in Preparing National Music Cadres], in *Komitasagan*, vol. 1, edited by Robert Atayan et al (Yerevan: ARMSSR Academy of Sciences, 1969): 239.

4. Mahler and Adler quoted in K.N. Kasbarian, "Komitas: Gensakragan Agnarg" [Komitas: Biographical Sketch], in K.N., Kasbarian ed., *Zhamanagagitsnere Komitasi Masin* [Contemporaries on Komitas], (Yerevan: Haybedhrad, 1960): 30.
5. *Ibid.*, 29.
6. *Ibid.*, 32–33.
7. Recent reissues of these recordings state that they were made in 1912. The Armenian press of the time, however, indicates that they were made in 1914.
8. Quoted in A. Oghlukian, ed., *Kragan Nêshkhark Komitas Vartabedi Peghun Kêrchen* [Literary Fragments from Komitas Vartabed's Prolific Pen], (Montreal: Canadian Diocese of the Armenian Church, 1994): 30.
9. D. Chengurian and P. Terlemezian, "Gronagan Zhoghovi Voroshume" [The Decision of the National Church Assembly], *Puzantion* (Constantinople), no. 5370 (1914): 2; Archag Tchobanian, "Angron Voroshum Me" [A Sacrilegious Decision], *Puzantion* (Constantinople), nos. 5384 and 5385 (1914): 1; Sadrushan, "Komitas Vartabede yev Gronagan Zhoghove" [Komitas Vartabed and the Church Assembly], *Puzantion* (Constantinople), no. 5393 (1914): 1; Levon Tchilingarian, "Komitas Vartabed," *Puzantion* (Constantinople), no. 5397 (1914): 1.
10. H.J. Siruni, "The Victory of Armenian Music: An Interview with Komitas," in *Hotvadzner yev Usumnasirutyunner* [Articles and Studies] (Yerevan: Haybedhrad, 1941): 198.
11. Ibid., 198.
12. Matevos Muratian, ed., "Komitasi Andib Namagnere" [Unpublished Letters of Komitas], *Badmapanasiragan Hantes* 17 (Yerevan), no. 1 (1958): 266.
13. Richard Hovannisian, "The Historical Dimensions of the Armenian Question: 1878–1923," in *The Armenian Genocide in Perspective,* edited by Richard Hovannisian (Oxford: Transaction, 1986): 25.
14. T. Akçam, *Türk Ulusal Kimligi ve Ermeni Sorunu* [Turkish National Identity and the Armenian Question] (Istanbul: Baski, 1992): 109.
15. H.J. Siruni, "Komitasi Hed" [With Komitas], *Etchmiadzin* (Etchmiadzin) (March 1968): 43.
16. H.J. Siruni, "Komitasi Hed" [With Komitas], *Etchmiadzin* (Etchmiadzin) (February 1968): 50. The "Ezan" is the Muslim call to prayer.

# 7

# Death-Camp and Breakdown 1915

Under this cloud of religious and political terror, Komitas, who had returned to Constantinople in October of 1914 after a month of freedom in Berlin, buried himself in work. In a letter to an acquaintance he wrote: "To spare my mind and my feelings as much as possible from the atrocities of these times, I am working incessantly. . . ."[1]

The presence of friends and colleagues made this anxious period bearable. Dikran Chituni, an Armenian who had recently moved to Constantinople, worked with him throughout December 1914, assisting him with his labor of love, the transcription of Armenian folk songs. It was not the first time the two had collaborated. Their friendship had begun five years earlier, during the ceremonies surrounding the elevation of Mateos II to the office of Catholicos in 1909, when Chituni came to Etchmiadzin as a delegate representing the Vasburagan region of Armenia. At the time they had quickly established the lively partnership that would flourish again in the dark days of late 1914. As Chituni recounts in his memoirs of Komitas,[2] the two had sat together for hours in Komitas's room in Etchmiadzin, surrounded by the monk's books, papers, and vast collection of musical instruments, while Chituni sang the many peasant songs he had learned in his native Vasburagan.

> I sang line by line and he transcribed . . . then he went to the piano and played what he had transcribed, and he wanted me to correct his transcriptions. At times he used the violin, or the duduk; often he just sang them himself . . . [3]

As the shadows of impending catastrophe gathered over Constantinople in 1914, Komitas and Chituni spent days immersed in the task at hand. Once again Chituni sang the peasant songs that he had learned, and Komitas, with his apparently inexhaustible energy, transcribed each of them. This time they developed the folk themes into songs for young children, managing to complete about forty of them.[4]

Komitas's frantic attempts to protect himself psychologically in an environment charged with the threat of communal madness and violence also propelled him to form a small chorus. In a public show of religious tolerance by the publicity conscious Turkish government, several of his pupils had been exempted from conscription on the grounds that they were deacons in the church. With the help of these students, Komitas devoted the early weeks of 1915 to reorganizing the choir of the Galata church, which he hoped to conduct during the approaching Easter celebrations.

In late March, only weeks before he would be swept up in the purges inflicted on Armenians, Komitas was invited to entertain the people who were about to betray him and his colleagues. As part of a campaign launched by the government of "Young Turks" to promote Turkish nationalism and identity, a group of Turkish intellectuals organized an evening of music, poetry and speeches. In many respects, it was an attempt to raise the international profile of the new Turkey, to show the world—and particularly Europe, where the perception of Turks as a rapacious people was widespread—that they were a people of high cultural attainment. Horrified by this invitation, Komitas felt he had no choice but to accept.

No other Armenian was offered an official invitation to this "celebration" of culture. Nevertheless, Hovaness Manoogian, an

Armenian doctor succeeded in obtaining tickets from a colleague, and years later, in a letter to the journalist H.J. Siruni, he described the events of that evening:

> The motorcades of the guests started to arrive . . . the hall was packed . . . the prince, Talaat Bey and other higher government functionaries were there . . . writers, scientists and Muslim clergymen came in one by one . . . I knew Komitas Vartabed from before . . . but he looked so changed, so pale and sad. The master of ceremonies, Hamdullah Subhi, introduced Komitas and said . . . "This son of Anatolia, an Armenian clergyman has, with his dedication and hard work, given wings to Armenian music . . . he ignored comfort and luxury and spent his time in the villages collecting folk songs . . . and presented those songs as part of the Armenian national heritage . . . . If only our clergy did the same thing. I wonder what treasures they would find, treasures that could elevate the value of the sensitive heart and the thinking mind of the Turkish nation . . . . The truth . . . is that the Armenian nation remains on the frontier of our cultural life. Wherever you go in Turkey, in any corner of Anatolia, the Armenian mind, the creative Armenian mind and hand will greet you and tell you 'I am here.' If you go to the palaces of the sultans, the architects are Armenians . . . . The tombstones of your loved ones, which are so finely carved, are the works of Armenian masters . . . . Armenian masters also make the world-famous jewelry boxes from Van. The founders of the medical school and the writers of scientific books are also Armenians . . . . These are the people with whom we have lived for centuries . . . ." Then Komitas sat at the piano and sang and played . . . . The hall reverberated with the ovations and applause . . . and you could hear shouting . . . "God save him from evil eyes . . . ."[5]

Only three weeks after this gathering, the government's genocidal campaign against Armenians was officially launched. Komitas found himself directly in its path, as did several thousand prominent Armenians in Constantinople. On April 24, 1915, Talaat Bey's Interior Ministry ordered the arrest of more than two hundred Armenian leaders suspected of harboring Armenian "nationalist sentiments." According to the sociologist Vahakn Dadrian, "in a matter of weeks 2,345 such leaders were arrested [in Constantinople] only to be executed subsequently in large part. A large number of them were neither nationalist nor in any way involved in politics. None of them was charged with wartime sabotage, espionage, or any other crime . . . ."[6] The "Red Harvest" of April 1915 had begun.[7]

Komitas's intuition had warned him of the coming terror. On the eve of his arrest, he had had a premonition in a dream that "something bad [was] going to happen." But his mood was fatalistic. He told Siruni of the dream and Siruni advised him to leave the city or, at the very least, to change his address, but he replied, "Let be what is going to be."[8] On the night of April 24, agents of the Turkish secret police descended on Komitas's house and arrested him without charges. He surrendered without protest, as if he had long expected their arrival.

During that night and over the course of the coming weeks, the strategy used by those who arrested Komitas was deployed on thousands of other occasions in thousands of other Armenian households. Aram Andonian, a young Armenian who was once arrested on the charge of spreading news of Turkish massacres,[9] expresses this in the powerful memoir he later wrote of the fate that he and Komitas shared during the "Red Harvest."[10]

> The arrest of Komitas Vartabed was not different in any way from many arrests carried out during that night. When I returned home, which was only a few blocks away from [Komitas's], my family did not know of anything. Usually, the arrests were made in a very courteous manner. An invitation was offered by a plain-clothes policeman to go to the local police station in order to answer a few questions for the police commissioner, which would not take more than five minutes . . .[11]

The following morning, Komitas's housekeeper, Varbed Garabed, went to the nearby house of Dr. Avedis Nakashian and informed him that Komitas had been taken away by the police.

Shocked by this news, Nakashian said he would go to the police station to inquire about the matter. Before he could do so, he too was arrested.

In this way, the majority of Constantinople's prominent Armenian citizens, on whom the Armenian population of Turkey depended for guidance and support, were rounded up: scholars and musicians like Komitas, parliamentary deputies and lawyers, writers and artists, doctors, journalists, and members of the clergy.[12] Andonian later noted that

> Some of us, like myself, suspected that these arrests would lead to exile. But we were not sure; our group was not homogenous. There were people with us whom we had never seen before. It was not possible that they played a role in national or governmental affairs.[13]

Among the most bewildered of the new prisoners was Dr. Dikran Allahverdi, a distinguished member of the Ittihad Party who, as Andonian explains, had raised large sums of money for the "Young Turks." Allahverdi was unable to recognize the gravity of the situation and asked a guard to inform the commissioner that given the lateness of the hour he would appreciate being asked the necessary questions so that he could return home to bed.[14]

No one in the group of roughly twenty prisoners—a group that now included Komitas, who was already being held at the station when Andonian arrived there—suspected the severity with which they were to be treated. Komitas, says Andonian, thought the whole thing was a "joke" that would be brought swiftly to an end by the allied intervention, the Armenian Patriarchate of Constantinople, the National Assembly, Armenian members of the Ottoman parliament, and foreign ambassadors. Indeed, it was Komitas's optimism that served to comfort Vahram Torkomian, a physician, who, ironically, was to become one of Komitas's chief caretakers when he descended into mental illness.[15] Torkomian had been frightened and depressed by the ordeal of his arrest and had spent the night in tears, convinced that he was to be among the first victims of whatever terrible fate awaited them.

The next morning, Andonian recalls, a Turkish functionary armed with a list of names appeared before the prisoners to take roll call. The men laughed when his inability to pronounce the Armenian names caused him to read them in ways that were often comical, and sometimes telling. When he came to Komitas's name, for example, he called out "Komitaji Rahib," meaning "revolutionary priest." Incensed by the mistake, Komitas responded with "*Mevdouj, mevdouj*," a sarcastic distortion of *mevjoud*, the word for "present." But the seriousness of the prisoners' situation soon became apparent. A portion of bread was allotted to each of them, a sure sign that their stay was not to be a short one, and that the policemen around them were their captors. Andonian remembers seeing Komitas at this moment, a piece of bread tucked under his arm, refusing offers of cheese, olives, dried figs, and boiled eggs that some of his fellow inmates had bought from the jail's supply store.[16]

It was then announced that each of the detainees would be permitted to write notes in Turkish to family members or friends, requesting food, money, extra clothing, bedding, and so on. Komitas sent two brief letters: one most probably to his housekeeper Varbed Garabed, the other to the American Embassy in Constantinople, which he hoped would negotiate his release.[17] As the hours passed, some of the prisoners began to joke about the events of the day and teased those among them who were most obviously stricken with fear and pessimism. Vahram Torkomian was one of the main targets of these jibes, and he later observed that he would not have been able to fend for himself had it not been for the kindness that Komitas had shown him the night before by staying awake and speaking calmly with him.[18]

As night set in, the hopes of the prisoners, many of who were now on the brink of despair, would be raised again when remarkable events took place outside in Constantinople. "That same night," Andonian recalls, "the city was bombed by the allied forces, English, French and Russians, increasing our hopes for the demise of the government and therefore for our freedom."[19] The prisoners, of whom there were now more than two hundred, settled in for the evening, lulled by a sense of false hope that was reinforced by the apparent leniency of the guards.[20] Andonian remembers seeing Dr. Torkomian "in the right corner of the hall," taking the coat his wife had brought to him earlier that day and spreading it over his bed in order to keep warm.[21]

Whatever respite they may have experienced was quickly disrupted. Two guards entered suddenly and ordered them to gather their belongings. When the bewildered prisoners asked what this meant, the guards repeated the order and left. "A cacophony had erupted in the courtyard of the jail," says Andonian,

> which was now crowded by prisoners from the Kovush [another of the prison's halls]. Those of us who had no luggage and had not yet gotten undressed were the first to join them . . . . There was a large crowd jammed near the door [that opened onto the courtyard] . . . . There were many lanterns lit in the courtyard, burning uselessly, but no one had thought of hanging any here . . . . The long and narrow hallway leading to the courtyard was dark as well. We had to pass through this hallway to arrive in the huge courtyard, where they were going to gather us and announce their decision.[22]

Agitated by the prospect of release, many of the prisoners began to press toward the narrow entranceway. "Finally, we were obliged to stop. It was impossible to move forward. But the pushing continued . . . the winemaker Onnig's voice was heard: 'What is your hurry?' he shouted, 'we're not going to a wedding.'"[23] It was then that Andonian saw Dr. Torkomian, who had taken time to dress himself carefully. "He looked completely confused, and was addressing this person and that for news about what was happening."[24]

"The joke was over," Andonian continues:

> The narrow hallway . . . was suddenly lit. And as best we could tell from a distance, soldiers lined the walls . . . guns in their hands with bayonets fixed to them. We saw a

> group of high-ranking officers in the middle of the hallway . . . I recognized three of them immediately. One was the director of the political division [*ghesme seyasi*], Reshad Bey; the other was Ibrahim, director of the central jail; and the third was the chief of police, Bedri Bey . . . .[25]

The prisoners were told to come forward when their names were called. Because the first to be called were well-known political activists, some of the remaining detainees began to hope that only these men would be held and the rest let go. But soon the names of non-activists were announced, and the faint possibility of release vanished. (This first group, numbering seventy-one in total, were eventually sent to a concentration camp at Ayash.)

After a pause of fifteen minutes or so, Andonian recalls, "it was our turn, and our names were read out by the men. First was Diran Kelegian, then the three clergymen, Balakian, Hovnan Garabedian, and Komitas, in that order."[26] When Andonian was called, he passed along the line of soldiers and entered the courtyard in time to see the tail end of a convoy of trucks carrying away the prisoners of the first group. Eventually, he says, "our group outnumbered the first. There were a further fifty-one of us. The calculation during the day brought [the total] number to one hundred and ninety-seven."[27]

The soldiers, having goaded the last of their charges into the courtyard, left the narrow entranceway and passed through the main gates of the prison, followed by a group of non-commissioned officers and prison guards. The order was then given for the prisoners to leave the courtyard. "There were exactly one hundred and twenty-two of us," Andonian writes, "and leaving wasn't an easy task, for everyone wanted to move through the door . . . ."[28] There were no trucks awaiting them outside. Instead, the road was lined on both sides by soldiers who brandished rifles equipped with serrated bayonets. These men, all of them graduates of the Harbiye military college and fervent Ittihadist nationalists, threatened and otherwise verbally abused the prisoners to "put our big disorderly group into order."[29]

It soon became clear that the prisoners were to make the half-hour march to Serayburnu, a small port town with a grisly reputation as a dumping-ground for those who displeased the "Young Turks": here disgraced government employees and undesirable women from the sultan's harems often were placed in bags filled with stones and thrown into the sea.[30] Realizing that Serayburnu was to be their destination, the prisoners began to panic, and many broke down in tears. With the order to march and the sound of the soldiers' boots "hitting the dry pavement with the unnerving, monotonous tick-tacking of a clock," the group moved forward "with the instinctual orderliness of sheep," devoid of will and courage. At this point, writes Andonian, "We had become puppets, manipulable to their satisfaction."[31]

Awaiting them at the docks of Serayburnu was a steamship that had been rented by the Ottoman government from the Shirketi Khayriye Company. Ironically, the vessel was one of the newest and most luxurious in the company's fleet. Shortly after midnight, the prisoners jostled and shoved as the soldiers prodded them on board, where they found the men of the first group—those who had been transported from the jail in trucks—being held.[32] Andonian succeeded in maneuvering himself into the first-class salon. There he found Komitas, with his carefully guarded air of stoicism, sitting alongside Dr. Torkomian, Diran Kelegian, and Hayg Khojasarian. Eventually they were joined by Puzant Kechian, the editor of the newspaper *Puzantion*. Agents of the secret police were now moving about the ship, cursing and threatening the prisoners.[33]

As the ship's whistle announced their departure, Torkomian gazed tearfully at the distant silhouette of Constantinople. "I won't see you again," he said. They sat him down beside Komitas, who had withdrawn completely into himself and stared at a point on the floor. Nearby, a man named Sako sat rocking back and forth. "We are in deep trouble, he repeated softly."[34]

They were being ferried eastward across the Bosporus, the strait that connects the Black Sea to the Sea of Marmara and divides the city of Constantinople in two.[35] The journey lasted three-quarters of an hour. When the ship docked at Haydar Pasha in the early-morning darkness and the men were ordered through the gangways and onto shore, they found themselves faced with soldiers in formation, lining the way from the dock to the large railway-station nearby. Andonian saw Ibrahim Efendi, the warden of the central jail, hurrying ahead of them. He also noticed that the high-ranking officers commanding the troops were standing in a position of salute, apparently in recognition of the row of dispirited prisoners—a bizarre detail that caused one of the prisoners to call out sarcastically, "What an honor, man!"[36]

The railway-station was brightly lit and filled with soldiers and policemen. All the exits had been blocked. The prisoners, most of whom were exhausted and hungry, now saw that exile was certain, but their destination remained the secret of their captors. Then, surrounded by guards, Ibrahim Efendi appeared in the center of the hall. His announcement was brief: only that their departure was imminent. Once again the men began to seek out friends and acquaintances, forming themselves into small tightly-knit groups. Komitas and his two fellow clergymen, Keropian and Balakian, along with Dr. Torkomian, Dr. Jevehirian, Dr. Nakashian, and the pharmacist Narkilejian stood together nervously. After less than an hour, the one hundred and ninety-three prisoners were loaded onto a train commandeered for the purpose, and began their journey of exile into the heart of the state to which they belonged as citizens.[37]

At sunrise the train came to a halt at the ancient city of Nicomedia (Izmit). Komitas and his fellow clerics, hoping that this was to be their destination, wrote out a letter to the government, requesting that they be housed in the nearby Armash Monastery.[38] It was not long before they realized the futility of this attempt to gain some control over their fate, for the train was soon moving again.

Night had fallen by the time they pulled into the city of Eskishehir. Soldiers surrounded the train and remained in place during the two hours that it sat in the station. Their intimidating presence was counterbalanced by the courageous intervention of Armenian railway-workers at the Eskishehir station. Realizing the nature of the train's "cargo," these men quietly collected the names of some of those on board, intending to notify the Patriarchate in

Aram Andonian

Constantinople. This extremely risky endeavor was repeated again and again over the course of the Genocide, and enabled the escape of a large number of Armenian exiles.

Not long after midnight the train was moving again, and rumors passed among the prisoners that they were headed for Ankara. A deep exhaustion had set in, and soon almost all of the men, along with several of their guards, were asleep.[39] When they awoke, the train had stopped short of Ankara, in a deserted area near Sinan Köy. On the unpaved road outside was a line of horse-drawn carts of the kind used to transport goods. At this moment, reappeared Ibrahim Efendi and read out a list of names, the same list that had been used to gather the initial group of seventy-one prisoners at the jail in Constantinople. These men, many of whom had been among the most outspoken and overtly political members of Constantinople's Armenian community, were ordered to leave the train and board the carts. They would carry them to Ayash, a town whose name was familiar to none of the captives. The carts were still being loaded when the train began to roll forward again; the prisoners who remained on board wondered what this division of their numbers meant.[40] Eventually, one of the guards told them that the men of the first group were being taken to the military base in Ayash.[41]

Another two hours brought the train to Ankara, a city with a large Armenian population, where the hopes of the prisoners were raised for the final time. At last they were allowed to leave the wagon cars in which they had been confined for almost a day and a half, and from the courtyard of the station they could see the city's vineyards, touching them with the hope that they would remain here to serve out their time for the crimes that their captors had yet to specify. The men were ushered into the station's two waiting-rooms (Ibrahim Efendi made a point of inviting the more prominent members of the group, including Komitas, into the first-class area), where responsibility for them was to be transferred to Ankara's chief of police, Behaeddin Bey, a man who was soon to gain a reputation for ruthlessness in robbing and killing the Armenians of Ankara and the surrounding regions.[42] Eventually, Behaeddin Bey's well-dressed silhouette appeared in the doorway, and the announcement was made that the group was to be exiled at Chankiri, 160 kilometers away. They were to travel there in carts, a journey that would take three days.

The name of the town was familiar to the Armenians, all of whom knew Dikran Chukhadjian's comic operetta *Leblebiji horhor agha*, in which one of the central characters hails from Chankiri. In a moment of frenzied humor, as the prisoners were led out to the line of forty-two carts that awaited them, a tune from the operetta rose from the group's back row. Komitas, who was walking near the front, kept turning repeatedly to look at the singers and encourage them with his smile.[43]

The sun was warm. Fifteen hours had passed since the prisoners had been allowed to eat, and none of them refused the portions of bread that the guards now distributed. The group was then told to

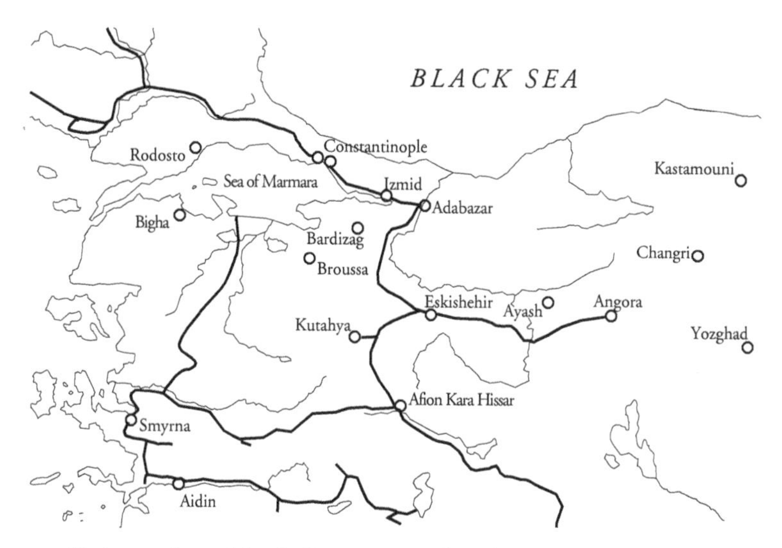


Path to exile and death. Route to Ayash and Chankiri, April 1915

board the carts, a few of which were relatively comfortable (including the one in which Komitas found himself seated); most were ramshackle affairs with wooden floors, so narrow that the men were forced to sit with their legs folded. Three prisoners were assigned to each cart, along with a soldier armed with a rifle and bayonet. Each of the drivers was also accompanied by a soldier brandishing weapons. As the convoy prepared to depart, local merchants approached offering boiled eggs, garlic, onions, olives, and halva. The policemen surrounding the carts encouraged the captives to buy as much as they could afford: the journey would be long and the opportunities to purchase food scarce.[44]

The caravan and its contingent of two dozen mounted gendarmes set out in the early afternoon. Andonian remembers that the two soldiers assigned to his cart, in which he sat with Hayg

Khojasarian and an old priest, poked fun at the ignorance of the government. The caravan made its way through the outskirts of Ankara and onto the road to Chankiri along a route obviously devised for the purpose of minimizing the number of witnesses to its passing. The first two hours of travel were not uncomfortable, says Andonian; the soldier sitting with them sang as they drove along smooth, well-maintained stretches of road. But soon the way became pitted with potholes and the men were often jolted from the floor of the cart, constantly trying to avert being thrown accidentally onto the soldier's exposed bayonet.[45] The road and the surrounding fields were virtually deserted. Brief moments of respite occurred when the caravan was halted because of a mechanical problem or a fallen horse.[46]

At four p.m. the caravan drew up to the first scheduled stop: Ravli Khan, a decrepit rest station where the drivers and gendarmes were to water their horses. The surrounding region was infamous for its bandits and smugglers. The station was a windowless two-story structure blackened by weather and neglect.[47] Andonian reports that by this point a number of the captives had begun to show signs of mental collapse. The behavior of one in particular, Dr. Krikor Jelali was deemed by the guards to be so potentially disruptive that it posed a threat to the safety of the group.[48] It was here too, as Andonian notes, that the "drama" of Komitas's breakdown began to unfold.[49]

The prisoners climbed down from the carts and sat in the breezy meadow by the station, rubbing their aching muscles. Hayg Khojasarian went into the station to buy provisions and returned with fresh bread, *khavurma* (fried meat), and *tahin halva* (a sesame sweet). No crushed salt was available for the meat, so the men used salt-crystals, and soon their thirst was overwhelming. There was only one well in the station's square, where an animated dispute had erupted between the drivers and the gendarmes over the order in which the horses (more than one hundred) should be allowed to drink. Seizing the opportunity presented by this distraction, two of the prisoners, Armen Dorian and Mihran Bastermajian, quietly walked away with a bucket of fresh water and brought it over to the group. Andonian remembers that Komitas seemed especially excited by this unexpected luxury, rubbing his hands together and staring at the bucket. But as his turn came to drink, and Dorian and Bastermajian raised the bucket to his lips, a mounted gendarme galloped toward the group. Reaching down from his horse, he wrenched the bucket away from Komitas's face, spilling water over him. "Komitas was stupefied," says Andonian, "unable to move, as if frozen, not noticing the handkerchiefs being offered to him to wipe his face. His eyes, filled with a surprised look, were fixed on the gendarme."[50] After the soldier rode away, Komitas had "an unusual look about him," as if he now regarded everyone around him with terror and suspicion.[51]

Dusk fell and the caravan set out in the direction of nearby Kalejik, where the exiles were to spend the night. Freezing in their thin clothes, the men believed that they would not survive to see Chankiri:

> It was not a road but a dark tunnel where the night was as black as asphalt, where the trees and the rocks on mountain-tops took on the shape of phantoms, and our imaginations turned them into the giants of legends or the monsters of fairy-tales.[52]

Komitas often lapsed into blind panic. Vartabed Krikoris Balakian, a priest who rode in the same cart, later wrote that Komitas "saw gendarmes hiding behind every tree" on the roadside, and that "he would cover his face with his hand and ask his colleagues to say prayers for him, hiding his head under his coat."[53] It was clear to all that he was not well.

They arrived at Kalejik after midnight. The local hostel, another ugly two-story structure, was filled with merchants. Ibrahim Efendi was infuriated and began barking orders to clear the building. As the soldiers moved in brandishing whips, many of the peasants fled without their belongings. The sickest of the prisoners were then taken up to the second floor, where a row of cell-like chambers, filled with smoke from oil lamps, served as bedrooms. Komitas's friends forced him to join this group, all of whom were placed under the care of Dr. Torkomian.[54]

When Komitas emerged from the building the following morning, his friends quickly saw that his behavior had become even more erratic. Standing in the square in front of the hostel, he seemed restless and upset, mumbling constantly to himself in a way that "nobody could understand."[55] When one of the gendarmes passed by, he bowed deeply. Soon he was bowing to others as well.[56] He became especially anxious when a messenger arrived from Ankara with orders that one of the prisoners, Ardzrouni, be transported back to Ankara and then to Ayash. Hearing of this, Komitas was stricken with fear, and asked again and again where the man was being taken. Soon afterwards, as he joined a group of prisoners, he called out suddenly, "Open the way, let him pass." The men turned to see a sickly donkey laboring along the road behind them. Komitas bowed formally to the animal and demanded that his friends do the same.[57]

At approximately eight o'clock on that gloomy morning, under the hardened gaze of the non-commissioned officers, the caravan set out on the twelve-hour trip to Chankiri.[58] During this time Komitas agonized aloud over the thought of the work, the piles of fragile paper, that he had been forced to leave behind in Constantinople, and he frequently cried out in pain. No one could calm him. It was disturbingly clear to those around him that he had been transformed: the man who had begun the ordeal by offering strength and encouragement to others—particularly to his friend Dr. Torkomian[59]—was now broken by feelings of terror and abasement. Decades later, Andonian remained perplexed by this seemingly sudden shift in Komitas's personality, but he was certain that it had begun when Komitas was assaulted by the mounted gendarme at the hostel in Ravli:

> The surprising thing was the difference in Komitas's behavior before the incident and after it. Before the incident with the gendarme, he was almost indifferent, showed no sign of panic . . . on the contrary, he often

> reassured others that it was all a big mistake, a misunderstanding, and would soon be corrected . . . . The incident with the gendarme demolished that calm . . . this was a mystery, difficult to understand . . . [60]

Finally, as dusk descended, the captives pulled into the remote town of Chankiri. Vartabed Krikoris Balakian later described what he and his fellow internees discovered at the end of their terrifying journey: the dark, cavernous basement of a military barracks, with nowhere to rest but a dirty floor.

> But how could we sleep on bare wood, when through the broken windows the freezing northern wind was blowing? Nature took over where human barbarism left off, for in this spring month it snowed, chilling us to our bones, which were already broken from the journey in the carts. But the nightmare of approaching death, like the ghost of a skeleton, was hovering in our confused imaginations.[61]

During the entire process of arrest and internment, the Turks employed the simple technique of unpredictability to inflict terror. Torn suddenly from their families and homes and cast into conditions of squalor and powerlessness, the prisoners were held in a constant state of suspense about their fate.

If the prisoners had known ahead of time what was to happen to them, they would not have been able to take it in. This much is clear in the case of Diran Kelegian. Before the "Red Harvest," he had been a respected university professor and the publisher of a popular Turkish-language newspaper, *Sabah.* He had been arrested in spite of his having taught only at Ottoman institutions and he had never worked for an Armenian newspaper. Arriving at Chankiri, Kelegian discovered that the camp's chief military officer, a man named Asaf, had once been a student of his at the university. Asaf greeted him with respect, Kelegian decided to speak with him privately in the hope of uncovering the motives for the experience he and his colleagues were enduring. According to Balakian Vartabed, who was present at the meeting, Asaf said:

> "Kelegian Efendi [Mr. Kelegian], find a way to get yourself out of here, for soon it could be too late." . . . [Asaf] then showed us a telegram he had received [from Interior Minister Talaat] which read: "Telegraph us immediately, saying how many Armenians are already dead, and how many still alive—Talaat." Then, when we had difficulty comprehending the meaning of the telegram, Asaf explained: "That simply means, how many have you killed so far . . . "[62]

Asaf's advice brought Kelegian to tears. It portended the terrible truth: the majority of the Armenian leaders arrested and interned in the months of April and May 1915, were eventually executed.[63] Kelegian himself was murdered on the way to Sivas, where he was told he was to be court-martialed.[64]

For the present there was the morbid atmosphere of the barracks, a group of buildings that had been deserted by the military after an outbreak of plague.[65] Puzant Kechian, the editor of *Puzantion*, later described how the prisoners tried to cope:

> One hundred and thirty Armenians on a cold night, under the flickering light of a little oil lamp, which deepened the shadows even more, hardly noticing each other . . . were celebrating mass . . . . Their souls completely melted, their senses numbed, the nightmare of uncertainty paralyzed their minds so that they could not guess or did not want to guess what kind of disaster tomorrow's light was hiding from them.[66]

* * * * *

Of the 291 Armenian men who were incarcerated at Chankiri over the course of the "Red Harvest," only forty survived. Komitas, as if by a miracle, was one of them. Abruptly and without official explanation, just thirteen days after his internment, he and seven of his fellow exiles were released from the camp and allowed to return to Constantinople. The reason for this remarkable turn of events remains a mystery. H.J. Siruni claims that the wife of Dr. Vahram Torkomian pleaded with Prince Mejid for the release of both her husband and Komitas. Prince Mejid knew the two prisoners personally: Komitas had been the music teacher of the prince's wife, and Torkomian his personal physician. According to rumor, the American Ambassador in Constantinople, Henry Morgenthau, also intervened on Komitas's behalf in response to the pleas of Arshag Schmavonian, the United States embassy legal adviser who had probably met Komitas when the priest performed there at the invitation of the Ambassador and his wife (it was to Schmavonian that Komitas had written while at the central jail in Constantinople).

For whatever combination of reasons, a coded telegram signed by Talaat himself was issued by the Ministry of the Interior on May 7, 1915:

> The following individuals among the Armenians sent to Kengiri [Chankiri] are to be notified that they are allowed to return to Istanbul [Constantinople]: Dr. Vahram Torkomian, Agop Nargileciyan, Karabet Keropeyan, Zare Bardizbanyan, Pozant Keciyan [Puzant Kechian], Pervant Tolayan, Rafael Karagozyan, and Komitas Vartabed.[67]

The prisoners were not notified of their good fortune until Sunday, May 9, when Komitas was celebrating mass at the Armenian Church in Chankiri where the Armenian inmates of the camp were allowed to attend weekly services. As Kechian later recalled: "While I was at the church and Komitas was celebrating mass, Yervant Tolayan [the prisoner named in the telegram as 'Pervant Tolayan'] informed me that the chief of police desired to meet with me."[68] This struck Kechian as ominous, reminding him of incidents on the journey to Chankiri when prisoners had suddenly been selected from the group and ordered back to Constantinople, to an unknown fate. He went immediately to the chief's office and found the mayor of Chankiri waiting for him there. The mayor handed Kechian the telegram, and said simply, "Your prayers have been answered."[69]

Komitas was still on the altar when Kechian returned to the church. He and Dr. Torkomian approached Komitas, and Kechian, while bowing to kiss the bible, from which the priest was reading out the final passages of the mass, whispered to him the news of their impending release. Komitas, still facing the congregation, was unable to disguise his emotions: his face radiated joy.[70]

Two days later, writes Kechian, "We left Chankiri with tearful eyes, half-happy, half-sad. The friends we left behind were encouraged that this was a good sign, the beginning of their release as well . . . ."[71] Once again seated in horse-drawn carts, the eight men—Komitas, Kechian, Dr. Torkomian, the Reverend Kerovpeyan, the manufacturer Yervant Tolayan, the pharmacist Rafael Karagozyan, the dentist Agop Nargilejian, and Zare Bardizbanian—traced in reverse the route they had taken weeks before. After spending the night in the house of an Armenian family in Kalejik, they set out for Ankara and arrived there late at night. They were taken to quarters prepared for them in the city's Armenian Church, where Komitas was welcomed as a cultural celebrity. The following day, he was invited to celebrate the Easter mass. The church was filled to capacity, as Armenians and Greeks from every sector of the city arrived to see and hear the famous monk. A reception was held in honor of the survivors, and they spent another night in Ankara before they moved on to Eskishehir. On the morning of Saturday, May 14, they boarded a train for Constantinople. They arrived that evening at the Haydar Pasha station, from which they had begun their journey. But their sense of relief had been tempered: on the way from Eskishehir they had heard from Armenian railway workers that Armenians were being taken on forced marches and massacred.

Komitas, Torkomian, and their six compatriots knew that only good fortune, perhaps in the guise of influential friends, had saved them from the fate awaiting those left behind. For these survivors, the knowledge became a crippling psychological burden, as the many later reports of Komitas's emotional state make clear.

One of those who met Komitas soon after his release was his old partner, Dikran Chituni. He had managed to escape the wave of arrests because the police had been unable to find him in

Constantinople. Hearing of Komitas's release, he hurried over to the Torkomian home, where Komitas was dining. Later, as he walked home with Komitas along an empty street where "both our shadows, cast by the moonlight, looked like ghosts from the cemetery," he saw how devastated his friend had been by the weeks in Chankiri. Komitas "was not the same person . . . . It seemed as though something deep down inside him was ruined . . . ."[72]

In her memoirs, Aghavni Mesrobian, a friend and fellow Armenian musician,[73] also describes the distraught, deeply saddened man Komitas had become. When she encountered him in the summer of 1915, he was "disheveled" and had "a horrified expression on his face."[74]

It was at this time that Komitas began a program of fasting, which he dedicated to the "thousands of mothers, sisters and children . . . dying of thirst and hunger" in exile. He also began taking "convoluted routes" through the streets of Constantinople in order to "avoid the possibility of being followed by the secret police."[75]

Now news of the mass deportation of Armenians circulated throughout Constantinople. Already wracked by guilt, images of the innocent trapped, tortured, and exiled, began to haunt him. One image in particular bordered on obsession, for he described it to Chituni on nearly every occasion that they met in the months that followed his return. Early one morning during the agonizing journey to Chankiri, he said,

> . . . I saw a caravan of thousands of displaced Armenians—children, women, old, young—who had spent the night on the hill singing a canticle in unison . . . "Blessed be the morning."[76]

This vision of helpless, frightened folks being led away to exile impressed itself deeply upon his imagination. He was never able to free himself of it. Its hold over him was ominous. But it was unlikely that Komitas actually witnessed this scene. The Ottoman government's program of deportations officially began on May 29,

1915,[77] over three weeks after Komitas was released from Chankiri. None of those who were transported to Chankiri with him—most notably Balakian Vartabed and Aram Andonian—reported seeing such a caravan. Komitas's impression of this scene was produced by reports of the deportations that he heard during and after his return to Constantinople—reports whose descriptions of emotional and physical brutality planted the seeds of detailed visual hallucinations in his unstable mind.

The deep trauma of his incarceration also began to exert a visible influence on his social relationships. When the wives and families of his exiled friends approached him in desperation for news of their loved ones, he was overcome by shame for his freedom and tried to avoid them. If any of his parishioners asked after the fate of the exiles, he would burst into tears and leave at once.

* * * * *

It is clear that during the terrible journey to the death-camp, which involved enough trauma to place enormous strains on even the most stable of psyches, Komitas suffered an episode of what is now called Acute Stress Disorder, a type of psychological stress reaction that is similar in many ways to PTSD but shorter in duration, more acute in onset, and quicker to appear. Just how closely the details of his behavior at this time match our understanding of Acute Stress Disorder is apparent by examining the symptoms that he displayed at this time.

A person afflicted by Acute Stress Disorder is someone who "experienced, witnessed, or was confronted with an event or events that involved actual or threatened death or serious injury to the self or others, and whose response to these events involved intense fear, helplessness, or horror."[78] There can be no question that Komitas had direct experience of such events when he was taken from his home in the middle of the night and brought to Constantinople's central jail, where he discovered that approximately two hundred other prominent Armenians had been arrested as well and charged with threatening the security of the state. As Aram Andonian remembers:

> We really didn't know our destination or our destiny... others in the group were convinced that this was a death sentence, and that sooner or later we were all going to be killed at any place, any time, with one or another excuse . . .[79]

Compounding Komitas's experience of horror was the incident at the rest stop on the road to Chankiri, when the mounted gendarme violently wrenched the bucket of water away from his face. This moment may well have left Komitas feeling as though he had been singled out for brutal treatment.

During or after the distressing event, the individual suffering from Acute Stress Disorder displays symptoms of dissociation—that is, a subjective sense of numbing or shock, a detachment from horrifying emotions and the surrounding environment. Andonian's description of Komitas's behavior immediately after the incident with the gendarme offers strong evidence of this phenomenon: "[Komitas] was frozen; he could not move . . . He was staring motionless at the gendarme who had whipped the bucket of water away... then his gaze froze, and he looked at the ground . . . He seemed calm . . . "[80]

A person suffering from Acute Stress Disorder will also undergo a persistent re-experiencing of the traumatic event; he or she will be haunted by images of it in vivid nightmares and waking "flashbacks" that are provoked by exposure to even the most trivial reminders. There was no shortage of such reminders in the circumstances in which Komitas was trapped. Shortly after the incident with the gendarme, Komitas wandered into the nearby rest-station, where he saw "a young Turkish fellow" wearing a bandage around his head: "Komitas, pointing at him, asked if the gendarme had done this . . . he repeated the same question several times . . . ."[81] Obviously, witnessing the physical suffering of another reminded Komitas immediately of the gendarme's assault, and forced him to relive the cruelty that had been inflicted on him only moments beforehand. The shock and fear that he felt after being assaulted was sustained by the sight of others being victimized. And everywhere he looked, he saw his tormentor pursuing him. According to Father Balakian, who rode in the same cart with Komitas, he began "mistaking the huge trees for lurking and marauding thieves . . . he was hiding his head under the hem of my coat . . . and pleading with me to pray for him, hoping to appease the immense anxiety that had overwhelmed him emotionally."[82]

Torments such as these will inevitably cause the person suffering from Acute Stress Disorder to avoid "stimuli that arouse recollections of the trauma." Again, in Komitas's case the onset of the symptom was virtually immediate. For a considerable period of time beginning shortly after the incident with the gendarme, he refused offers of water: "Komitas didn't want to drink any more and went into the station," Andonian tells us. "Even later, he did not drink when water was offered to him."[83] At this point, even water was a reminder of a significant moment of trauma. It had to be avoided for fear it would force him to relive the incident.

It is not difficult to imagine how a person so paralyzed by fear, so compelled by the desire to conceal himself and prevent any further harm from being done to him, would also display what we understand as symptoms of anxiety, not only about the present but also about what is to come. Komitas was certainly highly nervous throughout the ordeal. "He was worried about his papers and the works that he left behind, what was going to happen to them."[84]

All of these symptoms, says the DSM, combine to cause "clinically significant distress or impairment in social, occupational, or other important areas of functioning . . . ." It is clear from the accounts given of Komitas's behavior at this time, especially the description of him hiding in terror under the hem of Balakian's coat, that he was extremely distressed and socially dysfunctional. Indeed, he appeared completely lost.

Acute Stress Disorder, which typically arises within four weeks of the experience of trauma, can last for between two days and a month. Komitas's "disturbance" began immediately after his violent encounter with the mounted gendarme. The disturbed state continued for "two days and two nights, from April 27 to 29," until their arrival at the site of exile in Chankiri. "Komitas fell in and out of that state, hardly uttering a word."[85]

Finally, the DSM stipulates that in a case of Acute Stress Disorder "the direct physiological effects of a substance (e.g. a drug of abuse, a medication) or a general medical condition" must be ruled out. Komitas suffered no physical disorder before his arrest and exile, and never consumed tobacco, alcohol, or drugs.

All this confirms that at the time of his arrest and internment he suffered an episode of Acute Stress Disorder, a condition widely recognized as a harbinger of PTSD. Psychiatrist David Tomb contends that "those individuals who either acutely or chronically suffer from PTSD-like symptoms are those who had experienced noticeable shock [i.e. an emotionally overwhelmed response] at the time of their trauma."[86] Such a reaction, which has been widely observed in soldiers who have witnessed horrifying events on the battlefield, very often leads to the development of the more chronic symptoms of PTSD. This is precisely what happened to Komitas, and it left him mentally and emotionally disabled for the rest of his life.

* * * * *

Komitas was among the few who survived Chankiri. When he returned to Constantinople on May 15, 1915, the city was the bastion of a regime bent on ruling by terror. Although his exile was relatively short—only three weeks, after which he was officially "free"—he did not feel as though his persecution had ended. To him, Constantinople was a city seething with threats, teeming with undercover agents of a hostile government. "My house feels like a jail," he complained to friends.[87] It was only when he was in a friend's house, "hidden behind the gardens" on the outskirts of the city, that he felt "safe from the undercover agents . . . who are after me day and night . . . ."[88]

His fears were not entirely unfounded. Armenians in Constantinople remained in a state of virtual siege at the hands of the Ottoman government. Many of them were under the close surveillance of the secret police. Groups of them were "suddenly arrested on the streets."[89] Brutal attacks on Armenians by the Turkish police had become a commonplace occurrence in the city, even in broad daylight.[90] It is therefore not surprising that Komitas, whose residence was near the city's central police station where Armenians were routinely subjected to ruthless interrogations, experienced life in Constantinople as an extension of his imprisonment. Release from Chankiri had not brought an end to his trauma.

* * * * *

During this period Komitas's behavior and mental state fulfilled virtually all of the criteria for PTSD. Through nightmares and flashbacks he persistently re-experienced the events that had traumatized him.[91] Indeed, to the bewilderment of those around him, who saw only a friend behaving erratically, Komitas's emotional states were being dictated by events that he was reliving internally. His memories of horror and sadness caused him to display great fear and deep melancholy. To him, they were not recollections but *recurrences*, which were complicated by visual and auditory illusions: on one occasion, for example, he perceived the sound of rain beating on a window as "voices from the sky."[92]

These intense reactions to "cues that symbolize or resemble an aspect of the traumatic event" were in all likelihood not merely psychological but also physiological—for example shivering, becoming pale, and having palpitations. And, as can be expected in a case of PTSD, the "cues" themselves were both internal, in the form of memories, visions, hallucinations, and nightmares, and external. Thus, Komitas developed a "persistent avoidance of stimuli associated with the trauma and numbing of general responsiveness."[93] In an attempt to deaden his painful sensitivity to the world around him, he began to avoid friends and acquaintances that might bring news of the ongoing Genocide. As Garo Ushaklian remembers, with the passing of time Komitas "became more and more upset and silent . . . he received his friends with reluctance."[94] But no matter how great his efforts to elude reminders of the trauma—whether exiling thoughts, feelings, discussions, or even the mere presence of certain people—he could not succeed, for it took very little to reopen his psychological wounds:

> I went to see [Komitas] with a friend . . . [who] told us stories of the lives of deported Armenians. Then he asked Komitas to play for us. While playing, [Komitas] had a strange emotional reaction, although he was trying to keep his composure . . . .[95]

Komitas was suffering from what the DSM describes as "persistent symptoms of increased arousal."[96] He was emotional, irritable, easily distracted, and suspicious. On the increasingly rare nights that he was able to fall asleep, he would wake up suddenly and burst into tears.[97] Most tellingly, when he moved through the streets of Constantinople he was vigilant to the point of paranoia: "Komitas insisted on taking side-streets to avoid imaginary secret police and undercover agents," one of his contemporaries remembers.[98] All of this represented the "impairment in social, occupational, or other important areas of functioning" associated with Posttraumatic Stress Disorder.[99] The same mental disturbances that strained his social relationships also obstructed his creativity. Unable to concentrate, plagued by suspicions, he could no longer function professionally. Not only was he unable to continue his musical work, but he found that serious lapses in his concentration made it impossible for him to fulfill his offices as a priest of the Armenian Apostolic Church. Fear and distress enveloped him to the point that he could no longer feel empathy for those around him. Indeed, on one occasion he countered a request to pray for the sufferings of others with a plea of his own: " . . . but who is going to pray for my misguided soul, and give me some comfort . . . ?"[100]

*****

Komitas's lack of the support and care typically provided by close family relations, along with his deep financial difficulties, reinforced the effects of his trauma. The Armenian Patriarchate of Constantinople, overwhelmed by its role as the leading institution of a people who were being massacred, refused to help, on the grounds that he did not belong to their religious order. Others who survived Chankiri returned to their families and professions. Komitas came home to solitude and poverty.

One of those closest to him at this time was Dikran Chituni. Ten years Komitas's junior, he was the father of six children, the youngest of whom had been born shortly after Komitas returned from Chankiri. He made frequent visits to Chituni's home, where he took delight in the company of the children. The infant, especially, seemed to fascinate Komitas: he would hold her in his arms, stroking her hair and praising her dark, lively eyes. The Chituni's gave him the honor of naming her, and he chose "Hourig," meaning "born out of flames." She was christened on November 20, 1915, with Komitas as her godfather. Afterwards, he came regularly to the Chituni home so that he could play with the child and sing to her.[101] It was as if Hourig's innocence was a shield against the demons that haunted him when he was alone. As Chituni notes, Komitas constantly sought out the company of "humble Armenian families," whose homes he would visit "for supper, for tea, on Sundays and holidays, whenever he was free."[102]

But this was not enough to protect Komitas's fragile mental state from the terrible events unfolding around him. "Although Komitas had been freed from the claws of death and returned to his home," says Chituni,

> His flock was living through a catastrophe of deportation and death .... Seated on his balcony every day, the grief of his nation in his heart, the bloody images of genocide in his heart and mind ... *concerned about future surprises,* horrified at the possibility of being without income or home, Komitas was constantly regressing .... [103] [Chituni's emphasis].

The situation became increasingly grim when Chituni was forced to flee the city. By handing over large sums of money to Turkish officials over the course of many months, he had been able to avoid conscription—not into regular military service, but, like most Armenians, into one of the labor battalions, most of which worked under slave-like conditions and whose members were typically worked to death or executed. Realizing that each of his payments was inevitably followed by yet another notice of conscription, Chituni decided that the only way to prevent the systematic impoverishment of his family was self-imposed exile. He fled Constantinople in the spring of 1916, making his way to Bulgaria disguised as a German soldier on leave.

Shortly after this painful departure, Komitas paid one of his customary visits to the Chituni household. Though he tried to bring cheer to the family, the children stirred up sad memories of his own distant childhood. "He tried to pretend to be happy and cheer up the children," Chituni's wife remembers,

> But he could not keep this game up and broke into tears. He could not fathom this dangerous departure of the father of these young children, left behind without financial means and entirely abandoned [*ander* in Armenian, meaning "without master" or "belonging to no one"] ... He left the house hurriedly without touching any of the food, but promising to come again.[104]

Komitas's identification with the plight of Chituni's children—left *ander,* as he himself had been when his father died—was immediate and devastating. He was no less vulnerable than they were, for he was now virtually without any means of supporting himself.

Notes to Chapter Seven: Death-Camp and Breakdown, 1915

1. Komitas, Letter, 1914, doc. 1369, Komitas Archives, Charents Museum of Literature and Art, Yerevan.
2. Dikran Chituni, "Komitasi Hed" [With Komitas], *Hayrenik*, no. 2 (1936): 80–99.
3. *Ibid.*, 81.
4. *Ibid.*, 87.
5. Manoogian quoted in H.J. Siruni, "Komitasi Hed" [With Komitas], *Etchmiadzin* (Etchmiadzin) (March 1968): 45–46.
6. Vahakn Dadrian, *History of the Armenian Genocide* (Oxford: Berghahn Books, 1995): 221. According to a reliable contemporary source, the number arrested on the eve of April 24th alone was 270. See Teotig, *Amenouyn Daretsouyts* [Everyone's Yearbook] (Constantinople: M. Hovagimian, 1922): 114.
7. The term "Red Harvest" is a symbolic expression coined to reflect the horror of these arrests. The date, on which they began, April 24, is still observed by Armenians around the world as a day of commemoration for the events of the Genocide as a whole.
8. H.J. Siruni, "Komitasi Hed" [With Komitas], *Etchmiadzin* (Etchmiadzin) (January 1968): 48.
9. See: Viscount Gladstone, foreword to "The Memoirs of Naim Bey," by Aram Andonian, in *The Turkish Armenocide,* vol. 2 (Newton Square: Armenian Historical Research Association, 1965): xi-xii.
10. The first installment of Andonian's series of memoirs, *"Komitas Vartabed Aksori Metch: Inch Baymanneru Dag Haydnevetsav ir Mdkin Daknabe"* [Komitas Vartabed in exile: the conditions under which his mental distress appeared], was published in the weekly magazine *Arevmoudk* in December 1946, and the last in June 1947. There were twenty-five installments in all. Although the series appears to have been left unfinished. The vivid detail of Andonian's descriptions raises them to the historical importance of other first-hand chronicles of genocide, most notably Primo Levi's *Survival in Auschwitz.* Andonian was also responsible for publishing the invaluable memoirs of Naim Bey, a Turkish bureaucrat who reacted to the Armenian Genocide by handing over reams of incriminating government documents, telegrams, and decrees. "It is the voice of that conscience concerning the martyrdom that I am making heard in the present publication," wrote Andonian in a preface to this work. "It is a Turk who is going to speak through me—a Turk who was charged with the task of carrying out the policy of exterminating the whole Armenian nation, and through whose hands passed all the official orders of the deportations and massacres." See: "The Memoirs of Naim Bey," in *The Turkish Armenocide*, vol. 2 (Newton Square, Penn.: Armenian Historical Research Association, 1965): x. (For a scholarly discussion of this work, see: Vahakn Dadrian, "The Naim-Andonian Documents," *International Journal of Middle East Studies* 18 (1986): 311–360.)

11. Aram Andonian, "Komitas Vartabed Aksori Metch: Inch Baymanneru Dag Haydnevetsav ir Mdkin Daknabe" [Komitas Vartabed in Exile: The Conditions Under Which His Mental Distress Appeared], *Arevmoudk* (Paris), no. 5 (Dec. 15, 1946): 2.
12. Among those arrested were the dignitaries Vartkes Serengulian, Adom Yerjanian Siamanto, and Krikor Zohrab; the writers Agnuni, Rupen Sevag, Dikran Chegurian, and Taniel Varuzhan, and the actor Yenovk Shahen; the doctors Nazaret Daghavarian and Vahram Torkomian, who would be the man who would be crucial to Komitas's fate; the journalist Puzant Ketchian; and the clergyman Vartabed Krikoris Balakian, who later chronicled the entire series of events. See: Krikoris Balakian, *Hay Koghkotan: Têrvakner Hay Mardirosakrutyunen, Berlinen Der Zor 1914–1920* [The Armenian Golgotha: Episodes from Armenian Martyrdom: From Berlin to Der-zor, 1914–1920], vol. 1 (Vienna: Mkhitarian Press, 1922).
13. Andonian, "Komitas Vartabed Aksori Metch," no. 5 (December 15, 1946): 2
14. *Ibid.*, 3.
15. Andonian, "Komitas Vartabed Aksori Metch" no. 6 (Dec. 22, 1946): 2.
16. Andonian, "Komitas Vartabed Aksori Metch" no. 7 (Jan. 1, 1947).
17. *Ibid.*, 8.
18. Andonian, "Komitas Vartabed Aksori Metch" no. 8 (Jan. 12, 1947).
19. *Ibid.*
20. Andonian, "Komitas Vartabed Aksori Metch," no. 11 (Feb. 2, 1947).
21. Andonian, "Komitas Vartabed Aksori Metch," no. 12 (Feb. 9, 1947).
22. *Ibid.* 7.
23. *Ibid.* 7.
24. *Ibid.*, 8.
25. *Ibid.*, 8.
26. Andonian, "Komitas Vartabed Aksori Metch," no. 13 (Feb. 16, 1947): 7.
27. *Ibid.*, 7–8.
28. Andonian, "Komitas Vartabed Aksori Metch," no. 14 (Feb. 23, 1947): 7.
29. *Ibid.*, 7.
30. *Ibid.*, 7.
31. *Ibid.*, 8.
32. *Ibid.*
33. Andonian, "Komitas Vartabed Aksori Metch," no. 15 (March 2, 1947): 7.
34. *Ibid.*, 7–8.
35. The Bosporus has long served as one of the conceptual boundaries separating Europe from Asia.
36. Andonian, "Komitas Vartabed Aksori Metch," no. 16 (March 9, 1947): 7.
37. Andonian, "Komitas Vartabed Aksori Metch," no. 17 (March 16, 1947): 7.
38. *Ibid.*, 8.
39. Andonian, "Komitas Vartabed Aksori Metch," no. 18 (March 23, 1947): 7–8.
40. Andonian, "Komitas Vartabed Aksori Metch," no. 19 (March 30, 1947): 7–8.

41. Andonian, "Komitas Vartabed Aksori Metch," no. 20 (April 6, 1947): 7–8.
42. *Ibid.*, 7–8.
43. *Ibid.*, 7–8.
44. Andonian, "Komitas Vartabed Aksori Metch," no. 22 (April 20, 1947).
45. *Ibid.*
46. Andonian, "Komitas Vartabed Aksori Metch," no. 23 (April 27, 1947): 7.
47. Andonian, "Komitas Vartabed Aksori Metch," no. 24 (May 4, 1947): 7.
48. Indeed, Jelali's behavior was so erratic that he was eventually sent back to Constantinople.
49. Andonian, "Komitas Vartabed Aksori Metch," no. 23 (April 27, 1947): 7.
50. Andonian, "Komitas Vartabed Aksori Metch," no. 24 (May 4, 1947): 7–8.
51. *Ibid.*, 7.
52. Andonian, "Komitas Vartabed Aksori Metch," no. 26 (May 18, 1947).
53. Balakian, *Hay Koghkotan*, 92.
54. Andonian, "Komitas Vartabed Aksori Metch," no. 27 (May 25, 1947): 7–8.
55. Andonian, "Komitas Vartabed Aksori Metch," no. 28 (June 1, 1947): 7.
56. Andonian, "Komitas Vartabed Aksori Metch," no. 27 (May 25, 1947): 7–8.
57. Andonian, "Komitas Vartabed Aksori Metch," no. 28 (June 1, 1947): 7.
58. *Ibid.*, 7.
59. In the newspaper *Haratch*, Torkomian would later write that during the early days of exile Komitas "was my strength . . . . without him I felt that the enemy would take me away . . . . I felt safe in his arms and wanted to stay there . . . ." *Haratch* (Paris), Oct. 27, 1935.
60. Andonian, "Komitas Vartabed Aksori Metch," no. 29 (June 8, 1947): 7.
61. Balakian, *Hay Koghkotan*, 95.
62. *Ibid.*, 116–117.
63. Dadrian, *History of the Armenian Genocide*, 221.
64. Puzant Kechian, "Têrvak Aksori Sherchanen" [An Episode From Exile], *Amenun Daretsuytse* (Constantinople) (1922): 41.
65. *Ibid.*, 35.
66. *Ibid.*, 35.
67. Ahmet Altintas et al, eds., *Osmanli Belgelerinde Ermeniler* [The Armenians in the Ottoman Documents] *(1915–1920)* (Ankara: Basbakanlik, 1994). It was Puzant Kechian (listed here as "Pozant Keciyan") who informed Komitas of the release order: "[Komitas's] face brightened with an amazing glow . . . . He could not contain his happiness . . . which indicated how frightened he was by our ordeal." (Kechian, "Têrvak Aksori Sherchanen," 40).
68. Kechian, 40.
69. *Ibid.*, 40.
70. *Ibid.*, 40.
71. *Ibid.*, 40.
72. Chituni, 92.

73. Mesrobian was a pianist and music teacher who had met Komitas in Paris in 1907 and had later helped him select singers for the "Kusan" choir in Constantinople.
74. Aghavni Mesrobian, "Komitasi Gyanki Kidagtsagan Verchin Oreren" [From the Last Days of Komitas's Conscious Life], in *Zhamanagagitsnere Komitasi Masin* [Contemporaries on Komitas], edited by K.N. Kasbarian (Yerevan: Haybedhrad, 1960): 306–307.
75. Mesrobian, 307.
76. Komitas quoted in Chituni, 93.
77. Dadrian, *History of the Armenian Genocide*, 221.
78. All subsequent references to the DSM's diagnostic criteria for Acute Stress Disorder can be found on pp. 429–432 of *The Diagnostic and Statistical Manual of Mental Disorders*, 4th ed. (Washington, D.C.: American Psychiatric Association, 1994).
79. Andonian, "Komitas Vartabed Aksori Metch," 7.
80. *Ibid.*
81. *Ibid.*
82. Krikoris Balakian, *Hay Koghkotan: Têrvakner Hay Mardirosakrutyunen, Berlinen Der Zor 1914–1920* [The Armenian Golgotha: Episodes from Armenian Martyrdom: From Berlin to Der-zor, 1914–1920], vol.1 (Vienna: Mkhitarian Press, 1922): 92–93.
83. Andonian, "Komitas Vartabed Aksori Metch," no. 24, 7–8.
84. *Ibid.*
85. *Ibid.*
86. David Tomb, "The Phenomenology of Post-Traumatic Stress Disorder," *Psychiatric Clinics of North America* 17, no. 2 (1994): 241. Tomb goes on to explain that soldiers who "become overwhelmed on the battlefield typically become nonfunctional: they become exceptionally withdrawn or agitated, confused, paranoid, and disoriented; they display restlessness and signs of marked sympathetic overreactivity."
87. Aghavni Mesrobian, "Komitasi Gyanki Kidagtsagan Verchin Oreren" [From the Last Days of Komitas's Conscious Life], in *Zhamanagagitsnere Komitasi Masin* [Contemporaries on Komitas], edited by K.N. Kasbarian (Yerevan: Haybedhrad, 1960): 307.
88. *Ibid.*, 308.
89. Krikoris Balakian, *Hay Koghkotan* [Armenian Golgotha], vol. 2 (Paris: Arax, 1959): 165.
90. Reports of these occurrences are given in Chapter Nine of Part One. See also: H. Stuermer, *Two War Years in Constantinople: Sketches of German and Young Turkish Ethics and Politics*, translated by E. Allen and H. Stuermer (New York: George H. Doran, 1917): 62–63.
91. American Psychiatric Association, *Diagnostic and Statistical Manual of Psychiatric Disorders*, 4th ed. (Washington, D.C.: American Psychiatric Association, 1994): 428.

92. Garo Ushaklian quoted in H.J. Siruni, "Komitasi Hed" [With Komitas], *Etchmiadzin* (Etchmiadzin) (March 1969): 25.
93. *Diagnostic and Statistical Manual of Psychiatric Disorders*, 4th ed.: 428.
94. Cited in H.J. Siruni, "Komitasi Hed" [With Komitas], *Etchmiadzin* (Etchmiadzin) (March 1969): 24.
95. Ushaklian quoted in *Ibid.*, 25.
96. *Diagnostic and Statistical Manual of Psychiatric Disorders*, 4th ed.: 428.
97. See: H.J. Siruni, "Komitasi Hed" [With Komitas], *Etchmiadzin* (Etchmiadzin) (March 1969): 25.
98. Mesrobian, 307.
99. *Diagnostic and Statistical Manual of Psychiatric Disorders*, 4th ed.: 428.
100. Mesrobian, 308.
101. Chituni, 94.
102. *Ibid.*, 95.
103. *Ibid.*, 94.
104. *Ibid.*, 96.

# 8

# Mad in a Mad City 1916–1919

The fears paralyzing Komitas were not unfounded. Everywhere in Constantinople, Armenians carried out their daily lives under the watchful eye of the secret police. Every day there were sudden and unexplained arrests, deportations, and beatings.[1] The terror in the air was palpable, even to foreign observers. Harry Stuermer, a German newspaper correspondent who lived in Constantinople at the time, later described how the persecution of Armenians became routine:

> One day in the summer of 1916, my wife went out alone at about midday to shop in the *Grande Rue de Péra*. We lived a few steps from Galata-Seraï and had plenty of opportunity from our balcony of seeing the bands of Armenian deportees arriving at the police station under the escort of gendarmes . . . . On this particular day, my wife came back to the house trembling all over. She had not been able to go on her errand. As she passed by the "karakol" [police station], she had heard through the open hall door the agonizing groans of a tortured being, a dull wailing like the sound of an animal being tormented to death. "An Armenian," she was informed by the people standing at the door . . . "If such scenes occur in broad daylight in the busiest part of the European quarter of Péra, I should like to know what is done to Armenians in the uncivilized Interior," my wife asked me. "If the Turks act like wild beasts here in the capital, so that a woman

> going through the main streets gets a shock like that to her nerves, then I can't live in this frightful country." And then she burst into a fit of sobbing and let loose all her pent-up passion against what she and I had to witness for more than a year every time we set a foot out of doors.[2]

This was the atmosphere in which Komitas was struggling to recover from his experience in the death-camp. It was worsened by the fact that, during the year that followed his return from Chankiri, he could not find work. The activities he had always relied on to cope with psychological pain and anxiety were unavailable to him. Much of Constantinople's cultural life—the theater, literature, and music which comprised his world—had vanished under the pressures of war and repression. Unable to practice his profession, he was left alone with his fears of arrest and torture, alongside intense feelings of vulnerability and loneliness.

Soon his landlord was threatening to evict him for failing to pay rent, and the shame of homelessness and poverty that had plagued his childhood loomed once more. Komitas reacted by sinking into depression and anxiety, punctuated by dissociation and psychosis.

This condition, an exacerbated form of Posttraumatic Stress Disorder, continued to deteriorate with the arrival of the first anniversary of his arrest. A cherished companion, Bishop Hovsep Garabedian, remembers how Komitas had been invited to celebrate mass on Palm Sunday, 1916, one year after the beginning of the Armenian Genocide. "While chanting [the prayer] 'God open the doors,'" Garabedian says, "Komitas started to sob at the altar,"[3] overcome by memories so vivid that he seemed to be reliving the year-old terrors.

Komitas returned to his apartment in a fit of uncontrollable weeping. His old cook, deeply frightened, ran to the house of a neighbor, Terlemezian, to ask for help. "Come quick," he implored, "Vartabed is in a bad way, he cries and prays incessantly. . . ." Dr. Torkomian, with whom Komitas had been released from the camp at Chankiri, was also summoned. When Komitas was finally brought to the Terlemezian household, he refused the tranquilizers that Torkomian prescribed, though he agreed to take them later when they were offered by one of the Terlemezian children. (A child, in Komitas's opinion, was worthy of trust.) That night, Terlemezian's young daughter Arshaluys heard Komitas singing and went downstairs to see him. When she looked through the doorway she saw him weeping and praying before a portrait of Khrimian Hayrig, as if beseeching his old protector for help. Two weeks passed before Komitas began to emerge from this state of severe anxiety, which, as he later told his friends, was like having "a cat in my belly, scratching my insides."[4]

By early summer he had recovered enough of his strength and spirits to leave the city for the country residence of Asdvadzadur Harents, a prominent Armenian musicologist. "I invited him to be our guest in our country house," Harents remembers, "and he stayed with us almost three months. He recovered so well that he was able to work and harmonize the dances for which I still have the manuscripts . . . ."[5] A letter Komitas wrote to Arshaluys Sarkisian at the time confirms that he was enjoying a period of much-needed tranquillity: "I feel much better here. I eat, I drink, I stroll, and I sleep . . . . The Harents family is taking very good care of me. I feel lucky to be cared for by an Armenian family. I've decided not to work although I have the doctor's permission to do so."[6] He received a steady stream of visitors, among them Dikran Chituni, who had returned from his self-imposed exile in Bulgaria. Chituni "found him healthy, jolly and full of music . . . ." Komitas also declared his delight in having made a friend of Asdvadzadur's wife Arusyag, who often accompanied his songs on the piano. It seemed Komitas had fallen under the healing influence of another artistically talented woman who, like Margaret Babaian, could offer him the care and empathy that had been taken from him by the death of his mother. "The loving care of this cultured family," writes Chituni, "helped him a lot . . . . Recovered, he was able to work on piano harmonization's of his songs."[7]

Although he continued to be plagued by vivid flashbacks of Chankiri, he felt healthier: his sudden and unpredictable alterations of mood had vanished, his ability to concentrate had returned, and his sense of self had been restored by the love of a family. At the end of this placid summer he felt strong enough to return to his residence in Pera, in the center of Constantinople.

The intimation of renewal was, little more than a moment of calm before the eruption of a great storm that would ravage his remaining years. Just weeks after his return to Constantinople, Komitas succumbed to melancholic depression, which was probably precipitated by the arrival of yet another eviction notice. According to Asdvadzadur Harents, the darkness that engulfed him was intense: " . . . every week that passed he felt sadder . . . he was even angry at the sun . . . ."[8] He began to talk to himself. He stopped eating and refused to receive visitors. He was observed gazing silently into the well in the garden of his house, or crying out as if imaginary animals were attacking him. Eventually he took to his bed, pulling the blankets over his head and refusing to speak.[9] His ties to the outside world had been severed completely: he now lived in an internal realm governed by fears of persecution and abandonment.

Komitas's friends followed the progress of his illness anxiously. On the advice of a doctor, one of them, Garo Ushaklian, contrived to pass a night at Komitas's house in order to observe his increasingly erratic behavior: "It was midnight when [Komitas] sat up in his bed . . . I asked him if he was sick, he said no, he was just anxious and soon it would pass . . . . This was repeated throughout the night . . . ."[10] The following day he was completely withdrawn, refusing to communicate with anyone. Sensing that the situation was slipping from their grasp, his friends decided a drastic course of action. Through Dr. Torkomian, a police carriage was summoned to bring Komitas to Hôpital de la Paix, a sanitarium run by the Turkish military. In order to ensure that Komitas would comply, Torkomian instructed the officers to tell him that a government minister with whom he was acquainted, Nazir Bey, had some questions regarding a song.

When the carriage suddenly appeared, Komitas, who was understandably terrified of the police, submissively agreed to accompany the officers. The scenario must have struck him as a long and vivid echo of the fearful night of his detention a year and a half earlier. Clearly, he did not believe the story they were telling now of government ministers and songs, for he asked them if his cook, the only "family" that he had, could accompany him.

Hopital de la Paix in Istanbul Turkey today

It was an astonishingly inept and harmful way of ensuring that Komitas would acquiesce. His cook recalls that the deception was quickly discovered: "I got into the carriage with Komitas and we were driven in the direction of Shishli [where Hôpital de la Paix was located]. Komitas turned to the policeman driving the carriage and said, 'Sir, you lied to me, Nazir Bey does not live here."[11] Minutes later, enraged and helpless, he surrendered himself to the doctors who were awaiting him at the hospital doors.[12] He was once again a "captive" of the Turkish military.

Days later, several of his friends went to his apartment and placed his papers and valuables in boxes, which they sent to the Armenian Patriarchate of Constantinople for safekeeping.

Curiously, they neglected to seal any of the boxes. The rest of his belongings were sold to pay for his hospital expenses. This naive violation of his privacy—which, resulted in the mysterious loss of a number of his musical works—intensified the shame of hospitalization and the pain of having been deceived by friends. There can be no doubt that they believed themselves to be acting in Komitas's best interests, but their actions at this time only alienated their troubled friend more profoundly, with serious psychological consequences.

Dr. Vahram Torkomian

The chief psychiatrist at Hôpital de la Paix was Dr. Mazhar Osman Uzman; a man widely regarded as the founder of modern Turkish neuropsychiatry.[13] After graduating from the medical school of the Turkish military, Uzman had gone to Germany to study with some of the foremost thinkers in European psychiatry at the time, among them Kraeplin and Ziehen. In Komitas's eyes, however, Uzman was merely another powerful and therefore threatening Turk.

Two other psychiatrists were assigned to Komitas: his old compatriot Vahram Torkomian, and Dr. Konos, a Greek physician whose first name is not documented, but who was also a resident psychiatrist at a Greek hospital in Constantinople.

Partly as a result of being hospitalized against his will, Komitas was a stubbornly uncooperative patient. His life had been a series of struggles against the strictures of large and powerful institutions: the Armenian Church, which had repeatedly attempted to stifle important facets of his music, and the Turkish government, which had placed him, however briefly, in a situation that had threatened him with death. Now he was being confronted by a military-medical establishment that, in a single stroke, had taken away his home, and his work, his autonomy. Incredibly, it had done so on the advice of one of its "agents," Vahram Torkomian, whom he had once considered a close friend and with whom he had made the dreadful journey to Chankiri and back.

Before the terrors of the "Red Harvest," Torkomian had been a distinguished physician who lectured on hygiene and physiology at Constantinople's Berberian College and wrote extensively on the history of medicine. But by 1919 he had become a "thin, sickly, cautious old man,"[14] good-hearted but convinced that Komitas's only chance for recovery lay in complete isolation from the world and the pressures of creative work. Torkomian's judgment was certainly skewed by the fact that he was the archetypal "wounded healer," a man bearing his own scars from the trauma of Chankiri, involved with a patient whom he knew too intimately and wanted to heal too desperately. This was visible in an incident that took place during his treatment of Komitas at Hôpital de la Paix: discovering Komitas hard at work on some papers, Torkomian flew into a rage, yelling at his patient and tearing the sheets into pieces. To this sudden outburst, Komitas responded coldly: "Out, and don't come back."[15] Torkomian was now merely another enemy.

Fortunately, Komitas's relations with Dr. Konos were more amicable, and he spent many hours during the first six months of his stay confiding in the Greek psychiatrist. When Konos fell ill, however, Komitas was left in the hands of Dr. Uzman, with whom he was never more than courteous and reserved. Despite an excellent education and a reputation as one of the best psychiatrists in the city, Uzman was a Turk, and was a figure of terror for him.

Establishing a sense of trust, the crucial condition in any successful psychiatrist-patient relationship, became impossible for Komitas at Hôpital de la Paix. In his mind, Torkomian represented the friends who had deceived him; and Uzman the government that had tried to kill him. Given these stultifying relationships with some of the very people, who meant to cure him, he made little progress. In a letter Torkomian wrote to Archag Tchobanian on March 17, 1919, the exasperated doctor declares: "According to [Komitas], we are all enemies, especially me, and so are all those who care for him."[16]

### The Paradox of Komitas's Psychiatric Treatment

In any course of treatment for a case of PTSD caused by state terrorism, three interconnected issues are in play, each of such importance that it can determine whether or not psychiatric intervention is successful. The first is comprised of the personal factors present in the patient—the amalgam of genetic predisposition and personal experience that over the years have shaped the patient's internal world and his or her relationship with external reality. On the one hand, personal factors played a decisively negative role in Komitas's case. The social and psychological difficulties that pursued him through life—the deaths of his parents at a crucial stage in the formation of his personality, and his long struggle to endure the systematic contempt that his fellow clergymen showed for his "worldly" pursuits—left him extremely vulnerable to feelings of neglect, abandonment, and rejection. On the other hand, during his many years as a prominent artist, he had grown accustomed to the high degree of respect shown him by the Armenian public. Thus, with the startling violence of the gendarme's assault on the road to Chankiri, Komitas was brought to the unbearable realization that all of his immense psychological and professional efforts to overcome his childhood insecurities, to build a sense of self-worth, to establish himself as a valued member of society, had been suddenly stripped away. With the demeaning act of tearing a bucket of water away from lips, the anonymous gendarme also wrenched away all of the coping skills that Komitas had cultivated over the years—his sense of self-reliance, independence, and dignity—and returned him to the state of helplessness that he had endured as an orphaned child.

Komitas, Constantinople, 1917. Picture probably taken at the Hopital de la Paix

As the months passed and he grew less and less able to carry out his daily business, the attention that his increasingly erratic behavior drew from those around him made him feel utterly transparent to the outside world. Deprived of his ability to control himself, he was also deprived of his privacy. This only solidified his damaged sense of self, his intense feelings of humiliation and shame. The flood of disgrace peaked when he found himself tricked into being hospitalized, while the people he had once considered his friends and equals sold off his belongings and shuffled through his papers. Like an injured, battle-weary soldier, he had returned from Chankiri to find that none of his own people could appreciate what he had experienced, and (like many such soldiers) he became embittered, not only at the perpetrators of the violence, but at those close to him who could not recognize the terrible burdens he was forced to carry. Shielding himself with anger that gradually developed into rage, Komitas rejected them and the "treatment" they offered.

In many ways, Komitas's experience at this time resembles those described by recent studies of Posttraumatic Stress Disorder in American veterans of the Vietnam War.[17] Like these service people, Komitas suffered a psychological trauma that had two consecutive phases: the first occurred during his internment, and the second appeared with his return to society. When he returned to Constantinople after the horrors of the death-camp, he expected a more caring and respectful response from the Armenian community there. When this response did not occur, he was traumatized again. If the first facet of the trauma, the experience of the death-camp, robbed him of his mental health, the second led to the loss of his home and his freedom.[18]

These traumatic phases were catastrophic for him, and radically transformed his relationship with the world. The circumstances, under which he was hospitalized, along with the way his house and his belongings were disposed of by friends, severed his bonds to the very people whose care he required to get well. To spare himself further pain he withdrew completely: "He became more and more silent and sad . . . he didn't want to receive visitors . . . ."[19]

The second crucial issue in the treatment of traumatic stress is the institutional aspect of treatment. Unfortunately for Komitas, the institution chosen by his friends not only reinforced the impasse in his illness, but also complicated it. At the time of his hospitalization, Constantinople's Hôpital de la Paix was run by the Turkish military, the very arm of the government that had helped to inflict such suffering on him and his fellow Armenians. As Inger Agger and Søren Buus Jensen observe in their 1994 article "The Psychosexual Trauma of Torture," it is "difficult or even impossible to find a supportive institutional context in which victims of [any] dictatorship can receive treatment."[20] This is partly because therapists who work under the scrutiny of authoritarian governments risk being accused of treason if they attempt to help those who have been branded enemies of the state. This is also the result of the mental condition of the patients themselves. For Komitas, being institutionalized in a hospital run by the Turkish military was effectively no different from being held in a Turkish prison, in both situations he was in the hands of "the enemy." It is therefore not surprising that his condition failed to improve during his time at Hôpital de la Paix.

The last of the three treatment issues involves the personalities of the individual therapists. In Komitas's case, this became an issue of ethnicity: although it had been conducted under political pretenses, the persecution that Komitas experienced was "ethnic" in nature. Consequently the ethnic identities of his doctors at Hôpital de la Paix were highly significant, for it was uncertain as to what degree their actions were influenced by the anti-Armenian policies of the state. If they were in agreement with the government, were they active participants in its anti-Armenian policies? If they were opposed, how would they go about treating a case of madness that had been brought on by the calculated actions of the state? In Komitas's case, these issues require us to look closely at the ways in which the doctors at Hôpital de la Paix approached their traumatized patient, who was known to have become ill after his arrest by a government that was carrying out a campaign of genocide. In two cases out of three, the national identities of the physicians who treated Komitas at the hospital in

Constantinople placed insurmountable barriers between doctor and patient.

The instance in which a therapist's ethnic background did *not* create harmful complications in his relationship with Komitas was that of Dr. Konos, one of the hospital staff psychiatrists. Vahram Torkomian tells us that Konos and Komitas often held friendly conversations that lasted many hours.[21] Konos, it seems, was the one doctor at Hôpital de la Paix whom Komitas would not make every effort to avoid, evidence of a kind of therapeutic alliance that no other physician was able to form with the anguished and depressed composer. Why Konos? One clue may be that the psychiatrist belonged to Constantinople's large Greek community. As a member of a Christian community living in the Ottoman Empire—a community, which, like the Armenians, had long standing grievances against the ruling Turks—Konos was subject to the same unjust restrictions that had been imposed on Armenians.[22] And yet this community of Greeks to which Konos belonged had so far suffered none of the horrors that the government inflicted on Komitas and his people.[23] These circumstances allowed Konos to identify with Komitas's torments without feeling personally implicated in them, and thus he was able to strike the balance between empathy and objectivity that is critical to the success of a therapist's relationship with a patient. Unfortunately, not long after Komitas was admitted, Konos developed a case of typhus and became mentally ill, so was forced to leave his position at the hospital.

The trust that characterized Komitas's interactions with Konos stands in stark contrast to the deep suspicions that burdened his relationship with Dr. Mazhar Osman Uzman. From the outset, Komitas was unable to give Uzman the slightest trust. His position as the hospital's most prominent psychiatrist—indeed, a graduate of military medical school and one of the most renowned specialists in all of Constantinople[24]—in no way compensated for the fact that he was a Turk, a highly placed representative of the nation that was carrying out a savage attack on the Armenian people.

The Turkish medical establishment itself was not free of the government's intentions. Many Armenians suspected that, under the guise of an inoculation program, Turkish military doctors were infecting Armenian soldiers with strains of typhus for the sake of medical experimentation.[25] Some Turkish physicians were also implicated in organizing the mass annihilation of Armenians.[26] Whether Uzman was involved in such crimes is inconsequential here, as we have noted, for it was a feature of Komitas's illness that he reacted to specific stimuli with generalizations, which meant that any suspicions he harbored about Turkish doctors would inevitably be broadened to encompass Uzman as well.

Komitas's response to Uzman was a peculiar blend of extreme caution, compliance, and terror, which he displayed most clearly by refusing to speak anything but Turkish at the hospital. He obviously feared that identification with Armenian culture, or any culture other than Turkish, might be considered grounds for recommencing his punishment. He knew that he had been arrested because of his status as a cultured Armenian, so he attempted to play down his ethnic identity by concealing his knowledge of other languages. On one occasion, just before his discharge and voyage to Paris, he even went so far as to chide a group of Armenian visitors who had questioned him in their mother tongue about his cautious attitude, announcing loudly: "You devils, the language of your city is Turkish, don't you speak Turkish there?" This scene, which Komitas had apparently played out for the purpose of impressing Uzman with his conformity, was repeated when a group of four doctors came to examine him in order to prepare a medical certificate for his transfer to Paris. When one of the physicians, a Greek man, greeted him in French, Komitas turned on him: "What do you want, don't you know Turkish? Mazhar Bey [referring to Uzman, who was looking on] take these people away, they disturb me." Moments later, a doctor who had greeted him in Armenian—"*Parev Vartabed, inchbes es* [Hello Vartabed, how are you]?"—received an equally terse reprimand: "Here is another one, what do you want, man, who are you?" According to the account, after mocking the name of this Armenian physician, all the while speaking in Turkish, Komitas turned to Uzman and declared: "Osman Bey, take these people away, I wish to have my lunch . . . ."[27]

Evidently Komitas felt that he was again a prisoner—of the Turks in general, and of Uzman in particular—and that overt displays of submission offered the best chances of appeasing the anger and violence he perceived lurking in his "captors." The stress of the chronic fear[28] that Uzman's presence generated in him—stress that made him go to great lengths to convince the doctor that he trusted him—further entrenched his illness and lessened his chances of recovery.

Komitas's most complicated and highly charged therapeutic relationship at Hôpital de la Paix was with an Armenian doctor in whose company he had already experienced a great deal. Vahram Torkomian had been arrested alongside Komitas on the night that the "Red Harvest" began, and had undergone the same three-week-long ordeal at the death-camp. As we have seen, it was most likely the intervention of Torkomian's wife that secured the release of both Komitas and Torkomian from the death-camp.[29] Moreover, after their return from Chankiri, Torkomian was the psychiatrist who treated Komitas's episodes of mental illness in the spring and autumn of 1916. He was also instrumental in having Komitas hospitalized.

How did these painful experiences as prisoners of the Turks affect their relationship as doctor and patient? In the death-camp at Chankiri they had been equals in suffering. Now, in the Constantinople hospital, this bond no longer existed. Komitas could see that Torkomian was a "free" man, restored to his family and to the position of authority and respect that he had occupied in society before the arrests. Komitas himself, on the other hand, was ill and incarcerated; he had lost everything, even the most rudimentary ways of controlling his own future. Indeed, it was now Torkomian who had much of the decision-making power over Komitas's destiny.

While Komitas might not have been able to recognize it, both men still shared the burden that the recent past had placed on them. Torkomian, too, was faced with an institution that was directly linked to the regime that had terrorized him. And like Komitas, he was unable to give free expression to the anger, pain, and betrayal that he must have felt. This made the immense responsibility of caring for Komitas even heavier.

Mental health-care workers who have themselves been victims of state terrorism typically find it difficult to prevent feelings of aggression from entering their therapeutic relationships with other victims.[30] Often these therapists—who, like their patients, have been the defenseless targets of violence, and who are likewise denied the opportunity to express their pain in ways that would offer catharsis and a sense that the perpetrators had been brought to justice—redirect their feelings of anger either inwards upon themselves or outwards, upon patients who have had similar experiences. Just as often, therapists in this position attempt to repress or deny such feelings, for fear of perpetuating the victimization of their patients. In many cases, the vicious circle that is created in this way ruptures the therapeutic alliance. A benevolent, trusting relationship between doctor and patient, untainted by power struggles, becomes impossible.

The inability to cope with aggression severely damaged Torkomian's professional relationship with Komitas. While Komitas was at Hôpital de la Paix, Torkomian's overly protective feelings for his patient convinced him that the entire process of recovery would be jeopardized if Komitas were allowed to concentrate on musical projects. Torkomian, it seems, had come to believe that Komitas was suffering from exhaustion caused by working too hard. Clearly, at the root of this belief was a mixture of denial and extreme caution: the psychiatrist attributed his friend's breakdown to the relatively safe issue of overwork rather than to its actual cause, experiences of death-camp and genocide. Overwork could be controlled; one simply had to prevent the patient from working. Healing the psychological wounds of someone, who had been swept up in a genocidal campaign, as he himself had been, was a far more complex matter. It must have seemed to Torkomian that to go deeper into the real cause of his friend's illness would mean entering a realm that he himself wished to seal over to maintain his own stability. Thus, out of the pent-up frustrations created by his denial and his own deep feelings of helplessness, Torkomian finally lost control over his emotions and lashed out at Komitas: when he discovered that Komitas had ignored his orders and was sitting at a table working on some manuscripts, he flew into a rage, snatched the papers away, and tore them to pieces. The rift in the therapeutic relationship caused by this shocking incident was too large to be repaired. Years of friendship, during which the two men had also endured great suffering together, were brought to an end. Guiltily and with resignation, Torkomian wrote to tell Archag Tchobanian in Paris that "According to [Komitas], we are all his enemies, especially me . . . ."[31]

Clearly, Torkomian's outburst and Komitas's subsequent withdrawal caused the psychiatrist to reflect on the course their relationship had taken, and on the painful feelings that had long been preying on his psyche: guilt over the fact that, despite being indirectly responsible for Komitas's release from Chankiri, he was also responsible for Komitas's incarceration in an asylum; shame for Komitas's illness, an illness inflicted by the Ottoman government, and therefore a symbolic defeat for the Armenian struggle to survive as a nation. The Turks had scored a minor triumph by destroying one of Armenia's finest musical minds.

Torkomian was the paradigmatic "wounded healer." As a result of his own suffering and the sufferings of his people, he felt that his duties as a psychiatrist were far more demanding than the task of simply treating one patient, no matter how prominent. Indeed, he was on an all-embracing mission, one so enormous and burdensome that it was debilitating.[32] Torkomian's bond with Komitas—and the shattering of that bond—was the result of a state of "ethical nonneutrality" between therapist and patient, in which the therapist, seized by a sense of self as omnipotent rescuer, came to feel that responsibility for the success or failure of the entire healing process rested entirely on his own shoulders.[33]

That Torkomian had accepted too much of the burden became apparent when Komitas's friends proposed to rent and furnish Komitas's old apartment, allowing Komitas to return home under the supervision of a group of members of the Kusan choir, none of whom had been directly involved in the conflicts of his life. This plan to break the impasse in his illness and heal his injured pride was perhaps worth some consideration at this point, but Torkomian flatly witheld his consent. He was concerned, he said, that Komitas would not be able to cope with such a change.[34]

Komitas categorically refused to see most of his visitors. He made an exception for Dikran Chituni, probably for the reason that at the time of his hospitalization Chituni had again been in hiding from the Turkish authorities, and therefore had not been involved in the decision that landed Komitas in his present state. And Chituni was burdened by none of the feelings of guilt that no doubt haunted those who had made the decision, so trust and empathy seemed possible between them. When Chituni finally returned to Constantinople and arrived at the hospital, Komitas poured out his heart:

> [Komitas] received me with pleasure and we chatted for a long time . . . "I want to be with my people [he said] . . . I want my keys, I want my house, and I want my personal belongings . . . I want my desk . . . What happened to Panos's paintings? What happened to my cook? Where is my piano? Where are my students? Who gave them permission to do this?" He asked [these questions] repeatedly. He was deeply bitter about the people who were trying to take care of him . . . .[35]

It would be nearly two and a half years before Komitas finally left Hôpital de la Paix—not to resume his old role as one of the cultural leaders of the Armenian people, but to be shipped to Paris as a helpless psychiatric patient.

By early 1919 it was becoming clear to the friends and doctors caring for Komitas that he was making no progress in the Turkish hospital. They saw that his deep fears and suspicions showed no signs of abating. Indeed, he continued to speak only Turkish in the presence of Dr. Uzman, perhaps because he was terrified that a Turk in any position of authority might be convinced by the smallest "fault" in words or actions to send him back to Chankiri. Desperate for a solution, they considered sending him to the monasteries of Etchmiadzin or Jerusalem, but were quickly thwarted.[36] It was finally decided that Komitas's best chances for recovery lay in Paris, where there lived not only a great many of his close friends (among them Archag Tchobanian and, most importantly, Margaret Babaian), but also many renowned psychiatric specialists.

Terrified of change in any form Komitas resisted the transfer and demanded to be left alone. Repeatedly, almost obsessively, he demanded the keys to his apartment.[37] His friends, all of them now confused and ridden with guilt, once again felt the need to devise a "plot": this time they told Komitas that Tchobanian had written from Paris to invite him to a conference of the International Musical Society. It is almost certain that Komitas detected the lie long before he actually left Constantinople, and that this discovery deepened his sense of shame and humiliation: he was being treated like a fool, stripped of his autonomy.

A meeting was held between Komitas and a group of his doctors to discuss his possible transfer to Paris. He refused to cooperate, mocking one of the doctors, demanding constantly to be taken back to the apartment which was no longer his, and declaring that he would never leave the city. Once again he was brought against his will to the port of Constantinople. With him were Asdvadzadur Harents and a young student named Kevork

Kamlamayan, who was to accompany him on the journey.[38] Komitas and Kamlamayan boarded the Romanian passenger ship *Dachia*, which was bound for France. A group of Komitas's former students had assembled on the pier to see him off. They offered him flowers, and as a gesture of respect for the great teacher he had once been, they sang for him. But he only stared into the distance, as if he had already left the shores of his homeland for the last time.

Notes to Chapter Eight: Mad in a Mad City

1. Krikoris Balakian, *Hay Koghkotan* [The Armenian Golgotha], vol. 2 (Vienna: Mkhitarian Press, 1922): 165.
2. H. Stuermer, *Two War Years in Constantinople: Sketches of German and Young Turkish Ethics and Politics*, translated by E. Allen and H. Stuermer (New York: George H. Doran, (1917): 62–63.
3. Garabedian quoted in H.J. Siruni, "Komitasi Hed" [With Komitas], *Etchmiadzin* (Etchmiadzin) (March 1969): 24.
4. A. Sarkisian, "Sev Or Me, Komitas Gula Yev Gaghote . . . Husher Vartabedi Gyankits" [A Black Day, Komitas Cries and Prays . . . Memories of Komitas's Life], *Aztarar* (Constantinople), no.2741 (1935): 2.
5. Harents quoted in H.J. Siruni, "Komitasi Hed" [With Komitas], *Etchmiadzin* (Etchmiadzin) (March 1969): 29.
6. Sarkisian, 2.
7. Dikran Chituni, "Komitasi Hed" [With Komitas], *Hayrenik*, no. 2 (1936): 95.
8. Harents quoted in H.J. Siruni, "Komitasi Hed" [With Komitas], *Etchmiadzin* (Etchmiadzin) (March 1969): 30.
9. *Ibid.*, 29.
10. Ushaklian quoted in H.J. Siruni, "Komitasi Hed" [With Komitas], *Etchmiadzin* (Etchmiadzin) (March 1969): 30.
11. *Ibid.*, 31.
12. Unfortunately, details of Komitas's official status as a patient at Hôpital de la Paix are scarce; indeed, it is difficult to tell whether or not he was in fact "committed" at this time. His hospitalization was almost certainly, involuntary—this much is clear from the methods used to bring him to the hospital, and from his incessant and unheeded demands to be released. The fact that he had no immediate family to care for him must also have formed part of the reason for his detention. But because no mention of his status as a patient at the Hôpital de la Paix exists in the memoirs or letters of his

contemporaries, and because it is also unclear whether the Turkish health policies in place at this time required official commitment procedures in order to keep a patient in a psychiatric hospital against his will, the issue of whether or not Komitas was officially committed in Constantinople—as he would be later in France—remains a mystery. The hospital did not begin to maintain a complete archive of patient records until the 1930's. This information was acquired during the author's visit to the Hôpital de la Paix in Istanbul in October 1994.

13. D.V. Volkan, "Turkey," in *World History of Psychiatry*, edited by John G. Howells (New York: Brunner-Mazel, 1975): 391.
14. H.J. Siruni, "Komitasi Hed" [With Komitas], *Etchmiadzin* (Etchmiadzin) (March 1969): 30–31.
15. *Ibid.*, 30–31. Torkomian's granddaughter, Simone Torkomian Denis, remembers that the doctor was often angry and irritable after he returned from Chankiri, and that this behavior placed strains on his marriage. Such changes in personality are common in individuals who have undergone serious traumatic stress. Personal interview, July 1997, Paris.
16. *Ibid.*, 31.
17. See: Erwin R. Parson, "Posttraumatic Narcissism: Healing Traumatic Alterations in the Self through Curvilinear Group Psychotherapy," in *The International Handbook of Stress Disorders*, edited by John P. Wilson and Beverly Raphael (New York: Plenum Press, 1993): 821.
18. In his article, Parson concludes that "understanding the role of posttraumatic pathological narcissism (deregulated sense of self) is crucial to successful psychotherapy" for Vietnam veterans. Parson (822) locates the origin of the narcissistic vulnerabilities and pathology in the combination of psychic trauma in Vietnam and psychic trauma after returning home from combat. While making it clear that the form of narcissism being discussed in this context is an intrinsic aspect of human life and experience, and not necessarily a negative phenomenon or an illness to be overcome (i.e. that narcissism ranges from healthy to abnormal and pathological), Parson explains that within PTSD there is yet another, narcissistic disorder. Many Vietnam veterans became confused as to whether they should love or hate themselves for the actions they had been ordered to perform. Their own society's disapproval of the cause for which they had been sent to sacrifice their lives worked to distort their sense of self-worth and self-love.
19. Garo Ushaklian, *Aradzani* (Paris) (1940): 68–69.
20. Inger Agger and Søren Buus Jensen, "The Psychosexual Trauma of Torture," in *The International Handbook of Stress Disorders*, edited by John P. Wilson and Beverly Raphael (New York: Plenum Press, 1993): 272.
21. Vahram Torkomian, "Hushadedres" [From My Memoirs], *Vem* (Paris) (November-January 1938): 71.
22. A. Alaexandris, *The Greek Minority of Istanbul and Greek-Turkish Relations: 1918–1974* (Athens: Center for Asia Minor Studies, 1983).

23. This situation changed in 1922, when the Turks began deporting and killing large numbers of Greeks in Smyrna. See: Garabed Hatcherian, *An Armenian Doctor in Turkey: My Smyrna Ordeal of 1922* edited by Dora Sakayan (Montreal: Arod, 1997).
24. "Mazhar Osman Uzman was born in 1884, and graduated from Turkish Military Medical School in 1904, later studying under Kraeplin and Ziehen in Germany. . . . He held a variety of posts during his professional life, which spanned more than 40 years . . . . After the war of independence he became psychiatrist-in-chief of Topkapi Hospital. Uzman is often called the Pinel of Turkey." D.V. Volkan, "Turkey," in *World History of Psychiatry*, edited by John G. Howells (New York: Brunner-Mazel, 1975): 391–392.
25. K.M. Nersisian, ed., *Hayeri Tseghasbanutyune Osmanian Gaysrutyunum, Pasdatêghteri yev Nyuteri Zhoghovatzu* [The Genocide of Armenians in the Ottoman Empire, Collection of Documents and Material] (Yerevan: Hayastan, 1991): 520–524.
26. Vahakn Dadrian, "The Role of Turkish Physicians in the World War I Genocide of Ottoman Armenians," *Holocaust and Genocide Studies* 1, no. 2 (1986): 169–192. Among the most notorious of these physicians was Dr. Behaeddine Shakir, the Ottoman "Minister of Enlightenment," who played a central role in the plotting of the complex logistics of the Genocide.
27. Garo Ushaklian quoted in H.J. Siruni, "Komitasi Hed" [With Komitas], *Etchmiadzin* (Etchmiadzin) (April 1969): 37.
28. Inger Agger and Søren Buus Jensen, "Determinant Factors for Countertransference Reactions under State Terrorism," in *Countertransference in the Treatment of PTSD,* edited by John P. Wilson and Jacob D. Lindy (New York: Guilford Press, 1994): 280.
29. H.J. Siruni, "Komitasi Hed" [With Komitas], *Etchmiadzin* (Etchmiadzin) (October 1968): 54.
30. Agger and Jensen, "Determinant Factors," 285–286. In this article, Inger Agger and Søren Buus Jensen draw on their experiences as therapists in Chile, where an authoritarian government brutally oppressed a large portion of the country's population in the 1970s and 1980s.
31. Vahram Torkomian, "Hushadedres," 71.
32. As Agger and Jensen point out, "To be on a survivor's mission in Chile was not only a question of one's own survival but also of the survival of democracy and human dignity." Agger and Jensen, "Determinant Factors," 285.
33. *Ibid.*, 285.
34. Dikran Chituni, "Komitasi Hed" [With Komitas], *Hayrenik,* no. 2 (1936): 98.
35. Chituni, 97–98.
36. Precisely why the patriarch of Jerusalem refused is not documented, but by 1917 Etchmiadzin was in a chaotic state, produced by epidemics and the relentless influx of refugees fleeing massacres in Western Armenia.
37. Chituni, 97.

38. According to Margaret Babaian, Kevork Damlamayan was the student who accompanied Komitas to Paris. Yet in Komitas's medical file, this same student signs his name *Kamlamayan*. See footnote by Margaret Babaian in Thomas Hartman, "Komitas," in *Zhamanagagitsnere Komitasi Masin* [Contemporaries on Komitas], edited by K.N. Kasbarian (Yerevan: Haybedhrad, 1960): 61.

# 9

# The Lost Years 1918–1935

By the time of the armistice ending World War I in November 1918, Torkomian was exhausted, psychologically beaten by the huge, seemingly impossible task of restoring health to the fractured psyche of a man who was not only his friend but also a cultural icon. He had come to realize that from the night of the arrests onward he and his patient had been linked by some of the most complex and destructive of human feelings: fear, shame, and anger. With the war over, he knew that it was now time to see if the obstacles preventing Komitas from recovery could be removed by sending him far from home. The strain of caring for Komitas was apparent in the letter Torkomian wrote to friends in Paris at the time of Komitas's transfer there, in which he declared that his Parisian colleague, Dr. Cololian, "should follow [Komitas] as closely and with as much empathy as I have."[1]

During the arduous ten-day voyage to Paris, the young student Kevork Kamlamayan struggled with the enormous task of tending to a man who was both a delusional psychiatric patient and a national idol. Kamlamayan carried no medicine with him, only a letter and 1500 units of gold currency.[2] The letter was from Vahram Torkomian, and was addressed to Archag Tchobanian, who was to meet the two travelers upon their arrival. It read:

> . . . When [Komitas] arrives, do what is necessary to place him in a Maison de Santé on the outskirts of Paris . . . expenses have been looked after. 1500 [units of gold currency are] available. It is enough for a year. We are thinking about future expenses as well. According to [Komitas], we are all enemies, especially me and all others who have the title of "doctor." He has been in this situation for two years. His condition has changed for the better, but he still requires much care, which is not possible here. Until now he was treated at the Hôpital de la Paix in Shishli, but for a person suffering from neurosis [*chêghakarutyune*] we don't have the facilities. He should be treated by trying to change his ideas, taking him out to the garden, taking him for walks . . . . We had a Greek doctor in the hospital who used to spend lots of time with him, but unfortunately [the doctor] took ill . . . I would like to ask you to consult Dr. Gilbert Ballet with Dr. Cololian and, as they see fit, to let them treat him in an appropriate hospital. Four days ago, we had a meeting with the doctors [of Hôpital de la Paix] . . . and a report was signed. I beg you [to ensure] that Dr. Cololian follow him as closely and with as much empathy as I did.[3]

The letter has a tone of desperation, of wounded feelings caused by Komitas's rejection of Torkomian and others and by the failure of the treatment in Constantinople. While Torkomian claims to have noted some improvement—probably an alleviation of the symptoms of acute depression that prompted Komitas's hospitalization in August 1916—he makes no direct reference either to Komitas's persecutory delusions or to the experience of his internment. The transfer from Constantinople to Paris was part of the attempt at "trying to change his ideas"[4] by altering Komitas's environment, just as it was an acknowledgment that Constantinople offered neither the medical resources nor the political security that he needed to make a full recovery. Paris, with its progressive psychiatric institutions, its stable political environment, and its community of experts, was more promising. If only Komitas could be immersed in such a safe and therapeutic atmosphere and be freed of the constant reminders of genocide by a comprehensive program of treatment, then, thought

Torkomian, his scarcely suppressed rage might be dispelled and his sanity restored.

By the time Komitas arrived in Paris, his friends there had decided against hospitalizing him. They knew how greatly it had pained and angered him to be confined against his will to the hospital in Constantinople, and they did not want to rob him of his freedom a second time. It was decided to bring him to the

DÉPARTEMENT DE LA SEINE

RÉPUBLIQUE FRANÇAISE
LIBERTÉ - ÉGALITÉ - FRATERNITÉ

MAISON SPÉCIALE DE SANTÉ DE VILLE-ÉVRARD

DEMANDE DE PLACEMENT VOLONTAIRE

VOLONTAIRE

*Je, soussigné,* (1) K. Kamlamayan
*demeurant à* Paris
*âgé de* 29 *ans, profession d'* étudiant agricole *déclare*
*en ma qualité d'* ami *, que mon intention est de placer*
*dans la Maison spéciale de Santé de* Ville-Évrard *et prie en conséquence M. le Directeur dudit*
*établissement d'y recevoir pour l'y faire traiter de la maladie mentale dont est atteint* (2)
M Père Gomidas prêtre arménien
*âgé de* 50 *ans,*
*demeurant à* Constantinople *département d'* Turquie
*profession de* prêtre arménien.
*Fait à* , *le* 7 Avril 1919.
POUR COPIE CONFORME : *Le Directeur,*
Signé : Kévork Kamlamayan.

(1) Nom et prénoms de la personne qui fait la demande de placement.
(2) Nom et prénoms du malade dont l'admission est demandée.

Request for involuntary treatment, signed by Kevork Kamlamayan rectory apartment of the Jean-Baptist Armenian Church at 15 Rue Jean-Goujon, where he had stayed on many occasions during his trips to Paris. The place did not hold happy memories for him, however, for it was the same church whose administration had refused to hire him as choirmaster in 1906–07, a decision that deprived him of the chance to remain in Paris with his beloved Margaret. Because of this past rejection, and because he was becoming less and less capable of rational thought, Komitas did not want to stay in the rectory's apartment, insisting instead on walking the grounds during the day and sleeping in the dark, cold cellar at night, much to the dismay of those charged with caring for him.[5]

By this time his bitterness was spilling over to encompass virtually his entire Parisian social circle. He had long since realized that he had been duped once again, this time by tales of a nonexistent musical conference. Like his friends in Constantinople, his friends in Paris had deceived him and ignored his rights as an individual. Consequently, he refused to speak to the members of Paris's Armenian community involved in his care and expressed a malignant alienation and anger that was painful and frightening to them.[6] To Margaret Babaian, whom he had once adored as his closest, most trusted friend, he was now "indifferent . . . as if already in another world."[7] His intense embarrassment at what, in his own eyes, he had become—a tormented scarecrow of his former self—meant that he could not face her. Little was left of the brilliant music scholar, of the flirtatious and good-humored man who had tried to win the heart of a talented, spirited opera singer.

Puzzled by his harsh treatment of them, his friends were confronted with the agonizing dilemma of what to do next. His transfer to Paris was producing none of the beneficial effects they had hoped for, and pressure was mounting from all sides. Komitas's arrival had been widely publicized in the Armenian press, and the Armenian community in Paris, to whom he was a cultural icon, was demanding that he be given the best treatment and care available. To this end, Archag Tchobanian, Margaret Babaian, and an Armenian-born, French-educated psychiatrist, Dr. Paul Cololian, formed a group called "*Komitas Vartabedi Paregamneru Hantsnakhump*" ("Friends of Komitas") dedicated to raising money for his hospital expenses and collecting his works.[8]

Hôpital Villejuif, near Paris

Over the coming years many would volunteer to serve on this committee, but none would prove more devoted than Margaret Babaian, who was its first chairperson. Through the diligence of Margaret and the committee, Komitas was cared for until his death, and his musical manuscripts were either published or sent to Yerevan, where an archive was established for them at the Charents Museum of Literature and Art.

Given Komitas's hostility toward all who tried to care for him, the members of the group soon believed they had no alternative but to place him in a hospital. On the advice of Dr. Paul Cololian, they chose a first-class mental hospital located in a suburb of Paris: Maison Spéciale de Santé de Ville-Évrard.[9]

Established as an asylum in 1869, Ville-Évrard had built a reputation as a treatment facility for the wealthy. Patients were divided into three "classes." The members of the *première classe*, each of whom paid roughly twenty francs a day for the privilege, stayed in "Pavilion 1," which was fenced off from the rest of the hospital, offered private, comfortably furnished rooms, and served finely prepared meals accompanied by wine. They were not required to wear the uniform of the asylum and were permitted to receive guests daily (two hours on Thursdays and Sundays, one hour on all other days of the week); they were also allowed access to a private garden which overlooked a wooded area. It was to this relatively comfortable class of service that Komitas was assigned.[10]

## Komitas's French Psychiatrists and the Dilemma of His Diagnosis

The task of reviewing the medical files on Komitas in the archives of Ville-Évrard and Villejuif presented a number of challenges. Much of the diagnostic terminology that his French physicians used in their daily practice in the early part of the century was unfamiliar to me. This was an effect not only of time but also of place: I studied the history of psychiatry in North America, where the influence of German psychiatry has been pivotal.

At the time of Komitas's long stay in the asylums near Paris, French psychiatry was practiced in ways that made it distinct from the work being done in the rest of Europe, where most psychiatrists had begun to adopt the system of classification devised by the pioneering German psychiatrist Emil Kraeplin (1856–1926).[11] The French psychiatric community had been reluctant to accept Kraeplin's innovative work—perhaps, the historian Pierre Pichot suggests, because of the wave of nationalism sweeping through Europe at the time, which fueled French antagonism towards all things German.[12] In any case, the result was that "the rest of the world progressively accepted the ideas of the German school while French psychiatry became relatively isolated."[13]

* * * * *

The most informative psychiatric consultations date from the early years of Komitas's hospitalization in France (1919–1922), and were the work of three different psychiatrists: Paul Cololian, Maurice Ducoste, and Paul Guiraud. Taken together, these

The private pavillion of Ville-Évrard psychiatric hospital, as it stands today

clinical observations offer an invaluable portrait of Komitas's mental state at the time.

Dr. Paul Cololian, an Armenian-born psychiatrist living in Paris, was given the responsibility—indeed, the *moral duty*, according to Komitas's friends and admirers—of being the first physician to examine Komitas after the fifty-year-old monk's arrival in France. It was up to Cololian to answer the many urgent questions that Komitas's erratic behavior had provoked in his friends, and to recommend a course of action. As noted, a group of friends and acquaintances had at first decided against hospitalizing him in the hope that the damage inflicted by his confinement to Hôpital de la Paix would be undone by allowing him to live quietly in the rectory of Jean-Baptiste Armenian Church in Paris. It soon became clear that his mental condition was complex, and that he probably required the attention of a psychiatrist. Cololian undertook a detailed examination of Komitas on April 6, 1919—which was an exam conducted for legal purposes—and concluded that, for reasons of safety, he urgently needed to be hospitalized. The following day, Cololian, Kevork Kamlamayan (the student who had escorted Komitas on the voyage from Constantinople), and a small group of Komitas's friends brought him to la Maison Spéciale de Santé de Ville-Évrard. Cololian, who had received his psychiatric training in French hospitals, drew up the necessary medical certificate required for Komitas to be legally committed[14] for purposes of treatment.[15]

The story told by the file's legal and medical documents is complex. Looking closely at the certificate written by Dr. Cololian on the day of Komitas's admission to Ville-Évrard, we find the patient's basic background and place of residence ("15 Rue Jean-Goujon," the address of the Jean-Baptiste Armenian Church). And then in a brief paragraph in French, Cololian's diagnostic impressions of Komitas's illness:

> *. . . Dégénérescence mental avec délire polymorphe [underlined by Cololian]: délire d'interprétation, idées de persécution, idées mystiques, agitation par instant et dépression mélancolique par l'autre hallucination de l'ouïe probable.*[16]

The term *dégénérescence mental* was coined by Benedict-Augustin Morel (1809–1873), one of the great pioneers of French psychiatry and the first "psychobiologist" in the history of the field. Morel asserted that psychiatric diagnosis must take into account not only inherited biological factors but also external, environmental influences on the psyche; he attested that nature and nurture are given the same importance. For Morel and his followers, mental deterioration (*dégénérescence mental*) is the outcome of interaction between these two categories: "the double and potent influence of internal essential primary causes and external essential primary causes."[17] It occurs when "external" causes such as grief, poverty, or significant personal loss are brought to bear on a person who possesses some innate disposition towards mental illness, a disposition we now refer to as "biological vulnerability."

A pentioner's room at Ville-Évrard in the years 1910

The importance of "external factors" was later reinforced by proponents of Morel's theories, among them Victor Magnan (1835–1912), who emphasized the significance of violent psychic trauma in mental illness. Using Morel's theories, Magnan advanced explanations as to how people who had lived mentally healthy lives could abruptly become ill (e.g. delirious, melancholic, and/or manic)[18] when placed under the influence of violent and severe stress.[19]

Cololian's diagnosis thus did not focus solely on the severe psychological stress that had been inflicted on Komitas during his arrest and internment, but considered the aspects of his personal and family history—the "internal factors"—that may have rendered him vulnerable to the illness from which he was suffering. As we have noted, Komitas had approached the brink of emotional collapse, in both 1910 and 1912 and had retreated to a spa in the mountains near Kütahya. His parents, too, had displayed signs of deep emotional vulnerability: his father had lapsed into alcoholism in the final years of his life[20] and the circumstances surrounding the mysterious death of his mother, a woman prone to melancholy,[21] suggest that she may have succumbed to post-*partum* depression, a psychiatric illness that afflicts many women shortly after they give birth.

If we translate the nineteenth-century terminology, Dr. Cololian uses in his diagnostic formulation into the vocabulary of present-day North American psychiatric practice, we can say that Komitas was a biologically vulnerable person who developed a significant psychiatric disorder as a result of psychologically traumatic experiences.

The second term in Cololian's diagnosis, *délire polymorphe*, can also be traced to the work of Victor Magnan.[22] As used by French psychiatrists at the time, *délire* denoted the presence of delusions, or "false interpretations" of the real world. The term polymorphe indicates that the delusions took several forms. This diagnostic format—first naming the main category of illness and then indicating its most pronounced aspect in a given patient—is still in use today (for example, depression with psychotic features).

The rest of Cololian's description of Komitas on the Ville-Évrard certificate is given over to a list of symptoms intended to justify his diagnostic conclusions. *Délire d'interprétation*, which appears in the sentence immediately following the diagnosis, is especially noteworthy. Seriux and Capgras, the French psychiatrists who established this class of symptom in 1909,[23] described *délire d'interprétation* as occurring in psychiatric patients whose intelligence was for the most part unaffected by their illness. By using the term, Cololian indicates clearly that Komitas's intelligence and memory had remained largely intact, thus ruling out the possibility that the illness had some organic cause like syphilis, which was one of the most common causes of psychiatric illness at the turn of the century, and typically produced severe cognitive impairment.

Cololian goes on to offer an opinion about the actual causes of Komitas's illness, most significantly identifying his *idées de persécution,* first described in detail by the French psychiatrist Delasiauve,[24] who showed how these so-called "false beliefs" were often rooted in experiences of actual persecution—experiences that caused the moods of the afflicted person to be hyper-reactive to environmental stimuli, and forced him or her to lose trust in the intentions of others. In his opinion Komitas's delusions of being persecuted had their source in an actual traumatic experience, precipitated by the persecution that had been inflicted on him by the Ottoman government.

The subsequent reference Cololian makes to Komitas's *idées mystiques* reinforces this. The term reflects the elements of delusions that were shaped by his painful experiences as a clergyman: the attacks on his work by the conservative clergy and the malicious gossip of sexual misconduct that circulated through Etchmiadzin. Again, Cololian implies the sources of his illness do not lie entirely inside the patient's head, but in actual instances of victimization.[25]

Cololian goes on to describe Komitas's moods, noting *agitation par instant et dépression mélancolique par l'autre*, encapsulating the fact that Komitas could swing rapidly from states of high alarm to episodes of deep, heavy sadness. This lack of control over emotion (in psychiatric terminology, an inability to modulate affect) is common in people who have experienced severe trauma. Cololian adds that Komitas also may be suffering auditory hallucinations (*"hallucination de l'ouïe probable"*).

Having ruled out certain organic causes for the illness, Dr. Cololian identified precipitating factors based on knowledge of his patient's traumatic experiences, and described significant symptoms, both actual and possible, his recommendation for treatment being that it was urgent for Komitas to be in a specialized mental asylum.

*****

The next psychiatrist—in the terminology of the day, "alienist"—to examine Komitas was Dr. Maurice Ducoste, the emergency-room physician at Ville-Évrard. He carried out a psychiatric examination on April 7, the day of Komitas's admission to the hospital. His difficulty in examining Komitas is apparent in his report. To Cololian's observations, he adds only the general term *hypomanie* to indicate his belief that Komitas was suffering from a form of acute psychosis.[26] Because historians of French psychiatry do not give a precise explanation of the term, it can only be hypothesized that it was meant to indicate "mental alienation" of a relatively moderate intensity.[27]

Ducoste's detection of the "probabilité d'interprétations délirantes" supports Cololian's observation that Komitas was suffering from "delirious interpretations." Yet, Ducoste introduces an element of uncertainty, which may explain his use of the rather general term *hypomanie.* He seems to be avoiding a firm commitment to any specific diagnosis. Ducoste then refers to what he believes is Komitas's psychiatric history. "Aurait été, d'après les renseignements recueillis de ses compatriotes," he writes, "traité à diverses reprises dans des établissments turcs ou russes [According to his friends, he was treated many times in Turkish or Russian establishments]."[28]

He also implies that Komitas is unaware of his social and mental situation—In present-day terminology, that Komitas demonstrated a "lack of insight" into his own illness. Komitas's apparent inability to comprehend the fact of his illness may to some extent explain the descriptions in Ducoste's report, in which the psychiatrist notes that his patient "does not want to speak to doctors and refuses to sleep in a bed." Ducoste was unaware, however, that refusing the comfort of a bed was a habit Komitas had formed in his poverty-stricken childhood and had made a part of his ascetic practices as a monk.[29] The refusal may also have been a sign of lingering fear, of his readiness to escape if Turkish soldiers were suddenly to come for him again.

Ducoste concludes that Komitas requires the hospitalization requested by Dr. Cololian, and ends the certificate by noting that he is "to be maintained under observation." Fifteen days later, in accordance with the French laws governing hospitalization for psychiatric treatment, Ducoste performed another brief examination and detected little change in the mental status of the patient: "Continues to be hypomanic. No change since admission. Needs to stay."

It is likely that Ducoste was an extremely busy physician, a psychiatrist working in the crowded emergency ward of a psychiatric hospital.[30] To him, Komitas would have been merely one patient among many others requiring prompt attention. Any impression we may have of Ducoste's hastiness is also a result of the fact that diagnostic practices in the early part of this century were markedly different from what they are now. As historians examining the case books of nineteenth-century asylums have noted: "The process of diagnosis as a whole, and as seen in the light of modern categories, does not seem to have been precise or discussed in much detail."[31] This lack of precision was most likely due to a lack of specific treatments.[32]

In this light, Cololian's earlier diagnosis seems remarkably precise and complete. As we have seen, he identifies his patient, introduces a complex diagnostic impression, rejects medical conditions such as syphilis as causes of the illness, suggests that state terrorism may have been a precipitating factor, describes Komitas's moods, documents the possibility of hallucinations, and concludes with a proposed plan for treatment. Unlike his colleague, Cololian, an Armenian, *knew* Komitas, not only personally but also as an immensely important figure to the Armenian people. By this time, in Armenian communities everywhere, Komitas was being perceived as a living symbol of the sufferings endured by all victims of the Genocide.

As to what became of Komitas during his three-year stay at Ville-Évrard, the file is silent: it contains no record of examinations or attempted treatments.

A document in Komitas's file at the Ville-Évrard archives gives us a vivid description of him. Dated April 20, 1919, and entitled "Fifteenth-day questionnaire of M. Gomidas" (the French transliteration of his name), it is an invaluable summary of his condition and behavior during his first two weeks at the hospital:

1. The patient is docile, obedient and polite.
2. He is neither timid nor violent with the personnel, but has displayed hostility towards Dr. Lwoff and to other patients who wanted to converse with him.
3. His disposition seems to be normal but he seldom communicates.
4. The patient never sleeps in his bed; he takes his shoes off and sleeps on the *chaise-longue*.
5. Satisfies his needs regularly and appropriately [referring to bowel movements].
6. His appetite is excellent, he eats all his meals appropriately, does not use the napkins given to him.
7. Never goes to the park.
8. He goes for walks and he rests alternately in the garden and in the corridor, he has read or written nothing since he came here.
9. He has played music on only three occasions.[33]
10. He has not asked to go to Mass, nor have I seen him pray in any way.
11. He never speaks to Messieurs.[34]
12. Apart from some conversations with his doctors during his visit, he does not get involved with anyone.
13. The patient looks with indifference on external events, always refuses the magazines and books offered to him.
14. Apart from his mania [his sickness] of sleeping on the *chaise-longue*, he has not shown any bizarre behavior since his admission.

> 15. Does not show any appreciation for the care he receives, nor does he make any complaints.
>
> 16. He never spoke of his family nor of his friends, except for his comrades who brought him here.
>
> 17. Because he does not communicate much, I am unable to say what delusions [*délire*] he has; from some of the words he wanted to tell me it seems that he adores good music and [thinks that] bad music harms humanity; [he considers] his students who brought him here not to be his friends (he was very upset when he said this) and they are not honest with him.[35]

Komitas remained at Maison Spéciale de Santé de Ville-Évrard until July 31, 1922, a period of three years and four months. During this time, no significant improvement was observed in his mental health, despite the excellent living conditions at the asylum.[36] The fund raising efforts of his friends had not always been successful in meeting the costs of keeping him as a privileged patient in a private institution, and the committee of the "Friends of Komitas" decided with regret that the time had come to transfer him to the public Hôpital Villejuif.

Founded in 1884, Hôpital Villejuif is located on the outskirts of Paris, and remains in operation to this day, surrounded by green lawns and gardens, flowerbeds, statues, and fountains. Komitas would spend the next thirteen years, the rest of his troubled life here in this quiet and surprisingly pleasant institution, growing older and grayer as a ward patient in room No. 3, a small, sparsely furnished room overlooking the gardens.

The transfer note written in 1922, when Komitas was moved from Ville-Évrard to Villejuif, is of considerable interest. It further illuminates the nature of his illness and the ways in which it was perceived by physicians working in the early decades of the twentieth century.

The note, dated July 31, 1922, was written by Dr. Paul Guiraud, who was in all likelihood Komitas's treating doctor during the three years at Ville-Évrard. It reads:

> Persecutory and grandiose delusions are resulting from several bouts of periodic psychosis. He is withdrawn, isolated, mute and irritable. He has alternating inactivity and motor agitation. He believes that he is the victim of secret plots, and considers himself "initiated into the Mysteries of Nature and Life. Must remain interned. Can be transferred with a couple of chosen male nurses.[37]

When an anthology of memoirs written by Komitas's friends and colleagues was published in 1960,[38] most Armenians (including Armenian psychiatrists) who read the book immediately concluded that Komitas had suffered from either paranoid schizophrenia or manic-depressive psychosis. This opinion was based on the accounts of Komitas's delusions that were included in the memoirs, and grew in currency as a result of a lack of sustained, professional analysis—particularly analysis of his files at Ville-Évrard and Villejuif.

The prominent French psychiatrist who had treated Komitas was never identified, and as I researched Dr. Guiraud as a clinician,[39] I found that he preferred using older diagnostic terms in place of the various terms that were quickly coming into vogue through the influence of the German and Swiss schools. He would, for instance, use *hebephrenia* to denote what was then becoming more and more widely known as *schizophrenia*, the category of mental illness in which the Swiss psychiatrist Eugene Bleuler was doing influential work.[40]

What is important for our purposes here is not the fact that Guiraud favored one term over another, but that if he had detected in Komitas any sign of what we now call schizophrenia, he would have included the term *hebephrenia* in the transfer note. In doing so, he would have given credence to the widespread, long-standing assumptions about the nature of Komitas's illness.

As an opinion, of course, an assumption of schizophrenia was not entirely groundless. Even today, whenever a clinician encounters a patient who displays psychotic symptoms of the type that Komitas had—delusions (false beliefs) or hallucinations (hearing voices or seeing things that others do not)—he or she often places schizophrenia high on the list of possible diagnoses. But present-day practitioners know that psychotic symptoms can be produced by a great many factors other than schizophrenia, including depression, drug addiction, and trauma-related disorders.

Moreover, as the painter Panos Terlemezian observed on his visit to Ville-Évrard, Komitas never lost his capacity to use and understand abstraction, a crucial fact in determining whether his illness can be linked to schizophrenia.[41] His capacity for abstract thought and his ability to use symbols in a coherent manner in his responses to Terlemezian's questions indicate that he was not suffering from schizophrenia. His sophisticated comparison of Ville-Évrard to "a cemetery" and his use of the analogy of "peaches and apricots" to describe the relationship between Armenian and European musical forms show that his ability to think abstractly was undiminished.

Komitas's mental condition had not improved by the time he was transferred from Ville-Évrard to Hôpital Villejuif. The note written by Dr. Lwoff, the admitting physician at Villejuif,[42] dated August 6, 1922, observes:

> The patient is struck with persecutory delusions, with false interpretations and grandiose conceptualizations, mystical ideas, irritability, hostility toward physicians, resistance toward treatment.[43]

Two weeks later Komitas was reexamined by Dr. Ducoste, who apparently could find nothing to add to Lwoff's evaluation. By the middle of August, all the "alienists" who had met with Komitas had arrived at a consensus: the patient was psychotic and had to remain in "placement volontaire," "committed" to a hospital. Little or nothing could be done to help him.

For all its vaunted expertise, the French psychiatric system had produced no improvement in Komitas's condition in the three years he had spent in it. Bewildered and haunted by guilt, his friends now desperately began searching for alternative forms of treatment that might reestablish the ties that had been severed between Komitas and the society that revered him so deeply. Their inquiries soon directed them to Vienna, where Freud and his followers were attempting to treat psychological trauma using methods based on free association. Excited by the possibility of placing their troubled friend in the care of this famous innovator, they set about planning yet another transfer, and asked Dr. Lwoff for the required permission. His discharge note, written on August 5, 1922, remains part of Komitas's file at Villejuif:

> May be released under the care of the Armenian Committee [the "Friends of Komitas"] chaired by the Bishop of the Armenian Church of Paris who will be responsible for the patient . . . [Komitas] is a monk with no family. Mr. Komitas will be transferred to Vienna (Austria) under the care of the Committee. The Committee has taken all the necessary measures for his transfer under good conditions.[44]

Only two months after Komitas's admission to Villejuif, everything was in place for a move to Vienna. Yet the transfer never took place. Why? Surely many of the logistical problems involved in such a plan could have been overcome: the Mkhitarist Congregation of Vienna, whose abbey and properties were situated a mere ten-minute walk from Freud's clinic, would have been able to offer Komitas a place to stay. Was the plan aborted because of a lack of funds or a failure of nerve? The precise reasons are unknown. But whatever the case, the plan's failure doomed Komitas to languish in Villejuif until his death thirteen years later. What effect Freud's methods might have had on him, how successful they would have been in the face of Komitas's psychoses, is debatable, of course. Yet we cannot help but wonder how the great Viennese psychoanalyst would have responded to the sensitive and creative adult ravaged by catastrophic childhood losses and political persecution, a case, which had all but defeated Freud's eminent French colleagues.

Throughout the many years of his hospitalization—three and a half years at Ville-Évrard, and the thirteen years he was to spend at another Parisian hospital, Villejuif, very little in the behavior described earlier seems to have changed. He typically reacted in one of two ways to visitors whom he believed to have participated in the "plot" to hospitalize him: either he would display indifference and ask to be left in peace, or he would become agitated to the point that his guests would be driven away in confusion and fear. Komitas received great many visitors during these years. He might have had a great many more if word had not spread that his guests were seldom greeted warmly. For a time, the visits were banned altogether: according to a September 19, 1921 document in the Ville-Évrard file, Margaret Babaian, acting as treasurer of "the Armenian Society," requested that all future visitors be prevented from seeing Komitas—probably a reaction to the uproar that reports of the visits had created within the Armenian community.

Komitas's old friend and musical collaborator Dikran Chituni, who had moved to the safety of Paris not long after he did, waited eleven years before he visited.[45] Likewise, the journalist Siruni, who often passed through Paris, avoided visiting: "Although I had heard that Komitas dismissed his friends, I was not afraid of rejection. I was terrified of his eyes. Who knows how much anger and resentment he held in them?"[46] Eventually even Margaret stopped coming to the hospital.

What his friends and visitors did not know was that Komitas's puzzling behavior toward them was fairly typical of severely traumatized persons: not having control over one's thoughts and actions inevitably brings about overwhelming feelings of shame, fear, and helplessness. Anger and withdrawal are ways of defending against these feelings. While the traumatized person may long for intimacy, the fear of rejection and disappointment often forces him or her to behave in ways that produce the opposite result.

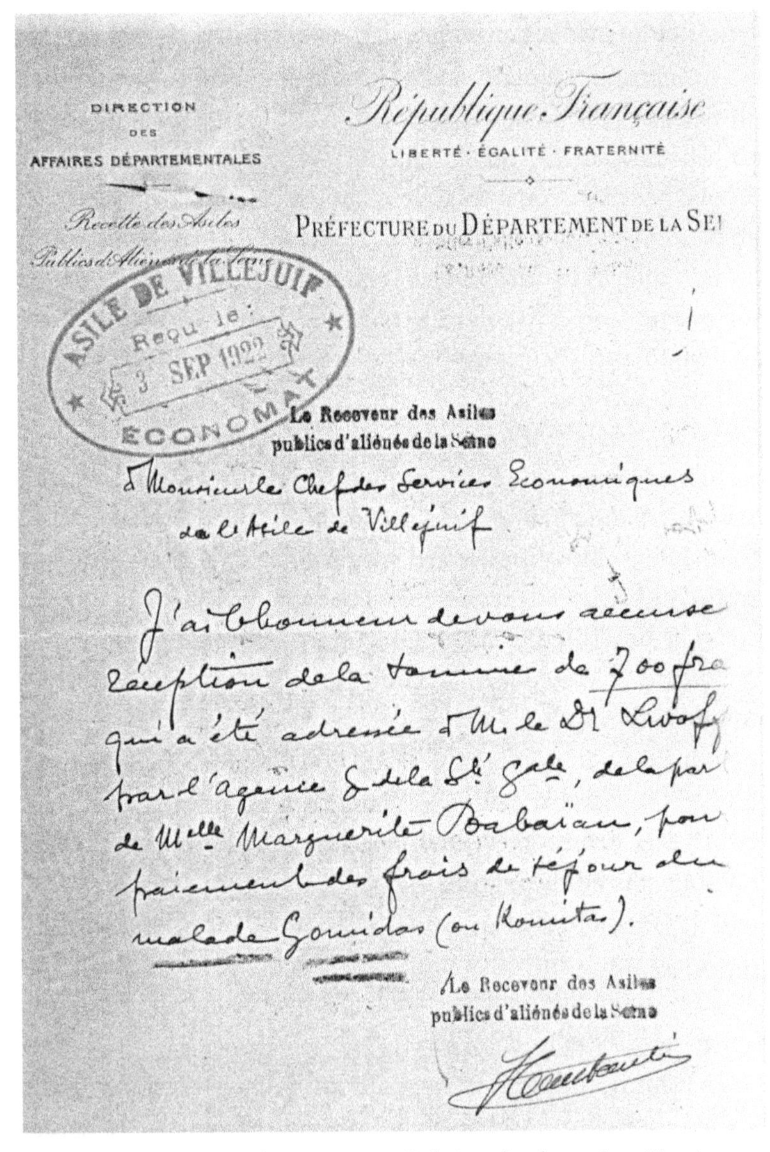

DIRECTION
DES
AFFAIRES DÉPARTEMENTALES

République Française
LIBERTÉ · ÉGALITÉ · FRATERNITÉ

Recette des Asiles
Publics d'Aliénés de la Seine

PRÉFECTURE DU DÉPARTEMENT DE LA SEI

ASILE DE VILLEJUIF
Reçu le:
3 SEP 1922
ECONOMAT

Le Receveur des Asiles
publics d'aliénés de la Seine

à Monsieur le Chef des Services Economiques
de l'Asile de Villejuif

J'ai l'honneur de vous accuser réception de la somme de 700 fr qui a été adressée à M. le Dr Lwoff par l'agence G de la Sté Gale, de la part de Melle Marguerite Babaïan, pour paiement des frais de séjour du malade Gomidas (ou Komitas).

Le Receveur des Asiles
publics d'aliénés de la Seine

A receipt for 700 FF from Margaret Babaian, for the patient Komitas, addressed to Dr. Lwoff, in Komitas's medical file in Paris

* * * * *

As years of research have shown, extremely traumatic experiences, such as being interned in a death-camp, cause profound alterations in the person's relationships to himself and those around him. "Along with the loss of the belief in a just or ordered world," writes Patti Levin, victims lose "the illusion of invulnerability." Often they also stop "reaching out to others," despite the "stronger needs for affective closeness" that the loss-stress relationship typically creates. Because the damaging consequences are reinforced by difficulties in controlling one's mood, by a decreased ability to experience feelings, and by the impulse to avoid any contact that may provoke anxiety," traumatized persons experience what Levin refers to as "trauma residue . . . [which includes] intensely painful feelings of terror, disgust, rage, anxiety, irritation and apprehensiveness."[47] Seen in this light, the seemingly "irritable" behavior that Komitas often displayed becomes fully comprehensible.

A select few were spared his anger. One of these was his former roommate from Pangalti Street in Constantinople, the painter Panos Terlemezian, whom Komitas received cordially. Terlemezian's memoirs of his 1921 visit to Ville-Évrard[48] provide us with a clear depiction of the speech and thought disorders, many of them symptomatic of psychosis, that afflicted Komitas at this time. Much of what he said seemed bizarre or incoherent. Asked for his views on painting, he replied that painting was not necessary: "light and nature" were the only things that were truly important. During a discussion of philosophical matters, he declared his belief that death did not exist. He followed this remark by opening the door of his room and saying, "If this is not a cemetery, what is it?" Later in the conversation, as Panos wondered whether Armenian music was better than European music, Komitas's words were again tinged with anger: "Brother, you cannot get the taste of peach from an apricot—each has its place." When Panos asked him if he still sang, Komitas said that now he sang only "very low and for myself." Although he made it clear that he did not want his friend to leave: "Why don't you stay, since you have come here!" His quick temper, his sadness, and his other volatile emotions were never far below the surface. After conversing for another half-hour, he became visibly upset. He went to the window, put his face to the glass, and fell silent. When Panos finally arose and left he made no sound.[49]

His medical file makes no mention of psychiatric treatment being offered to him during this time. His negative attitude toward the psychiatrists caring for him, which may have become even more entrenched after the transfer from Ville-Évrard, had so alienated them that they abandoned their attempts to help. Or did the fact that electroshock therapy was not in common use, and pharmacological treatments were not yet devised, mean that patients committed to long-term stays in psychiatric wards had no remedy available to them but custodial care?[50]

Five years after he had been taken there, the wisdom of placing Komitas in the custody of an asylum was publicly questioned by Asadur Navarian, a well-known Armenian writer who had been born in Komitas's home town of Kütahya and had later moved to Paris. It was a challenge that spawned great public controversy. Navarian, accompanied by the Torosian sisters (former members of one of Komitas's choirs), went to visit Komitas at Villejuif in December 1927. A month later he published two articles in *Haratch*, an Armenian-language daily based in Paris.

According to Navarian's account, when the visitors kissed Komitas's hand in observance of the traditional Armenian protocol for greeting clerics, he returned the gesture by kissing the hands of the young women, as if he were participating in a grand-salon. He then sat on the edge of his bed, a thin, stooped figure in a black clerical habit, which Navarian describes as "tragic," his hair and beard completely gray but his face still radiating dignity. His responses to the questions and comments of his guests were often incoherent, in the course of the conversation he mentioned his time in Chankiri, a statement that shattered a very old silence.

Komitas was now fifty-seven and this is his first recorded mention of the place where over twelve years before, his sanity had begun to give way. After this, he continued to ramble, returning again and again to the idea of "home":

> The universe is very wide [said Komitas]. Everyone has his own place in it. [The Primate of Romania] should stay in his own home and I'll stay in mine . . . This is what we should do in order to understand life. Our homes are our national soul . . . The home is the cornerstone of the social unit . . . Sometimes a flood, a bloody flood, comes and sweeps away our homes . . . [51]

Navarian concluded his articles by suggesting not only that the psychiatrists' diagnosis of Komitas's illness might have been wrong, but that Komitas had been thrown into the public asylum for the sake of saving fifteen francs (*ancien*) a day, presumably the difference in cost between Ville-Évrard and Villejuif.[52] He asserted that Komitas's recovery was being impeded by the condescending attitude of his friends, who, he charged, were treating him unjustly as an irreversible mental case. Although he conceded that Komitas showed some signs of mental illness, Navarian did not request them as anything other than the predictable and treatable effects of the great hardships that Komitas had endured in life.

Navarian's articles, the first in a long series of speculative attempts made by various people to understand the nature of Komitas's illness, had an enormous impact on Armenian communities around the world. The Friends of Komitas were quick to publish a rebuttal in the Armenian press; their statement, presumably written by Tchobanian, declared that the opinions of Navarian lacked "seriousness and credibility," and asserted that the committee was doing everything it could to help the tormented patient.[53]

This defense was not powerful enough to alter the widespread belief among Armenians that the committee of "Friends" bore at least some responsibility for Komitas's plight. As Siruni noted, after reading Navarian's assertions and the committee's response, the strange discrepancy between Komitas's hostile behavior toward friends and his cordial response to strangers implied to the public that he was profoundly angry with his friends, that he had never forgiven them for depriving him of his home and belongings by hospitalizing him against his will. Siruni's own conclusion, expressed years later in an article written in 1969, was that Komitas's anger encompassed humanity as a whole.

* * * * *

As controversial as his articles on Komitas were, Navarian was right to remark on the powerful effects of his past tragedy on his present predicament. Indeed, many of the hardships that Komitas had endured over the course of his life—the early death of his mother, his father's alcoholism and death, his complete lack of immediate family, his internment in Chankiri—were alive and vivid in one of his last recorded conversations. It took place in March 1933, when his old friend Armenag Shahmuratian and four others paid him a visit.

> [Komitas] saw Shahmuratian and said . . . "Armen is that you? Where were you all this time?" . . . With perfect memory, he mentioned some names and asked for news of them. . . . We all sat around a table, and at times he asked very coherent questions. At other times he said incomprehensible things and launched into long monologues. . . . Then he advised us . . . "If you have nice faces like this, you will have unity in your homes . . . otherwise your families will be destroyed" . . . We asked him how he spent his time . . . did he write, read or work? He answered . . . "No, as long as I stay here and don't have my wife and my children with me, and no longer have a home, I can't work . . . I still have lots of work here . . . lots of soldiers which I have to watch . . . work is hard . . . very hard . . . I just finished that work . . . you came later . . . I finished earlier . . . ."[54]

Komitas now lived in an internal world governed by the ineradicable images of his past. Long stretches of time had collapsed to form a tightly linked chain of sad events, which remained fixated in his mind: his tragic childhood, his life without a family or home, his exhausting fear of "soldiers." Eighteen years had passed since his arrest and internment at Chankiri, yet he still

RÉPUBLIQUE FRANÇAISE
LIBERTÉ - ÉGALITÉ - FRATERNITÉ

1er feuillet

Préfecture du Département de la Seine

Placement VOLONTAIRE

ASILE DE VILLE ~~JUIF~~ — Évrard

Copie des Certificats médicaux

N° M[le] P.V.

concernant l'aliéné ~~R. Père~~ Gomidas
Prêtre arménien

Asile de Ville Évrard. — Immédiat — 7 avril 1919

Paraît atteint d'hypomanie, probabilité d'interprétations délirantes. Aurait été, d'après les renseignements recueillis de ses compatriotes, traité à diverses reprises dans des établissements turcs ou russes. Inconscient de sa situation, ne veut pas parler aux médecins, refuse de se coucher dans un lit. A maintenir en observation.
Signé : Dr Ducoste

Asile de Ville Évrard. — Quinzaine — 22 avril 1919

Est atteint d'hypomanie. Pas de modification depuis l'entrée. Doit être maintenu.
Signé : Dr Ducoste

Asile de Ville Évrard. — Transfert — 31 juillet 192[illegible]

Est atteint de délire de persécution et de grandeur consécutif à plusieurs accès de psychose périodique.
Repliement sur lui-même, mutisme et instabilité, inactivité alternant avec de l'agitation motrice.
Se croit victime de machinations secrètes et se considère comme "Initié" aux Mystères de la Nature et de la Vie.
Réactions vives à l'égard des pensionnaires et des médecins.
Doit être maintenu interné. Peut être transféré par deux infirmiers choisis.
Signé : Dr Paul Guiraud

(Voir 2e feuillet)

PRÉFECTURE DU DÉPARTEMENT DE LA SEINE
[illegible]
VILLEJUIF

Pour copie conforme :
Le Directeur de l'Asile de Villejuif

Official form containing handwritten copies of the medical certificate for Komitas's admission to Ville-Évrard, the report of an examination carried out fifteen days later, and a transfer note signed by Dr. Paul Guiraud feared that at any moment policemen might reappear at his door and drag him back down into the horrors of the Genocide.

Memory would also bring the occasional moment of healing, however, and Komitas's old humorous and compassionate self would briefly be restored. At the end of his meeting with Shahmuratian, for example,

> He saw us to the garden. We hugged him and kissed him again and again.... The girls kissed his hand... Vartabed told them to give his greetings to the "Kertenkellas" [a type of lizard] as he jokingly called his students and friends in the old days....[55]

As his life drew to a close, these moments of respite became more frequent, the passing of time finally closed some of his old wounds and allowed him to resolve his anger. This explains the atmosphere surrounding his last recorded meeting with friends, which took place in May 1935, only five months before he died. By this time a severe and painful foot infection, from which he had been suffering for months, despite surgery and various treatments, had begun to spread and was ravaging his health. Bedridden and very weak, he nevertheless conversed pleasantly and willingly with his visitors and asked each of about their families. As if aware of his approaching death, he reminisced about Kütahya and Etchmiadzin. But he appeared to think little of his own life, and instead advised his visitors "to take care of the children of the Armenian nation... to love each other, to love a lot so you can live...."[56] Later he asked them to kneel by his bed and blessed each one with his weak hands.

It is not known if any of his friends was present when, at five minutes after four on the afternoon of October 20, 1935, Komitas succumbed to "*cachexie organique*" (wasting caused by vascular illness), and his remarkable and deeply troubled life finally came to an end.[57]

* * * * *

Komitas's funeral was held on Sunday, October 27, 1935, in the Jean-Baptist Armenian Church on Rue Jean-Goujon in Paris. He had lain in state there for three days, in an oak casket with a small glass window through which his emaciated face could be seen. The crowd of mourners that gathered for the funeral was probably more than a thousand strong and spilled out of the church's doors. During the funeral mass, Armenag Shahmuratian sang Komitas's "God, Bestow on Us Your Mercy." Karekin Khachaturian, an Armenian bishop visiting from California, read the eulogy. Twelve other dignitaries also read eulogies, describing Komitas as an artist and a scholar who had introduced Armenian music to Armenians and foreigners alike. He was celebrated as a teacher whom thousands followed, a source of inspiration to Armenians everywhere.[58]

In May 1936, Komitas's embalmed corpse was transferred to Armenia, and was put to rest at the Armenian Pantheon in Yerevan. Until an official memorial to the Genocide was finally erected in Yerevan in 1967, his tomb served as a cenotaph around which Armenians would gather every April 24 to commemorate the one and a half million people who perished in the terrors that began with the "Red Harvest" of 1915.

## Notes to Chapter Nine: The Lost Years, 1918–1935

1. Vahram Torkomian, "Hushadedres," 71.
2. The money was probably in *mejidiye*, the Turkish currency.
3. H.J. Siruni, "Komitasi Hed" [With Komitas], *Etchmiadzin* (Etchmiadzin) (April 1969): 38.
4. The terms "ideas" and "idea-changing" are verbatim translations of *kaghapar*, by which Torkomian implies that Komitas was obsessed by persecutory ideas derived from his experiences in the death camp.

5. Visitors to the church can descend to this cellar where Komitas isolated himself. It is now a depository for old books and journals. With its steep stairs and small window, it is dark, cold, and eerie.
6. Darryl Watts and Gethin Morgan, "Malignant Alienation," *British Journal of Psychiatry* 164 (1994): 11–15.
7. Margaret Babaian, "Husher Komitas Vartabeden" [Memories of Komitas], *Arevmoudk* (Paris), no. 5 (1946): 147.
8. Although this group went under many names over the years, we refer to it as the "committee" of the "Friends of Komitas." The group originally dubbed "*Komitas Vartabedi Bashdban Hantsnakhump* [Committee for the Protection of Komitas Vartabed]." Later it also referred to itself as "*Komitasian Khênamadar Hantsnakhump* [Komitas Curatorial Committee]" and "*Parisi Komitasian Hantsnazhoghov* [Komitas Commission of Paris]." By 1953 its letterhead read simply "*Comité du Père Komitas.*" These changes reflected the evolving demands placed on the group. Its first task was finding a safe haven for Komitas, but as the years of his hospitalization passed, his most pressing need was the support of dedicated friends. After his death the committee helped establish an archive of his works in Yerevan, and between 1925 and 1951 was responsible for releasing a series of seven booklets which contained most of his published works.

   On a recent trip to Paris, I visited the Armenian General Benevolent Union's Nubar Library and discovered that it had served for decades as a meeting place for Paul Cololian, Archag Tchobanian, Margaret Babaian, Aram Andonian (who was director of the library from 1928 to 1951), and Vahram Torkomian, who moved to Paris from Constantinople in 1922, after the massacre of Greeks and Armenians in Smyrna. Many of the decisions regarding Komitas and his work must have been made here. Even after Komitas's death, the group would gather at the library to discuss literature, politics, and issues concerning refugees of the Armenian Genocide.
9. I gathered much of the information given below during a visit I made to Ville-Évrard during the summer of 1997, when I also met with Gilbert Leon, a historian of psychiatry in Paris. Ville-Évrard kept record-books in which each patient's demographic, personal, medical, and diagnostic information was accorded two pages.
10. Medical File of Komitas, from Maison Spéciale de Santé Ville-Évrard, Docs. 2, Société d'études et de Recherches Historiques en Psychiatrie, Paris. Komitas's Ville-Évrard file is presently stored as a historical document by the Société d'Etudes et de Recherches Historiques en Psychiatrie (SERHEP). It was this organization that made the file available to me.
11. Pierre Pichot, "Historical Introduction to Psychiatry," in *The Scientific Basis of Psychiatry*, edited by Malcolm P.I. Weller and Michael W. Eysenck (London: W.B. Saunders, 1992): 43.
12. *Ibid.*, 43.
13. *Ibid.*, 43.

14. Cololian played a critical role in organizing medical assistance for Armenian expatriates and refugees. In 1919 he established a union of Armenian medical doctors, which later became known as the UMA (*Union Médicale Arménienne*). In collaboration with Vahram Torkomian, he also founded the Armenian Red Cross. These two organizations were soon working in tandem with members of the UMA assisting the Armenian Red Cross by offering free consultations and medication to the wave of refugees that arrived in Paris at the time. Cololian's union (now called the UMAF) remains a vital resource for Armenians. In particular, their work in the aftermath of the 1988 earthquake in Armenia was invaluable.
15. Leon Murard and François Fourquer, eds., "Histoire de la psychiatrie de secteur, ou le secteur impossible," in *Recherches* 17 (Vaille: Torrubis, 1975): 52.
16. Paul Cololian, Report, 6 April 1919, Medical file of Komitas [Gomidas], Archives of Hôpital Villejuif, Paris.
17. R. Friedlander, *Benedict-Augustin Morel and the Development of the Theory of Dégénérescence* (Ann Arbor, Mich.: University Microfilms International, 1979): 111.
18. Contemporary psychiatry now refers to these states as "confused," "depressed," and "psychotic-agitated," respectively.
19. Yves Pelicier, "France," in *World History of Psychiatry*, edited by John G. Howells (New York: Brunner-Mazel, 1975): 130.
20. Arnag, "Komitas Vartabed," *Hayrenik* (Boston), no. 3 (January 1936): 73.
21. K.N. Kasbarian, "Komitas: Gensakragan Agnarg" [Komitas: A Biographical Sketch], in *Zhamanagagitsnere Komitasi Masin* [Contemporaries on Komitas], edited by K.N. Kasbarian (Yerevan: Haybedhrad, 1960): 8.
22. J. Postel and C. Quétel, eds., *Nouvelle histoire de la psychiatrie* (Toulouse: Editions Privat, 1983): 338.
23. *Ibid.*, 339.
24. *Ibid.*, 339.
25. *Ibid.*, 340.
26. Copie des certificats medicaux, Medical file of Komitas [Gomidas], Archives of Hôpital Villejuif, Paris. The term *hypomanie* has a long and complex history in psychiatric practice. Philippe Pinel (1745–1826), who is widely considered to be the father of French psychiatry, first employed it. Pinel gained notoriety for refusing to allow his patients to be bound in chains, which at the time was standard practice in Bicêtre, the prison-like asylum in Paris where he worked. In the psychiatric lexicon that Pinel developed, the term *manie* simply denoted "mental alienation"—that is, madness in all its forms. By adding prefixes, Pinel's followers—most notably Esquirol (1772–1840)—used this term for specific diagnostic purposes. *Monomanie* was used in the diagnosis of illnesses that produced chronic psychosis with delusions, and *lypémanie* to diagnose depressions such as melancholic sadness. See: Philippe Pinel, *Traité médico-philosophique sur alienation mentale, ou la*

*manie* (Paris: Richard, Caille, 1801); J. Postel and C. Quétel, eds., *Nouvelle histoire de la psychiatrie* (Toulouse: Editions Privat, 1983): 159.

27. The Latin prefix *hypo-* means "to a lesser degree." In contemporary North American psychiatry, *hypomania* is part of the terminology used in diagnosing a milder form of manic phase in manic-depressive psychosis.
28. Here Ducoste is only partially correct. Before being admitted to Ville-Évrard, Komitas had spent time in only one psychiatric hospital, Hôpital de la Paix in Constantinople; he had never been treated in any other institution.
29. The Ville-Évrard files contain a document in which a psychiatric nurse attendant describes Komitas's preference for sleeping in a chaise longue, fully clothed but for his shoes.
30. In 1881, not long before Ducoste's time, there were only 120 psychiatrists in France—one for every 300,000 inhabitants. See: Pierre Pichot, "Historical Introduction to Psychiatry," in *The Scientific Basis of Psychiatry*, edited by Malcolm P.I. Weller and Michael W. Eysenck (London: W.B. Saunders, 1992): 39.
31. Trevor H. Turner, *A Diagnostic Analysis of the Casebooks of Ticehurst House Asylum, 1845–1890* (Cambridge: Cambridge University Press, 1992): 33.
32. *Ibid.*, 34.
33. Komitas probably played the piano in the hospital's lounge.
34. Possibly "Messieurs" refers to members of the hospital staff, e.g. orderlies.
35. Medical File of Komitas, from Maison Spéciale de Santé Ville-Évrard, doc. 19, Société d'Etudes et de Recherches Historiques en Psychiatrie, Paris.
36. According to his records at Ville-Évrard (doc. no. 15), Komitas weighed only 57 kilograms when he was admitted. One year later his weight had risen to 72 kilograms.
37. Paul Guiraud, Report, 31 July 1922. Medical file of Komitas [Gomidas], Archives of Hôpital Villejuif, Paris.
38. Kasbarian, *Zhamanagagitsnere Komitasi Masin* [Contemporaries on Komitas], 8.
39. Pelicier, "France," 133.
40. Even now, a given mental illness may go under two different names in two different countries. Efforts have therefore been made to universalize psychiatric terminology, in order to facilitate exchanges of research information at the international level. Two important examples of such efforts are the International Classification of Diseases (ICD) developed in Europe and the Diagnostic and Statistical Manual of Psychiatric Disorders (DSM) developed in North America.
41. See: Frank J. Fish, *Clinical Psychopathology Signs and Symptoms in Psychiatry* (Bristol: Wright, 1967): 49.
42. Lwoff's first name is not given in the file.
43. Dr. Lwoff, Report, 6 August 1922, Medical file of Komitas [Gomidas], Archives of Hôpital Villejuif, Paris.
44. Dr. Lwoff, Report, 5 October 1922, Medical file of Komitas [Gomidas], Archives of Hôpital Villejuif, Paris.

45. Dikran Chituni, "Komitasi Hed" [With Komitas], *Hayrenik*, no. 2 (1936): 99.
46. H.J. Siruni, "Komitasi Hed" [With Komitas], *Etchmiadzin* (Etchmiadzin) (May 1969): 22.
47. Patti Levin, "Assessing Post-Traumatic Stress Disorder with the Rorschach Projective Technique," in *The International Handbook of Traumatic Stress*, edited by John P. Wilson and Beverley Raphael (New York: Plenum Press, 1993).
48. Terlemezian does not mention the reason for his being in Paris.
49. Panos Terlemezian, "Komitasi Masin" [On Komitas], in *Zhamanagagitsnere Komitasi Masin* [Contemporaries on Komitas], edited by K.N. Kasbarian (Yerevan: Haybedhrad, 1960): 186–197.
50. During Komitas's years at Villejuif, a number of attempts were made to transfer him to other treatment facilities. Only two months after his admission to Villejuif, his friends, seeing that no improvement in his condition was imminent, tried to have him transferred to Vienna. Whether this plan failed for medical or financial reasons is unknown. The next attempt, in the summer of 1933, was made for administrative reasons. Because of overcrowding at Villejuif, the hospital's administration wished to transfer a number of patients to a provincial asylum in Dordogne, and Komitas was among those listed for the move. The committee of "Friends" opposed this transfer; Asdvadzadur Harents, then the treasurer of the committee, pleaded with the administration to allow Komitas to remain at Villejuif. The administration consented. See: Medical file of Komitas [Gomidas], Archives of l'Hôpital Villejuif, Paris.
51. Asadur Navarian, "Tibvatz Te Abakinum" [Coincidence or Recovery], *Haratch* (Paris), no. 531 (1927): 2.
52. The "Friends of Komitas" committee continued its efforts to find money throughout the years of Komitas's hospitalization. In a letter dated September 11, 1926, Archag Tchobanian pleaded with a friend to forward any funds that might be raised from the sale of Russian translations of Komitas's work. In the same letter Margaret Babaian asks if the Academy Choir in Leningrad could organize a special fundraising concert of Armenian music. See: Archag Tchobanian and Margaret Babaian, Letter, 11 September 1926, doc. 70, Komitas Archives, Charents Museum of Literature and Art, Yerevan. The cost of caring for Komitas was twenty francs *ancien* a day. The perception of this cost can be gauged by noting that the typical wage of a nurse at the time was three francs a day.
53. H.J. Siruni, "Komitasi Hed" [With Komitas], *Etchmiadzin* (Etchmiadzin) (May 1969): 24.
54. K. Alemshah, "Ayts me Vartabedin" [A Visit with Komitas], *Haratch* (Paris), no. 50 (1976): 116–117.
55. *Ibid.*
56. H. Garabedian, "Verchin aytselutyun me Komitas Vartabedin" [Last Visit to Komitas Vartabed], *Gochnag* (New York) (14 December 1935): 1185. See

also: Henry Krystal, "The Aging Survivor of the Holocaust: Integration and Self Healing in Posttraumatic States," *Journal of Geriatric Psychiatric* 14, no. 2 (1981): 165–189.

57. Here are the details of Komitas's death and funeral arrangements, as they appear in his medical file of Komitas [Gomidas], Archives of l'Hôpital Villejuif, Paris:
    (1) On October 16, 1935, a telegram was sent to Ms. Magasian at 242 rue de Courcelles, Paris, warning her of Komitas's grave health.
    (2) The death certificate issued on October 21, 1935 specifies the date of the death as October 20, 1935, at 16:00 hours and 5 minutes. The cause of death was identified as "Cachexie Organique."
    (3) A telegram was sent to Asdvadzadur Harents, announcing Komitas's death and requesting clothing for the deceased.
    (4) Two days after Komitas's death, permission was granted to Mr. Alemshah to take an imprint of the face.
    (5) The body was embalmed at 2 p.m., Wednesday October 23, 1935.
    (6) In a document issued by the funeral home, which refers to itself as "Pompes Funèbres Générales," the casket is described as being made of hard oak with metal corners.
58. "Komitas Vartabedi Taghume Metz Shukov Gadarvetsav [The Funeral of Komitas Vartabed Was Carried Out With Great Fanfare]." *Haratch* (Paris), no. 9–11 (1935): 567–569.

# 10

# Epilogue
# Creativity and Mourning

For decades the nature of Komitas's creativity has been debated and discussed by scholars,[1] but this investigation marks for the first time the details of his inner life and mental illness, and subjects them to rigorous psychological analysis. Nor has his scholarly and artistic output been viewed from a psychoanalytic perspective until now. [2]

A psychoanalytic examination of Komitas as a creative artist is, by definition, an examination of the ways in which core psychological issues supplied his art with an overriding purpose and also interfered with his ability to express himself freely. As we shall see, these psychoanalytic vantage points open onto uncharted territories. Using the psychoanalytic method, the core issues conceptualize the conflicts at the core of Komitas's psyche—not only the personal conflicts resulting from his childhood losses and his early ignorance of the Armenian language, but also certain "nationalist" conflicts stemming from the linguistic, religious, and cultural oppression inflicted on Armenians by their Ottoman rulers.

In the tradition of investigating the effects of childhood trauma on the lives and creativity of artistic people, I propose that Komitas's drive to uncover the roots of Armenian national music was in large part a sublimated attempt at mourning—indeed, at symbolically resurrecting—the parents he lost in childhood. The mental illness that struck him later in life, in response to the new and immense trauma of Chankiri, brought an end to this innately creative approach to mourning.

Komitas's creativity was crucial to his mental stability. His stunning restoration of the foundations of Armenian music opened a way for him to move through the consecutive phases of mourning (widely characterized as denial, anger, sadness, and resolution),[3] but his inability to respond creatively to the enormity of internment and genocide, a trauma so dire as to be virtually beyond mourning, brought about psychological disaster. This nightmarish turn of events deprived him of the very instrument of sublimation that he relied upon to heal him of grief and protect him from psychopathology, and its absence propelled him into severe Posttraumatic Stress Disorder complicated by psychotic symptoms.

*****

Komitas's profoundly creative method of coping with grief was one he depended on throughout his most productive years. Three important factors came into play when he was brought to Etchmiadzin as a boy of twelve. First, he was introduced into a highly stimulating cultural environment, presided over by the dynamic personality of Kevork IV. The Catholicos's fervent interest in the preservation of Armenian ecclesiastical music inspired him deeply, to the point that he recognized this great task as his own. Second was his beautiful singing voice, the gift of natural aptitude and family background that won him a place in the Seminary and the admiring attention of the Catholicos. Finally there was the psychological "baggage" he carried with him to the Seminary: orphanhood, poverty, and neglect, all suffered during the formative years of his life.

These factors combined to produce Komitas's unique genius, the first two guiding him to his lifelong vocation and providing him with powerful psychological tools for coping with the third.

The result was music of great importance and beauty—immortal music. As psychoanalyst Howard Gardner has observed:

> Extreme creative behavior is so unusual that perhaps it can occur only under very special circumstances . . . . There is necessity for "co-incidence"—that conjunction of genetic, familial, motivational, and cultural factors which must all be present if the efforts of an Einstein, a Darwin, or a Beethoven are to come to fruition.[4]

In his article "The Mourning Process, the Creative Process, and the Creation," George Pollock reinforces Gardner's point—as well as our synopsis of Komitas's experience at Etchmiadzin—by suggesting that the conversion of grief into powerful works of art is driven by a synthesis of inborn talent and cultural environment.[5]

* * * * *

As we saw, Komitas became an orphan at a very young age, losing his mother when he was six months old and his father when he was ten. It has long been observed that losses of this type, apart from causing acute grief, often provoke intense desires to restore the severed relationship in any possible way. Such attempts at restitution, using whatever psychological or symbolic process available, are meant not only to end the pain of grieving but also to perpetuate the "life" of the lost person. In gifted individuals, they often involve acts of *re-creation* that allow the wounded self to shed the emotional handicaps caused by the trauma of loss.[6]

This process of adaptation and transformation has biological roots. It is universal and as old as humanity, having evolved to sustain individuals as they move through the fundamentally difficult transitions of grieving.[7] Versions of it exist in nearly every culture and religion: Christians believe in the resurrection of Christ and his followers; Buddhists avow the concept of rebirth; and Muslims place their faith in the garden of heaven, to which the souls of martyrs go directly. Restoration of the dead, whether through resurrection, rebirth, or rehabitation, is an ancient and essential component of human belief. It is a "magical" way of coping with the pain of loss and the irreversibility of death. Because earthly restitution is impossible, the process is carried out on a highly abstract level.

An individual who is inherently creative will often use his or her work to construct symbolic surrogates of a relationship that has been dissolved by death.[8] This reconstructive, creative process of grieving takes many forms: as psychoanalyst G.W. Niederlander points out, re-creation can take place "through externalization on canvas, stone, paper, marble, or even the little black dots in musical composition, [which] can turn into rousing, 'living' symphonies or operas."[9] Whatever its form, the object in which this process culminates will contain symbolic representations of the lost figure.

* * * * *

Psychoanalysis, remarks Howard Gardner, is concerned with how "the individual's societal concerns grow out of his own personal and familial conflicts."[10] This insight certainly applies to Komitas, whose relentless efforts to preserve Armenian cultural heritage were fueled by the tumultuous events of his own life. The finality of death was unacceptable to him; indeed, he never spoke of his own mortality, even during the most trying periods of his troubled life. His obsessive transcribing of every fragment of peasant music he encountered was in large part a symbolic attempt to preserve the music of his parents, and, in doing so, to preserve a vital part of them. In his mental and emotional world, his lost parents were transformed into "songs," for he had inherited little else from them other than the ability to perform and create music. In an effort to immortalize them, he devoted himself to ensuring the permanence of the songs of the Armenian folk. If he did not, the music itself might prove to be as transient as the lives of his loved ones. Komitas did in fact transcribe sixty of his parents' songs, all of which he heard when he returned to Kutahya in 1893, after an absence of eleven years.

The same can be said of his obsession with restoring Armenian ecclesiastical music, a monumental task that flowed directly from the loss of his adoptive "father," Catholicos Kevork IV. The Catholicos's reverence for the music of the church inspired Komitas to embark on the project of reviving the long-dead *khaz* system of musical notation. In the mind of the young monk, success in this endeavor would represent not only a triumph for

Statute of Komitas in the park in Yerevan named after him. It faces the state conservatory of music

Armenian sacred music, but also a fulfillment of his deeply seated, unconscious drive to please the Catholicos, to remain the "favorite son" even though the powerful father-figure had gone forever. Like an archeologist, Komitas assiduously tried to reconstruct the past; both personal and historical, in order to give it new life.

The confluence of the personal and the historical in Komitas's art points to one of the major reasons for its enduring importance to the Armenian people. As Howard Gardner notes: "The ideological innovator contrives a meaningful personal solution which, in light of widespread cultural concerns during his lifetime, happens to make profound sense to an entire population."[11] This astute observation distills Komitas's artistic achievement: the remedy he applied to his own wounds also helped to heal the wounds inflicted by history on the Armenian people as a whole. The psychological traumas that Komitas suffered early in life set his great talent to the task of *re-creation*, and furnished him with a lifelong mission that made "profound sense" to his beleaguered countrymen. His desire to rescue Armenian folk music from the threat of oblivion was a faithful echo of the desires of the Armenian nation as a whole, which had found itself repeatedly placed on the brink of assimilation and extinction.

In his long search for an adoptive family, Komitas was eventually led by his innately therapeutic vocation to view himself as a member of the broader Armenian "family"—just as, through his music, Armenians came to regard him as one of their greatest "sons." As we have seen, this search involved a series of ever-widening turns, from his yearnings in childhood ("Grandma, did anyone ask for me?"), to his identification with Kevork IV and the Seminary in Etchmiadzin (as seen in his passing habit of signing his name "Kevorkian"),[12] to his eventual empathy for Armenian culture as a whole. By the end of his search, which began in the confusion and rootlessness of orphanhood, Komitas had become an exalted member of the *kusan* tradition, a "wandering balladeer"[13] who would be welcomed as family by any of the world's scattered Armenian communities.

* * * * *

The various themes of Komitas's grief work grew out of the different nature of the losses he endured. The loss of his parents inspired his secular-folkloric creativity. The loss of his adoptive parent-figures in the church (especially Kevork IV) formed his spiritual-ecclesiastic interests. And his awareness of national losses—of the fact that Armenians had not been an independent people for nearly six hundred years—provided the impetus for his cultural and national concerns.

Thus, the process of mourning his personal losses came to include issues of national identity and culture (as well as the cultural issues of neighboring peoples).[14] "While harmonizing the songs," writes musicologist Robert Atayan, Komitas "paid special attention to preserve the authentic character and pure national color, style and spirit of Armenian folk songs."[15] It was this drive to give expression to authentically Armenian musical forms that inspired Komitas's plans to write operas based on Armenian legends.[16]

This aspect of Komitas's work sheds light upon another of the subtle personal issues that affected him in the early stages of life: the matter of the Armenian language itself. Like most Armenians in Kütahya, his family spoke only Turkish, and when he first arrived in the ecclesiastic stronghold of Etchmiadzin he suffered intense feelings of embarrassment and guilt over his own ignorance and the ignorance of his parents.[17] "If you can't speak Armenian, why did you come?" asked the imposing figure of Kevork IV, who had expressed reservations about admitting a turkophone pupil to the Seminary. In certain respects, the reluctance of the Catholicos was understandable: the church represented the only sphere of Armenian life in which the languages of the ruling powers, Turkish and Russian, did not hold sway. At the Seminary, Komitas was taught the importance of sustaining spoken Armenian in the struggle against assimilation. His subsequent preoccupation with the language can be seen as an expression of guilt, an attempt at repenting the "sin" that he felt he and his parents had committed by speaking and singing only in Turkish. It became a way for him to mourn the deprivation of their freedom to learn and speak their mother tongue.[18]

The unconscious factors that interfered with Komitas's work provoked a good deal of confusion and misunderstanding among the scholars studying his contribution to music.

What are we to make of Komitas's seeming inability to take full credit for his work, and thus for his own creativity? Regardless of the extent to which a given song was the result of his own genius, he invariably signed it with the phrase "Harmonized by Komitas Vartabed [*Tashnagets Komitas Vartabed*]." This practice has misled scholars for decades. As Nigoghos Tahmizian notes, "from the beginning it presented itself as an intricate and confusing issue . . . . It took a long time to recognize the magical power of those words and to emerge from it . . . ."[19]

It is likely that many of the musicologists studying Komitas were ill served by the immense respect they had for his opinions and statements: they simply took the master at his word. The misinterpretation was further reinforced by passages in his letters, in which he complains of being unable to create.[20] Various commentators have devised their own solutions to this mystery: for example, out of deference to Komitas's view of his own work, Tahmizian refers to him as "the ingenious editor of folkloric creations."[21] Conversely, one of Komitas's contemporaries, the music scholar Thomas Hartman, who was not bound to him by national or emotional ties, suggests that he made a mistake by not publishing the original transcriptions of the songs alongside their harmonized counterparts: had he done so, says Hartman, the discrepancies would be enough to make it clear that he was "first and foremost a composer."[22]

Robert Atayan enters this debate firmly on Hartman's side. Like him, Atayan draws attention to the great disparity between unadorned Armenian folk music and Komitas's presentation of it. "After all," he writes, the versions that Komitas produced "were not very accessible to simple folks." These songs, taken "from the mouths of the villagers" and transformed into meticulously orchestrated pieces, "drew sensational reactions from audiences in Europe," who would not likely have been so impressed if they had been presented with a collection of fragments of folk songs.[23] Yet Komitas steadfastly refused to claim authorship. Apparently frustrated with Komitas's persistent self-denial, Atayan goes on to suggest with considerable irony that even if Komitas had completed work on the *Anush* opera (which remained unfinished at the time of Komitas's death), the monk would have accepted credit only for "organizing the musical part from folk themes with very refined editorial work."[24]

Berlin Opera House, September 1999

Komitas's practice here was not simply an expression of humility, for he was certainly aware of the momentous contribution he was making to Armenian musical culture. In large part, his attachment to the phrase "harmonized by . . . " arose from the sanctions against secular pursuits that the Armenian Church imposed on its monks. As we have seen, he first confronted serious criticism of his work in 1895, when he published a collection of music that included love songs. As one commentator has put it, this event "opened the . . . gates of hell upon him."[25] Although he repeatedly and bravely asserted that he would continue no matter what the opposition, he was in all likelihood terrified of punishment at the hands of the church fathers,[26] and was deeply worried that the more "free-spirited" or "secular" aspects of his work would be perceived by those in authority as expressions of his innermost thoughts and feelings.[27] The words "harmonized by Komitas Vartabed" were a way of saying "do not persecute me, for I am not the real author; these are the works of the Armenian people." They obscured his actual contribution to the music and shielded him against the powerful and psychologically devastating criticism being directed at him by certain segments of the clergy. With these words, he took refuge among his people.[28]

Another much-debated matter concerning the psychological hindrances to Komitas's creativity is "his so-called failure to produce large-scale works—more specifically his unfinished opera *Anush,* 'so-called' here because the debate so far has overlooked his masterly re-harmonization of the Armenian Divine Liturgy, a large-scale work by any standard."[29] From the outset, Komitas's trepidation about associating himself with the operatic form was evident. Although he spoke often of *Anush* and his hopes for its completion,[30] he avoided referring to the work as an opera,[31] an omission that indicates conflict. The Armenian Apostolic Church has traditionally forbidden its clergy from even attending theatrical performances, let alone composing them. Komitas himself observed this rule at one time: as a student in Berlin, he turned down an opportunity to sing in the Berlin Opera, despite the fact that he was in dire need of money.[32]

A second reason for his apprehensions about *Anush* was the explicitly secular subject matter of the work. The original poem, written by one of his great contemporaries, Hovaness Tumanian, tells the story of an ill-starred love affair between a peasant girl, Anush, and a shepherd-boy named Saro, a friend of her brother Mosi. During a playful wrestling match, Saro, spurred on by his love for Anush, overpowers Mosi and throws him to the ground. Mosi's honor is so deeply wounded by this act that he avenges himself by killing Saro. Anush, torn between anger and grief, commits suicide in the hope that she will be reunited with Saro in death.

This was the tale brought to Komitas in 1904 by Tumanian's daughter Mariam, who wanted the poem turned into an opera based on folk forms. But there was a strange note of ambivalence

ԿՈՄԻՏԱՍ ՎԱՐԴԱՊԵՏ

ԵՐԳԵՑՈՂՈՒԹԻՒՆՔ ՍՐԲՈՅ ՊԱՏԱՐԱԳԻ

Վերատեսեալ ի ձեռն
ՎԱՐԴԱՆ ՍԱՐԳՍԵԱՆԻ

ՓԱՐԻԶ
1933

Tous droits de traduction et de reproduction réservés pour tous pays.

Title page of the 1933 publication of Komitas's rendering of the Divine Liturgy in Komitas's seemingly enthusiastic acceptance of the project: in a letter to Mariam, he demands many changes to the libretto and emphasizes that he is extremely busy, has a great many other commitments, and "cannot promise when [the score] will be ready"—even that he "[does] not have the appropriate musical instrument on which to test what I have written."[33] No doubt he was drawn psychologically to the conflict portrayed in *Anush,* yet his demands and complaints suggests a weighty sense of reservation about involving himself in it.

According to the notes he wrote on his drafts of *Anush*, Komitas envisioned a significantly altered version of the story, one which he had reoriented (more or less unconsciously) to address the conflicts at the core of his own psyche. In it, Anush kills herself not out of madness and grief but out of "defiance of the unfair treatment to which her worldly love was subjected."[34] The work therefore becomes a metaphor for Komitas's own struggles, with an authority figure (Mosi) destroying romantic love for the sake of honor, and a victim of this act (Anush) taking control—in an extreme manner, to be sure—of her own destiny.[35] Komitas almost certainly saw this as a compelling allegory of his fate at the hands of the church, which had explicitly attacked his secular love songs and implicitly proscribed his strong feelings for Margaret Babaian. For the sake of its honor, the church had betrayed his trust, a stance for which he harbored a sense of deep resentment and defiance.

With all these factors in play, it was psychologically impossible for Komitas to complete work on *Anush*, despite his conscious, genuine desire to do so. The fact that the operatic form itself was forbidden to him by the church, coupled with the overtly secular nature of the story, formed a psychological barrier too strong for him to overcome. Although he did manage to resolve many of his deepest psychological conflicts through symbolic re-creations of lost relationships, he was unable to quell the inner turmoil caused by the incompatibility of celibate priesthood and worldly love.

*Anush*, his only attempt at opera, became one of the victims of this conflict.

He was, however, able to write five songs that were to be included in the opera. In one of them, entitled "*Asum en urin, aghchig er ints bes* [They Said the Willow Tree was a Maiden Like Me]," Anush sings the mythical tale of how a young, romantic girl was transformed into a willow tree, hunched over with the pain of unrequited love. Komitas expresses here how he was attracted by the idea of transformation, through pain, from one form of being to another. This psychological-symbolic game, a type of psychological defense mechanism, also can be seen in his poem "My Mother's Lullaby," described earlier, in which he transforms his mother into a dove. This is also visible in the poem he wrote to Margaret Babaian, in which Margaret becomes a music box to which Komitas speaks. In his final years, this fascination with imaginative transformations took on a pathological tone: in an attempt to achieve his unfulfilled dreams, he imagined a wife and children for himself, thus reviving and perpetuating his struggle against death and loss.

Komitas's creative life ended with his hospitalization in 1916, an event that came on the heels of the attempted annihilation of Armenians in the Ottoman Empire. His art had been rooted in the attempt to restore life to his people, first to his deceased parents and then to Armenian music itself. The deaths of so many of his "family" meant the death of his creativity, his reason for living.[36] His mind was filled with ineradicable images of his experiences in the death-camp. His memory-clock stopped. He became frozen in time. Although he had spent so much of his life grieving, he could no longer mourn. With only anger and defiance available to him, he retreated from the real world into a realm where there could be no more losses, no more pain. He escaped the burden of extreme anxiety, the pain of uncontrollable feelings and unavoidable thoughts, by lapsing into the unreal world of psychosis, in which unrealized dreams sometimes come true.

Komitas performed no miracles in his lifetime, but his music had a profoundly healing effect on the psychological wounds of the Armenian people. Indeed, its restorative powers are still felt by Armenians to this day. His personal, highly creative method of mourning played an integral role in healing an entire nation. What he gave to the Armenian people is similar to what Bartok gave to the Hungarians—the voice of a nation's spirit.[37] Through Komitas and his work, Armenians were able, both consciously and unconsciously, to liberate themselves from the pain and injustice inflicted on them by history.

Notes to Chapter Ten: Creativity and Mourning

1. R. Terlemezian, *Komitas* (Yerevan: Academy of Science of Armenia, 1992); Nigoghos Tahmizian, "Nertashnagyal Badarake yev Hokevor Ayl Yerkeri Tashnavorumner" [The Harmonized Divine Liturgy and Harmonization of Other Spiritual Songs], in *Komitase yev Hay Zhoghoverti Yerazheshdagan Zharankutyune* [Komitas and the Musical Heritage of the Armenian People] (Pasadena: Trazarg, 1994) A. Shahverdian, *Komitas i Armianskaya Musikalnaya Kultura* [Komitas and Armenian Musical Culture] (Yerevan: Haybedhrad, 1956).
2. On p. 3 of the introduction, Tahmizian notes that "the psychology of creative issues" is one of the areas requiring further attention in studies of Komitas.
3. George H. Pollock, "The Mourning Process, the Creative Process, and the Creation," in *The Problem of Loss and Mourning: Psychoanalytic Perspectives,* edited by David R. Dietrich and Peter C. Shabad (Madison, Conn.: International Universities Press, 1990).
4. Howard Gardner, "Creativity in the Adult Years," in *Art, Mind and Brain: a Cognitive Approach to Creativity* (New York: Basic Books, 1982): 356–357.
5. Pollock, 30.
6. Sigmund Freud, *The Complete Psychological Works of Sigmund Freud,* standard edition, vol. 14 (London: Hogarth, 1961): 244–245.
7. Pollock, 27.
8. David R. Dietrich, "The Scope of the Problem of Loss and Mourning," in *The Problem of Loss and Mourning: Psychoanalytic Perspectives,* edited by David R. Dietrich and Peter C. Shabad (Madison, Conn.: International Universities Press, 1990): 2.

9. William G. Niederland, "Trauma, Loss, Restoration, and Creativity," in *The Problem of Loss and Mourning: Psychoanalytic Perspectives*, edited by David R. Dietrich and Peter C. Shabad (Madison, Conn.: International Universities Press, 1990): 79.
10. Gardner, 356.
11. Ibid, 356.
12. Komitas was able to detach himself psychologically from Etchmiadzin and the Kevorkian Seminary only after the election of Mateos II in 1909. During the terms of Kevork IV and Khrimian Hayrig, Komitas enjoyed the favor of the Catholicos, and thus felt himself to be a "son" of the Kevorkian Seminary. This was the reason why he changed his family name from "Soghomonian" to that of the Seminary itself—"Kevorkian." After Khrimian Hayrig's death, Komitas reverted to the practice of referring to himself by the name "Soghomonian." Thus, it was at this relatively late stage in life, at the age of thirty-nine, that he entered the separation/individuation phase of psychosexual development.
13. Ryszard Kapuscinski, *Imperium*, translated by Klara Glowczewska (New York: Knopf, 1994): 45.
14. Komitas was interested in preserving not only the musical heritage of the Armenians, but also those of the Turks and the Kurds. K.N. Kasbarian, "Komitas: Gensakragan Agnarg" [Komitas: Biographical Sketch], in *Zhamanagagitsnere Komitasi Masin* [Contemporaries on Komitas], edited by K.N. Kasbarian (Yerevan: Haybedhrad, 1960): 10.
15. Robert Atayan, "Komitasi *Anush* Anavard Operayi Urvakrere" [The Draft of Komitas's *Anush* Opera], in *Komitasagan*, edited by Robert Atayan, vol. 2 (Yerevan: ARMSSR Academy of Sciences, 1981): 49.
16. Pakhtiar Hovagimian, "Komitasi Taderagan Ashkharhe" [The Theatrical World of Komitas Vartabed], in *Komitasagan*, edited by Robert Atayan, vol. 2 (Yerevan: ARMSSR Academy of Sciences Publication, 1981): 243.
17. When I was a child I experienced similar feelings of guilt and embarrassment whenever my father, a native of the Turkaphone city of Aintab in Lesser Armenia, spoke Turkish.
18. Komitas's love of Armenian extended to literature. One of his idols was the early nineteenth-century novelist Khachadur Apovian.
19. Tahmizian, 41.
20. Matevos Muratian, ed., "Komitasi Andib Namagnere" [Unpublished Letters of Komitas], *Badmapanasiragan Hantes* 17 (Yerevan), no. 1 (1958): 259.
21. Tahmizian, 36.
22. Thomas Hartman, "Komitas," in *Zhamanagagitsnere Komitasi Masin* [Contemporaries on Komitas], edited by K.N. Kasbarian (Yerevan: Haybedhrad, 1960): 56.
23. Atayan, "Komitasi *Anush*," 47.
24. *Ibid.*, 52.
25. Kasbarian, "Komitas: Gensakragan Agnarg," 10.

26. This fear is a deep-seated one, and has provided the thematic underpinnings for many great artistic works. Mozart's *Don Giovanni*, with its tale of a son haunted by the ghost of his father, is just one prominent example.

27. On the other hand, in the privacy of his own home, Komitas seemed to lose this inhibition and give free reign to his emotions. Evidence for this can be found in his notebook of poetry, which contains many love songs. The notebook was found among his belongings after he had been hospitalized, and was published in 1939. Komitas, *Knarerkutyunner* [Poetry] edited by Toros Azadian (Constantinople: Mêshaguyt, 1939).

28. Komitas was not the only cleric-composer to suffer persecution at the hands of his own church. In many respects, the career of Antonio Vivaldi (1678–1741) mirrors that of Komitas. Like him, Vivaldi was ordained at the age of 25 and worked as a music director and choirmaster, most notably at the Ospedale orphanage in Venice. Bored by his duties (just as Komitas would be, two centuries later in Etchmiadzin), Vivaldi cultivated the "secular" side of his personality, composing explicitly worldly pieces and befriending female opera singers. Apparently, this lifestyle eventually caused him to be brought before a court of the Inquisition, which dismissed him as a mere "musician idiot." Like his Armenian counterpart, Vivaldi at one time received a decree from the highest echelons of the church forbidding him to perform his work in particular settings. And just as his tainted relations with the Armenian Apostolic Church forced Komitas to leave Etchmiadzin, Vivaldi eventually felt compelled to forsake Venice for Vienna, where (like Komitas) he died in poverty. W. Kolnder, *Antonio Vivaldi: His Life and Work* translated by Bill Hopkins (Los Angeles: University of California Press, 1970).

29. Nigoghos Tahmizian, "Nertashnagyal Badarake yev Hokevor Ayl Yerkeri Tashnavorumner" [The Harmonized Divine Liturgy and Harmonization of Other Spiritual Songs], in *Komitase yev Hay Zhoghoverti Yerazheshdagan Zharankutyune* [Komitas and the Musical Heritage of the Armenian People] (Pasadena: Trazarg, 1994): 243–278.

30. Hovagimian, 242–260.

31. Atayan, 49.

32. Hrachia Ajarian, "Husher Komitasi Masin" [Memories of Komitas], *Etchmiadzin* (Etchmiadzin) (1953).

33. Komitas, Letter to Mariam Tumanian, 1904, doc. 4, Komitas Archives, Charents Museum of Literature and Art, Yerevan.

34. Atayan, "Komitasi *Anush*," 78.

35. Komitas's identification with the character of Anush can also be seen in the fact that he scored one of the opera's songs with a transcription he had made years before while listening to an Armenian orphan girl sing as she worked on a village rooftop. (See: Atayan, "Komitasi *Anush*," 76.) Earlier we noted Komitas's deep empathy for the sufferings of this girl. Here in the opera we have a creative mingling of Komitas's own painful experiences with those of the orphaned stranger and the fictional heroine. In his eyes, all three had been treated unfairly by life.
36. Albert Nalchajian, *The Psychology of Death* (Yerevan: Punik, 1992): 17.
37. E. Haraszti, *Bela Bartok: His Life and Works* (Paris: The Lyrebird Press, 1938): 18.

# Appendix
# Komitas's Publications

## WORKS COLLECTED AND DISCUSSED BY ROBERT ATAYAN

Over a period of more than twenty years, the distinguished Armenian musicologist Robert Atayan collected and edited Komitas's entire *oeuvre*, which was published in six volumes entitled *Yergeri Zhoghovadzu* [Collected Works].

Komitas. *Yergeri Zhoghovadzu, Arachin Hador: Menerkner* [Collected Works, First Volume: Solo Songs]. Edited by Robert Atayan. Yerevan: Haybedhrad, 1960.

The first volume is comprised of forty solo songs, many of which were initially published by Komitas himself in the collections *Hay Knar* and *Hay Keghchug Yerker.* It also contains songs that the "Friends of Komitas" committee published in a series of seven booklets entitled *Hay Zhoghovertagan Yerazheshdutyun.* A comparison of Komitas's concert programs with the list of songs published in this volume indicates that several of his folk pieces have disappeared. Either they are in some archive or private collection or they have been permanently lost. (*Yergeri zhoghovadzu* 1:8).

According to Robert Atayan, two reasons account for why Komitas did not publish more of his work during the productive period of his life. The first arose from the severe financial constraints of these years; the second, more importantly, was because Komitas was extremely demanding of his own work, publishing only those pieces he deemed to be as close to perfection as he could bring them. Only the songs of *Hay Knar* and *Hay Keghchug Yerker*, therefore, can be considered truly finished. The remaining songs, such as "Dun Ari," "Lusnage Sari Dagin," "Mogats Mirza," and "Oror," were only partially harmonized by Komitas, and so must be classified as works in progress (1:8). Atayan includes these in the volume "because they portray the composer's fine taste, his original and valuable thoughts, certain elements of his creative style"—a unique style which according to Atayan first emerged in 1900, when Komitas returned to Armenia from Berlin (1:8).

Komitas and Manoog Apeghian first published the lyrics for most of the songs during the years 1903–1905, in the form of two volumes entitled *Hazar u mi Khagh*. Each of the volumes contained fifty poems meant to be sung (1:12).

——. *Yergeri Zhoghovadzu, Yergrort Hador: Khêmperker* [Collected Works, Second Volume: Choir Pieces]. Edited by Robert Atayan. Yerevan: Hayasdan, 1969.

The second volume of Atayan's collection is devoted to choral pieces created from folk songs. These works form the largest segment of Komitas's *oeuvre*. That Komitas focused so much of his creative energy on composing for choir was a consequence of conditions in Armenian communities at the time. Political oppression in the Armenian homelands, along with sociopolitical circumstances in the communities of the Diaspora, meant that it was impossible to sustain large, state-funded musical organizations like opera companies and symphonic orchestras. Choirs were therefore the most available way of making music on a large scale. "Choral music performed *a cappella*," writes Atayan, "became the medium through which Komitas expressed, evaluated, and sharpened his unique artistic vision, becoming in the process a world-class choirmaster" (2:1). Komitas found that he could use the form to achieve very different artistic goals, from his modernization of the ancient music of the Armenian Church to his innovative interpretations of popular works based on folk melodies (2:1). The choirs themselves were altered as Komitas proceeded with his musical explorations. He conducted all male, all female, and mixed choirs (2:2). He used so-called "high-volume" and "low-volume" choirs and experimented with many kinds of quadraphonic ensembles. From these he coaxed an enormous array of effects, ranging from the witty mimicry of natural sounds or musical instruments to sublime renditions of well-known melodies (2:2).

Another distinctive feature of Komitas's choral work is the way in which he often grouped songs in pairs, so that they would always be performed one after the other. Joining a song of the same name with another entitled "Sari Sovor," for example, created the pair "Keler Tsoler." "The results of this process were not so much songs as choral poems," says Atayan (2:7). "Komitas would also form suites of vocal music by placing songs in his repertoire in very specific orders, numbering them *1a*, *1b*, *1c*, and so on, in his concert programs. Thus, for instance, 'Alakyaz' would be followed immediately by 'Khengi Tzar,' 'Sareri Vrov Knats,' and 'Yeri, Yeri.' Only one of these multi-part suites, a series of wedding songs, has been published to date."

Still other musical experiments are known to have been conducted by Komitas only because they are mentioned in the programs of his concerts. As Atayan explains, the repertoires of the composer's later concerts "featured the *double choir* form, clearly the result of his admiration of Wagner, who employed double choirs in the operas *Danhauser* and *Flying Dutchman.*" Indeed, Komitas arranged an entire series of folk dances for double choir. Unfortunately, the manuscripts of these works have been lost (2:6).

The songs that Komitas harmonized for his choirs have become classics of Armenian music. As a group they express the full spectrum of human emotions. "'Karun a' communicates strong feelings of tragedy," remarks Atayan, "which are counterbalanced by the humor of 'Khumar' and the lyricism and lucidity of 'Guzhn ara.' The magnificence and enthusiasm of the work song 'Loru Kutanerke' are enlarged to the scale of glorious ceremony in 'Aravodun Pari Luyse' and to martial urgency in 'Sipana Kacher'" (2:2)

——. *Yergeri Zhoghovadzu, Yerrort Hador: Khêmperker* [Collected Works, Third Volume: Choir Pieces]. Edited by Robert Atayan. Yerevan: Hayasdan, 1969.

The third volume of Atayan's massive compilation houses seventy choral pieces divided into categories of "wedding," "folk," and "dance," as well as seventy-two variants. All of these pieces came directly from a collection of manuscripts, notebooks, and unbound papers Margaret Babaian contributed that in 1955. The posthumous appearance of these works was a significant addition to Komitas's legacy of choir music (3: "Foreword").

——. *Yergeri Zhoghovadzu, Chororrt Hador: Khêmperker yev Menerker* [Collected Works, Fourth Volume: Choir Pieces and Solo Songs]. Edited by Robert Atayan. Yerevan: Hayasdan, 1976.

The fourth volume contains further twenty-six choral songs composed during the long period of creativity between the 1890s and 1914. Nineteen of the songs are accompanied by alternate versions. The volume also offers additional four solo songs and a series of drafts considered valuable in themselves. Most of these fifty-six pieces were found among Komitas's manuscripts. Others made their way into the personal libraries of friends and associates like Margaret Babaian. Very few of them were fair copies, so that deciphering them often presented significant difficulties. For the most part, the works are concerned with nationalistic or patriotic subjects (4:5–13).

——. *Yergeri Zhoghovadzu, Hinkerort Hador: Menerker yev Khêmperker* [Collected Works, fifth volume: Solo Songs and Choir Pieces]. Edited by Robert Atayan. Yerevan: Sovedagan Krogh, 1979.

The one hundred songs of the fifth volume, most of them rather modest in scale, are related to Komitas's career as a teacher in Etchmiadzin and Constantinople. Slightly over half of them are alternate versions of songs collected in the first four volumes. Most were reconstructed from copies that Komitas made in pencil. This volume also contains songs that were discovered after the publication of the previous volumes.

——. *Yergeri Zhoghovadzu, Vetserort Hador: Tashnamurayin Sdeghdzakordzutyunner* [Collected Works, Sixth Volume: Piano Pieces]. Edited by Robert Atayan. Yerevan: Sovedagan Krogh, 1982.

The sixth volume is devoted to the pieces written for piano, which are referred to as "Dances." Although these works comprise the smallest category of Komitas's *oeuvre*, Atayan notes that "their uniqueness is expressed through Komitas's use of the piano's special effects to convey folk-music ideas" (6:7). Many of these works illuminate particular areas of Komitas's life and work. "Mêsho Shorer" is a rigorously traditional dance, which he believed to be rooted in ancient, pre-Christian times. A number of these piano pieces had been performed by Margaret Babaian's sister Shushanig during the concert in Paris in December 1906, and were first published in 1925 by the "Friends of Komitas" committee. As a result they were quickly integrated into various prominent repertoires, such as those of the French pianist Lazar Levi, and the Artists' Society of the Soviet Socialist Republics. They have since been arranged for orchestra and have been performed often by the renowned "Komitas String Quartet."

Also included in this volume are the seven songs "Yot Yerk," short songs he wrote while vacationing with Margaret Babaian on the Isle of Wight. The "Mangagan Nvakner" [Children's Tunes] were written as pedagogical aids: Komitas used them to introduce Armenian folk music to his pupils in Constantinople.

## PUBLICATIONS PERSONALLY OVERSEEN BY KOMITAS

Komitas. *Shar Agna Zhoghovertagan Yerkeri, Tsaynakrets Komitas Vartabed* [Series of Folk Songs of Agn, Transcribed by Komitas Vartabed]. Etchmiadzin: Etchmiadzin Publishing House, 1895.

——. and Manoog Apeghian. *Hazar u mi Khagh: Zhoghovertagan Yerkaran Arachin Hisnyag, Khempakretsin Komitas Vartabed yev Manoog Apeghian* [One Thousand and One Couplet: Folkloric Songbook, First Fifty, Edited by Komitas Vartabed and Manoog Apeghian]. Vagharshabad, 1904.

——. and Manoog Apeghian. *Hazar u mi Khagh: Zhoghovertagan Yerkaran Yergrort Hisnyag, Khempakretsin Komitas Vartabed yev Manoog Apeghian* [One Thousand and One Couplet: Folkloric Songbook, Second Fifty, Edited by Komitas Vartabed and Manoog Apeghian]. Vagharshabad, 1905.

——. *Hay Knar: Keghchug Yerker, Havakets, Tashnagets Komitas Vartabed* [Armenian Lyre: Rustic Songs, Transcribed and Harmonized by Komitas Vartabed]. Paris, 1907.

——. *Hay Keghchug Yerker no. 13–22, Kri Arav yev Tashnagets Komitas Vartabed* [Armenian Rustic Song's no. 13–22, Transcribed and Harmonized by Komitas Vartabed]. Leipzig: Druck von Brietkopf und Härtel, 1912.

——. *Hay Keghchug Yerker no. 23–32, Kri Arav yev Tashnagets Komitas Vartabed* [Armenian Rustic Song's no. 23–32, Transcribed and Harmonized by Komitas Vartabed]. Leipzig: Druck von Brietkopf und Härtel, 1912.

## PERSONAL JOURNALS AND PROGRAM SCORES OF KOMITAS'S VARIOUS WORKS (FROM THE KOMITAS ARCHIVES, CHARENTS MUSEUM OF LITERATURE AND ART

Komitas. *Parisian Dedr. 1906, Tegdemper 1–*. [Parisian Journal for Concert on December 1, 1906].

——. *Tserats Dedrag Hay Keghchug Hamerki, vor Ghegavarutyamp Komitas Vartabedi yev Sirahozhar Masnagtsutyamp ir 300 Yergser Yerkichneru, Mard 20/2 Abril, 1911: Khêmpakrets Hamarod Neratzutyamp Komitas Vartabed* [Journal of Armenian Rustic Concert, under the direction of Komitas Vartabed with 300 singers, March 20/2 April 1911: Harmonized with Short Introduction by Komitas Vartabed]. Constantinople.

——. *Tserats Dedrag Hay Sêrpazan yev Keghchug Hamerki, Khêmpakrets Hamarod Neratzutyamp Komitas Vartabed* [Journal of Armenian Sacred and Rustic Concert, Edited with a Short Introduction by Komitas Vartabed]. Alexandria, 1911.

——. *Tserats Dedrag 1913, Mayisi 12/25i Hamerki Hay Keghchug Yerkeri Hamarod Ampopume, Krets Komitas Vartabed* [Journal for May 12/25 1913 Concert of Armenian Rustic Songs, Brief Summary, by Komitas Vartabed]. Constantinople.

## PARISIAN PUBLICATIONS BY "KOMITAS VARTABEDI PAREGAMNERU HANTSNAKHOUMP [THE FRIENDS OF KOMITAS VARTABED COMMITTEE]"

Komitas. *Hay Zhoghovertagan Yerazheshdutyun Nor Shark Kri Arav yev Tashnakets Komitas Vartabed* [Armenian Folkloric Music, New Series, Transcribed and Harmonized by Komitas Vartabed]. Paris: Comité du Pere Komitas.

[This is a series of seven booklets published in Paris over the course of twenty-six years. The booklets were labeled "A" through

"H," and were published in the following years, respectively: 1925, 1925, 1928, 1930, 1933, 1937, and 1951].

——. *Tashnavoryal Yerketsoghutyunk Srpots Badaraki, Hayasdanyats Arakelagan Surp Yegeghetsvo, Vasn Miaser Aragan Khêmpi* [Harmonized Chantership of the Holy of Holies Mass of the Armenian Apostolic Holy Church, for Male Choir]. Edited by Vartan Sarxian. Paris, 1933.

## ARMENIAN SOVIET SOCIALIST REPUBLIC PUBLICATIONS

Komitas. *Zhoghovertagan Yerker, Azkakragan Zhoghovadzu* [Folk Songs, Ethnographical Collection]. Translated to European notation, with a forward and annotations by Spiriton Melikian. Yerevan: Haybedhrad, 1931.

——. *Hay Zhoghovertagan Yerker yev Barerker, Azkakragan Zhoghovadzu, Hador 2-rt* [Armenian Folk and Dance Songs, Ethnographical Collection, Second Volume]. Collected by M.Gh. Aghayan, edited by Kristapor S. Kushnarian. ARMSSR Academy of Sciences, Haybedhrad, 1950.

### Posthumously Published Folkloric Couplets—in collaboration with Manoog Apeghian

Komitas. *Zhoghovertagan Khaghigner* [Folkloric Couplets]. Edited by Manoog Apeghian. Yerevan: Haybedhrad, 1940.

### Collected Writings

Komitas. *Hotvatzner yev Usumnasirutyunner* [Articles and Studies]. Yerevan: Haybedhrad, 1941.

# Bibliography

## PERIODICALS

"Bedk e Kachalerel, Te Voch" [Should We Encourage Him or Not?]. *Daraz* (Tbilisi), no. 32 (1904): 294–295.

"Haygagan Nvakahantes i Paris" [Armenian Concert in Paris]. *Anahid* (Paris), no. 10–12 (1906): 240.

"Komitas Vartabedi Hamerke" [The Concert of Komitas Vartabed]. *Puzantion* (Constantinople), no. 4289 (1910): 2.

"Komitas Vartabedi Hamerke" [The Concert of Komitas Vartabed]. *Puzantion* (Constantinople), no. 4290 (1910): 4.

"Komitas Vartabed yev Hay Yegeghetsagan Yerazheshdutyun" [Komitas Vartabed and Armenian Church Music]. *Puzantion* (Constantinople), no. 4156 (1910): 1, and no. 4157 (1910): 1.

"Komitas Vartabedi Arachin Adenapanutyune" [First Public Lecture of Komitas Vartabed]. *Dajar* (Constantinople), no. 34 (1910): 698.

"Komitas Vartabedi Hamerke Bolsum" [The Concert of Komitas Vartabed in Constantinople]. *Luys* (Nor-Nakhichevan), no. 44 (1910): 12–13.

"Komitas Vartabedi Hokevor-Zhoghovertagan Hamerke" [The Ecclesiastic-Folk Concert of Komitas Vartabed]. *Mshag* (Tbilisi), no. 62 (1905): 1–2.

"Komitas Vartabedi Nvakahantese Parisum" [Komitas Vartabed's Concert in Paris]. *Husharar* (Tbilisi), no. 4 (1906): 59.

"Komitas Vartabedi Taghume Metz Shukov Gadarvetsav" [The Funeral of Komitas Vartabed Was Carried Out With Great Fanfare]. *Haratch* (Paris), no. 9–11 (1935): 567–569.

"Komitasi Hamerke Masnagtsutyamp Yergser Khêmpi, Paghgatsatz 300 Yerkichnerits" [The Concert of Komitas, with the Participation of 300 Male and Female Choir Members]. *Dajar* (Constantinople), no. 33 (1910): 746.

Letter to the editor. *Nor-tar* (Tbilisi), no. 110 (1903): 2–3.

"Mer Aracharge: Komitasin Hravirel Tiflis, ir Khêmpov Hamerkner dalu" [Our Proposal: to Invite Komitas and his Choir to Tbilisi for a Concert]. *Daraz* (Tbilisi), no. 34 (1904): 327–328.

* * * * *

Ajarian, Hrachia. "Husher Komitasi Masin" [Memories of Komitas]. *Etchmiadzin* (Etchmiadzin) (1953).

Alemshah, K. "Ayts me Vartabedin" [A Visit with Komitas]. *Haratch* (Paris), no. 50 (1976): 116–117.

Allodi, F.A. "Post-Traumatic Stress Disorder in Hostages and Victims of Torture." *Psychiatric Clinics of North America* 17, no. 2 (1994): 279–288.

Arnag. "Komitas Vartabed." *Hayrenik* (Boston), no. 3 (January 1936): 73.

——. "Nisher Varbedin Gyanken" [Notes from Varbed's Life]. *Amenun Daretsuytse* (Venezia) (1924): 305–307.

Anais. "Kegharvesdagan Dbavorutyunner" [Artistic Impressions]. *Puzantion* (Constantinople), no. 4305 (1910): 1.

Andonian, Aram. "Komitas Vartabed Aksori Metch, Inch Baymanneru Dag Haydnevetsav Ir Mdkin Daknabe" [Komitas Vartabed in Exile, the Conditions Under Which His Mental Distress Appeared]. *Arevmoudk* (Paris), no 5 (15 December 1946), no. 6 (22 December 1946), no. 7 (1 January 1947), no. 8 (12 January 1947), no. 9 (19 January 1947), no. 10 (26 January 1947), no. 11 (2 February 1947), no. 12 (9 February 1947), no. 13 (16 February 1947), no. 14 (23 February 1947), no. 15 (2 March 1947), no. 16 (9 March 1947), no. 17 (16 March 1947), no. 18 (23 March 1947), no. 19 (30 March 1947), no. 20 (6 April 1947), no. 21 (13 April 1947), no. 22 (20 April 1947), no. 23 (27 April 1947), no. 24 (4 May 1947), no. 25 (11 May 1947), no. 26 (18 May 1947), no. 27 (25 May 1947), no. 28 (1 June 1947), no. 29 (8 June 1947).

Babaian, Margaret. "Husher Komitas Vartabeden" [Memories of Komitas]. *Arevmoudk* (Paris), no. 5 (1946): 92.

——. "Hay Yerazheshdutyune yev Komitas Vartabed" [Armenian Music and Komitas Vartabed]. *Amenun Daretsuytse* (Constantinople) (1921): 489.

Blank, A.S. "Clinical Detection, Diagnosis and Differential Diagnosis of Post-Traumatic Stress Disorder." *Psychiatric Clinics of North America* 17, no. 2 (1994): 351–383.

Chengurian, D. and P. Terlemezian. "Gronagan Zhoghovi Voroshume" [The Decision of the National Church Assembly]. *Puzantion* (Constantinople), no. 5370 (1914): 2.

Chituni, Dikran. "Komitasi Hed" [With Komitas]. *Hayrenik*, no. 2 (1936): 80–99.

Dadrian, Vahakn. "The Naim-Andonian Documents." *International Journal of Middle East Studies* 18 (1986): 311–360.

——. "The Role of Turkish Physicians in the World War I Genocide of Ottoman Armenians." *Holocaust and Genocide Studies* 1, no. 2 (1986):169–192.

Eitinger, Leo. "Pathology of the Concentration Camp Syndrome." *Archives of General Psychiatry* 5 (1961): 79–87.

Foa, Edna B., U. Feaske, T.B. Murdoch, M.J. Kozak, and P.R. McCarthy. "Processing of Threat-Related Information in Rape Victims." *Journal of Abnormal Psychology* 100 (1991): 156–62.

Garabedian, H. "Verchin Aytselutyun me Komitas Vartabedin" [Last Visit to Komitas Vartabed]. *Gochnag* (New York) (14 December 1935): 1185.

Ghadirian, Abdul-Missagh, Heinz Edgar Lehmann, Maurice Dongier, and Tom Kolivakis. "Multiple Personality in a Case of Functional Psychosis." *Comprehensive Psychiatry* 26, no. 1 (1985): 22–28.

Gorst-Unsworth, C. and E. Goldenberg. "Psychological Sequelae of Torture and Organized Violence Suffered by Refugees from Iraq." *British Journal of Psychiatry* 172 (1988): 90–4.

Helweg-Larson, P. et al. "Famine Disease in German Concentration Camps." *Acta Psychiatrica Scandinavica,* Suppl. 83 (1952).

Jerrakian, L. "Komitasi Hayatsknere Haygagan Yerazheshdutyan Vra (Ir Isg Haydararutyunnere)" [The Views of Komitas on Armenian Music (His Own Views)]. *Jamanak* (Constantinople), no. 584 (1910): 1.

Kalayjian, S. Anie et al. "Coping with Ottoman Turkish Genocide: An Exploration of the Experience of Armenian Survivors." *Journal of Traumatic Stress* 9, no. 1 (1996): 87–97.

Kechian, Puzant. "Khêmpakragan Bahbanoghaganutyun, te Khavaramêdutyun. Komitas Vartabedi Hamerkin Tem Gêgheramid Arkelknere. Yergu Khosk Badriarkagan Pokhanortin Hastseyin" [Editorial Conservatism or Obscurantism? The Clerical Obstacles to Komitas Vartabed's Concert. Two Words Addressed to the Deputy Patriarch]. *Puzantion* (Constantinople), no. 4293 (1910): 1.

Kechian, Puzant. "Têrvak Aksori Sherchanen" [An Episode from Exile]. *Amenun Daretsuytse* (Constantinople) (1922): 33–45.

Khojasarian, H. "Komitas Vartabed Antsnagan Husheres" [Komitas Vartabed, Personal Memories]. *Hayastani Gochnag* 1 (1936): 11.

Klein, M. "Mourning and its Relation to Manic-Depressive States." *Intentional Journal of Psychoanalysis* 21, no. 2 (1940): 125–153.

Komitas. "Franz Liszt." *Daraz* (Tbilisi), no. 19 (1904): 173–174.

——. "Hay Keghchug Yerazheshdutyun" [Armenian Rustic Music]. *Anahid* (Paris) (January-March 1937): 29–30.

——. "Giuseppe Verdi." *Daraz* (Tbilisi), no. 23 (1904): 208–209.

Krystal, Henry. "The Aging Survivor of the Holocaust: Integration and Self Healing in Posttraumatic States." *Journal of Geriatric Psychiatric* 14, no. 2 (1981): 165–189.

Muratian, Matevos, ed. "Komitasi Andib Namagnere" [Unpublished Letters of Komitas]. *Badmapanasiragan Hantes* 17 (Yerevan), no. 1 (1958): 245–267.

Navarian, Asadur. "Tibvatz te Abakinum" [Coincidence or Recovery]. *Haratch* (Paris), no. 531 (1927): 2.

Nader, Amir, Jane Stafford, Melinda S. Freshman, and Edna B. Foa. "The Relationship between Trauma Narratives and Trauma Pathology." *Journal of Traumatic Stress* 11, no. 2 (1998): 385–92.

Nimant. "Etchmiadzni Mêtnolordits" [From Circles of Etchmiadzin]. *Mshag* (Tbilisi), no. 40 (1909): 2.

Ohanian, A. "Letter from France: Komitas's Armenian Concert in Paris." *Mshag* (Tbilisi), no. 265 (1906): 3–4.

Platz, W.E., and A.F. Oberlander. "On the Problems of Expert Opinion on Holocaust Survivors Submitted to the Compensation Authorities in Germany." *International Journal of Law and Psychiatry* 18, no. 3 (1995): 305–321.

Sadrushan. "Komitas Vartabede yev Gronagan Zhoghove" [Komitas Vartabed and the Church Assembly]. *Puzantion* (Constantinople), no. 5393 (1914): 1.

Sarkisian, A. "Sev or me, Komitas Gula yev Gaghote . . . . Husher Vartabedi Gyankits" [A Black Day, Komitas Cries and Prays . . . . Memories from Komitas's Life]. *Aztarar* (Constantinople), no.2741 (1935): 2.

Schwartz, E.D., and D.B. Perry. "The Post-Traumatic Response in Children and Adolescents." *Psychiatric Clinics of North America* 17, no. 2 (1994): 311–326.

Seeman, Kenneth, Leslie Widrow, and Jerome Yesevage. "Fantasized Companions and Suicidal Depressions." *American Journal of Psychotherapy* 38, no. 4 (1984): 133–156.

Shahen. "Bolsagan Namagner Gosdandinoubolis 23e Noyemperi" [Letters from Constantinople, 23rd of November]. *Mshag* (Tbilisi), no. 272 (1910): 2.

Siruni, H.J. "Komitasi Hed" [With Komitas]. *Etchmiadzin* (Etchmiadzin) (January 1965): 35–39, (May-July 1965): 165–176, (August-September 1965): 74–79, (October 1965): 17–25, (March 1967): 36–45, (April 1967): 37–49, (May 1967): 37–45, (June 1967): 39–49, (January 1968): 43–48, (February 1968): 43–51, (March 1968): 43–49, (July 1968): 5–12, (October 1968): 52–56, (March 1969): 22–31, (April 1969): 30–38, (May 1969): 16–28.

Stengel, Erwin. "On the Aetiology of Fugue States." *Journal of Mental Sciences* 87 (1941): 572–599.

——. "Studies on the Psychopathology of Compulsive Wandering." *British Journal of Medical Psychology* 18 (1939): 250–254.

Tashjian, S. "Was Soghomon (Komitas Vartabed) a destitute, miserable and abandoned child after his parents' death? Was he left with no family to care for him?" *Hem Yeramia* (New York) (July-September 1996): 13–16.

Tchilingerian, Levon. "Komitas Vartabed." *Puzantion* (Constantinople), no. 5397 (1914): 1.

——. "Komitas Vartabed yev Haygagan Yerazheshdutyune" [Komitas Vartabed and Armenian Music]. *Jamanak* (Constantinople), no. 592 (1910): 1.

Tchobanian, Archag. "Angron Voroshum me" [A Sacrilegious Decision]. *Puzantion* (Constantinople), nos. 5384 and 5385 (1914): 1.

——. "Komitas Vartabed." *Anahid* (Paris) (June-July 1901): 141–144.

——. "Komitase yev Hay Yerazheshdutyune" [Komitas and Armenian Music]. *Anahid* (Paris), no.1–2 (1931): 103–127.

Trautman, E.C. "Fear and Panic in Nazi Concentration Camps." *International Journal of Social Psychiatry* 10 (1964): 134–141.

Torkomian, Vahram. "Hushadedres" [From My Memoirs]. *Vem* (Paris) (January-March 1938): 71.

Tomb, David. "The Phenomenology of Post-Traumatic Stress Disorder." *Psychiatric Clinics of North America* 17, no. 2 (1994): 237–250.

Ushaklian, Garo. *Aradzani* (Paris) (1940): 68–69.

van der Kolk, Bessel A., and Onno van der Hart. "The Intrusive Past: the Flexibility of Memory and the Engraving of Trauma." *American Imago* 48, no. 4 (1991): 425–454.

Watts, Darryl, and Gethin Morgan. "Malignant Alienation." *British Journal of Psychiatry* 164 (1994): 11–15.

## ESSAYS IN BOOKS

Agger, Inger and Søren Buus Jensen. "Determinant Factors for Countertransference Reactions under State Terrorism." In *Countertransference in the Treatment of PTSD.* Edited by John P. Wilson and Jacob D. Lindy. New York: Guilford Press, 1994.

——. and ——. "The Psychosexual Trauma of Torture." In *The International Handbook of Stress Disorders.* Edited by John P. Wilson and Beverly Raphael. New York: Plenum Press, 1993.

Andonian, A. "The Memoirs of Naim Bey." In *The Turkish Armenocide* 2. Newton Square, Pennsylvania: Armenian Historical Research Association, 1965.

Apeghian, Manoog. "Hishoghutyuner Komitasi Masin" [Memories of Komitas]. In *Zhamanagagitsnere Komitasi Masin* [Contemporaries on Komitas]. Edited by K.N. Kasbarian. Yerevan: Haybedhrad, 1960.

Atayan, Robert. "Komitas." In *New Grove Dictionary of Music and Musicians.* Edited by Stanley Sadie. New York: Groves Dictionaries of Music, 1980.

——. et al, eds. *Komitasagan* 1. Yerevan: ARMSSR Academy of Sciences, 1969.

——. "Komitasi *Anush* Anavard Operayi Urvakrere" [The Draft of Komitas's *Anush* Opera]. In *Komitasagan.* Edited by Robert Atayan. Vol. 2. Yerevan: ARMSSR Academy of Sciences, 1981.

——. "Margaret Babaian." In *Haygagan Sovedagan Hamaynakidaran* [Soviet Armenian Encyclopedia]. Edited by B.A. Simonian. Vol. 2. Yerevan: ARMSSR Academy of Sciences, 1976.

Babaian, Margaret. "Dbavorutyunner Komitasi Antsin yev Kortzin Shurch" [Impressions of Komitas and his Work]. In *Zhamanagagitsnere Komitasi Masin* [Contemporaries on Komitas]. Edited by K.N. Kasbarian. Yerevan: Haybedhrad, 1960.

——. "Husher Komitas Vartabeden" [Memories of Komitas Vartabed]. In *Zhamanagagitsnere Komitasi Masin* [Contemporaries on Komitas]. Edited by K. N. Kasbarian. Yerevan: Haybedhrad, 1960.

——. "Komitas Vartabed ir Namagneri Michov" [Komitas Vartabed Through His Letters]. In *Zhamanagagitsnere Komitasi Masin* [Contemporaries on Komitas]. Edited by K.N. Kasbarian. Yerevan: Haybedhrad, 1960.

Boydstun, James, and Carlos J.G. Perry. "Military Psychiatry." In *Comprehensive Textbook of Psychiatry.* Edited by Harold I. Kaplan, Alfred M. Freedman, and Benjamin J. Sadock. Vol. 3. Baltimore: Williams and Wilkins, 1980.

Brewin, R.C. "Psychology and Psychiatric Symptoms: An Information Processing Account." In *The Scientific Basis of Psychiatry.* Edited by Malcolm P.I. Weller and Michael W. Eysenck. London: W.B. Saunders, 1992.

Davidson, Jonathan, and Edna B. Foa, eds. *Post-Traumatic Stress Disorder: DSM-IV and Beyond.* Washington, D.C.: American Psychiatric Press, 1992.

Eitinger, Leo. "The Concentration Camp Syndrome and its Late Sequelae." In *Survivors, Victims, and Perpetrators: Essays on the Nazi Holocaust.* Edited by J.E. Dimsdale et al. Hemisphere, 1980.

Gardner, Howard. "Creativity in the Adult Years." In *Art, Mind and Brain: a Cognitive Approach to Creativity.* New York: Basic Books, 1982.

Hartman, Thomas. "Komitas." In *Zhamanagagitsnere Komitasi Masin* [Contemporaries on Komitas]. Edited by K.N. Kasbarian. Yerevan: Haybedhrad, 1960.

Hovagimian, Pakhtiar. "Komitasi Taderagan ashkharhe" [The Theatrical World of Komitas Vartabed]. In *Komitasagan.* Edited by Robert Atayan. Vol. 2. Yerevan: ARMSSR Academy of Sciences Publication, 1981.

Hovannisian, Richard. "The Historical Dimensions of the Armenian Question, 1878–1923." In *The Armenian Genocide in Perspective.* Edited by Richard Hovannisian. Oxford: Transaction, 1986.

Hummer, Karita M., and Arnold Samuels. "The Influence of the Recent Death of a Spouse on the Parenting Function of the Surviving Parent." In *Childhood Bereavement and its Aftermath.* Edited by Sol Altschul. Madison, Conn.: International University Press, 1988.

Kasbarian, K.N. "Komitas: Gensakragan Agnarg" [Komitas: A Biographical Sketch]. In *Zhamanagagitsnere Komitasi Masin* [Contemporaries on Komitas]. Edited by K.N. Kasbarian. Yerevan: Haybedhrad, 1960.

Komitas. "Hay Keghchug Yerazheshdutyun" [Armenian Peasant Music]. In *Hotvadzner yev Usumnasirutyunner* [Articles and Studies]. Yerevan: Haybedhrad, 1941.

——. "Hay Zhoghovertagan yev Yegeghetsagan Yerkere" [Armenian Folk and Ecclesiastic Songs]. In *Hotvadzner yev Usumnasirutyunner* [Articles and Studies]. Yerevan: Haybedhrad, 1941.

——. "Hayots Yegeghetsagan Yerazheshdutyune Dasneinnerort Tarun" [Armenian Church Music of the 19th Century]. In *Hotvatzner yev Usumnasirutyunner* [Articles and Studies]. Yerevan: Haybedhrad, 1941.

——. "Wagner." In *Hotvadzner yev Usumnasirutyunner* [Articles and Studies]. Yerevan: Haybedhrad, 1941.

Kushnarian, Kristapor S., Matevos H. Muratian, and Kevork Keotagian, eds. *Agnarg Hay Yerazheshdutian Badmutian* [Overview of the History of Armenian Music]. Yerevan: ARMSSR Academy of Sciences, 1963.

Levin, Patti. "Assessing Post-Traumatic Stress Disorder with the Rorschach Projective Technique." In *The International Handbook of Traumatic Stress*. Edited by John P. Wilson and Beverley Raphael. New York: Plenum Press, 1993.

Levonian, Karekin. "Mer Komitase" [Our Komitas]. In *Zhamanagagitsnere Komitasi Masin* [Contemporaries on Komitas]. Edited by K.N. Kasbarian. Yerevan: Haybedhrad, 1960.

Mesrobian, Aghavni. "Komitasi Gyanki Kidagtsagan Verchin Oreren" [From the Last Days of Komitas's Conscious Life]. In *Zhamanagagitsnere Komitasi Masin* [Contemporaries on Komitas]. Edited by K.N. Kasbarian. Yerevan: Haybedhrad, 1960.

——. "Vramsabuh Kibariane Komitasi Masin" [Vramsabuh Kibarian on Komitas]. In *Zhamanagagitsnere Komitasi Masin* [Contemporaries on Komitas]. Edited by K.N. Kasbarian. Yerevan: Haybedhrad, 1960.

Murard, Leon, and François Fourquer, eds. "Histoire de la psychiatrie de secteur, ou le secteur impossible." *Recherches* 17. Vaille: Torrubis, 1975.

Muratian, Matevos. "Azkayin Yerazheshdagan Uzheri Badrasdman Komitasian Tsêrakrere" [Komitas's Plans in Preparing National Music Cadres]. In *Komitasagan*, vol. 1. Edited by Robert Atayan et al. Yerevan: ARMSSR Academy of Sciences, 1969.

——. "The Armenian Music Culture During the First Half of the Nineteenth Century." In *Agnarg Hay Yerazheshdutian Badmutian* [Overview of the History of Armenian Music]. Kristapor S. Kushnarian, Matevos H. Muratian, and Kevork Keotagian, eds. Yerevan: ARMSSR Academy of Sciences, 1963.

——. "Hay Yerazheshdutyune XIX Tarum yev XX Tari Êsgezpum" [Armenian Music in the Nineteenth and Early Twentieth Centuries]. In *Agnarg Hay Yerazheshdutian Badmutian*. [Overview of the History of Armenian Music]. Edited by Kristapor S. Kushnarian, Matevos H. Muratian, Kevork Keotagian. Yerevan: ARMSSR Academy of Sciences, 1963.

Nersessian, Vrej, ed. *Essays on Armenian Music*. London: Kahn & Averill, 1978.

Nersisian, K.M., ed. *Hayeri Tseghasbanutyune Osmanian Gaysrutyunum, Pasdatêghteri yev Nyuteri Zhoghovatzu* [The Genocide of Armenians in the Ottoman Empire, Collection of Documents and Material]. Yerevan: Hayastan, 1991.

Niederland, William G. "Trauma, Loss, Restoration, and Creativity." In *The Problem of Loss and Mourning: Psychoanalytic Perspectives*. Edited by David R. Dietrich and Peter C. Shabad. Madison, Conn.: International Universities Press, 1990.

Parson, Erwin R. "Posttraumatic Narcissism: Healing Traumatic Alterations in the Self through Curvilinear Group Psychotherapy." In *The International Handbook of Stress Disorders.* Edited by John P. Wilson and Beverly Raphael. New York: Plenum Press, 1993.

Pelicier, Yves. "France." In *World History of Psychiatry.* Edited by John G. Howells. New York: Brunner-Mazel, 1975.

Pichot, Pierre. "Historical Introduction to Psychiatry." In *The Scientific Basis of Psychiatry.* Edited by Malcolm P.I. Weller and Michael W. Eysenck. London: W.B. Saunders, 1992.

Poladian, Sirvat. "Komitas Vartabed and his Contribution to Ethnomusicology, Komitas the Pioneer." In *Essays on Armenian Music.* Edited by Vrej Nersessian. London: Kahn & Averill, 1978.

Pollock, George H. "The Mourning Process, the Creative Process, and the Creation." In *The Problem of Loss and Mourning: Psychoanalytic Perspectives.* Edited by David R. Dietrich and Peter C. Shabad. Madison, Conn.: International Universities Press, 1990.

Postel, J., and C. Quétel, eds. *Nouvelle histoire de la psychiatrie.* Toulouse: Editions Privat, 1983.

Sheskous, R. "Komitas Berlinum" [Komitas in Berlin]. In *Komitasagan.* Edited by Robert Atayan. Vol. 2. Yerevan: ARMSSR Academy of Sciences Publication, 1981.

Simpson, Michael A. "Traumatic Stress and the Bruising of the Soul: the Effects of Torture and Coercive Interrogation." In *The International Handbook of Stress Disorders.* Edited by John P. Wilson and Beverly Raphael. New York: Plenum Press, 1993.

Siruni, H.J. "Hay Yerazheshdutyan Haghtanage" [The Victory of Armenian Music]. In *Hotvatzner yev Usumnasirutyunner* [Articles and Studies]. Yerevan: Haybedhrad, 1941.

Tahmizian, Nigoghos. "Nertashnagyal Badarake yev Hokevor ayl Yerkeri Tashnavorumner" [The Harmonized Divine Liturgy and Harmonization of Other Spiritual Songs]. In *Komitase yev Hay Zhoghoverti Yerazheshdagan Zharankutyune* [Komitas and the Musical Heritage of the Armenian People]. Pasadena: Trazarg, 1994.

Terlemezian, Panos. "Komitasi Masin" [On Komitas]. In *Zhamanagagitsnere Komitasi Masin* [Contemporaries on Komitas]. Edited by K.N. Kasbarian. Yerevan: Haybedhrad, 1960.

Terlemezian, Rupen. "Komitasi Arvesde: Desagan, Kênnatadagan Verlutzutyun" [Komitas's Art: Theoretical and Critical Review]. In *Zhamanagagitsnere Komitasi Masin* [Contemporaries on Komitas]. Edited by K.N. Kasbarian. Yerevan: Haybedhrad, 1960.

Volkan, D.V. "Turkey." In *World History of Psychiatry.* Edited by John G. Howells. New York: Brunner-Mazel, 1975.

## BOOKS

Aghayan, Tz. B. et al, eds. *Hay Zhoghoverti Badmutyun* [History of Armenian People]. Vol. 2. Yerevan: ARMSSR Academy of Science, 1984.

Alaexandris, A. *The Greek Minority of Istanbul and Greek-Turkish Relations, 1918–1974.* Athens: Center for Asia Minor Studies, 1983.

Alexander, Edward. *A Crime of Vengeance: An Armenian Struggle for Justice.* New York: Free Press, 1991.

Altintas, Ahmet et al, eds. *Osmanli Belgelerinde Ermeniler* [The Armenians in the Ottoman Documents] *(1915–1920).* Ankara: Basbakanlik, 1994.

Akçam, T. *Türk Ulusal Kimligi ve Ermeni Sorunu* [Turkish National Identity and the Armenian Question]. Istanbul: Baski, 1992.

Azadian, Toros. *Komitas Vartabed.* Constantinople: Gutenberg, 1931.

Balakian, Krikoris. *Hay Koghkotan: Têrvakner Hay Mardirosakrutyunen, Berlinen Der Zor 1914–1920* [The Armenian Golgotha: Episodes from Armenian Martyrdom: From Berlin to Der Zor, 1914–1920]. Vol.1. Vienna: Mkhitarian Press, 1922.

——. *Hay Koghkotan* [Armenian Golgotha]. Vol. 2. Paris: Araxnes, 1959.

Balakian, Peter. *The Black Dog of Fate: A Memoir.* New York: Basic Books, 1997.

Dadrian, Vahakn. *History of the Armenian Genocide.* Oxford: Berghahn Books, 1995.

Edgarian, Carol. *Rise the Euphrates.* New York: Random House, 1994.

Erikson, E.H. *Eight Stages of Men in Childhood and Society.* New York: Norton, 1950.

Fish, Frank J. *Clinical Psychopathology Signs and Symptoms in Psychiatry.* Bristol: Wright, 1967.

Freud, Sigmund. *The Complete Psychological Works of Sigmund Freud.* Standard edition. Vol. 14. London: Hogarth, 1961.

Friedlander, R. *Benedict-Augustin Morel and the Development of the Theory of Dégénérescence.* Ann Arbor, Mich.: University Microfilms International, 1979.

Hampartsumian, H.V., ed. *Haygagan Sovedagan Hamaynakidaran* [Armenian Soviet Encyclopedia]. Vol. 3. Yerevan: ARMSSR Academy of Sciences, 1977.

Haraszti, E. *Bela Bartok: His Life and Works.* Paris: The Lyrebird Press, 1938.

Janikian, Hovsep. *Hnutyunk Agna.* Tbilisi: 1895.

Kapuscinski, Ryszard. *Imperium.* Translated by Klara Glowczewska. New York: Knopf, 1994.

Keushgerian, Arminé, Araxi Kestekian, and Hagop Kestekian, eds. *Khrimian Hayrig.* Montreal: Canadian Diocese of the Armenian Church, 1994.

Kolnder, W. *Antonio Vivaldi: His Life and Work.* Translated by Bill Hopkins. Los Angeles: University of California Press, 1970.

Komitas Vartabed. *Knarerkutyunner* [Poetry]. Edited by Toros Azadian. Istanbul: Mêshaguyt, 1939.

Levonian, Karekin. *Husher* [Memoirs]. Yerevan: Haybedhrad, 1959.

Morgenthau, Henry. *Ambassador Morgenthau's Story*. New York: New Age, 1975.

Nalchajian, A. *The Psychology of Death*. Yerevan: Punik, 1992.

Oghlukian, Abel., ed. *Kragan Nêshkhark Komitas Vartabedi Peghun Kêrchen* [Literary Fragments from Komitas Vartabed's Prolific Pen]. Montreal: Canadian Diocese of the Armenian Church, 1994.

Pinel, Philippe. *Traité médico-philosophique sur alienation mentale, ou la manie*. Paris: Richard, Caille, 1801.

Pollock, G., ed. *The Mourning Liberation Process*. Madison, Conn.: International Universities Press, 1989.

Prudian, Tsitsilia. *Komitas*. Yerevan: Hayastan, 1969.

Sevag, Baruyr. *Anlreli Zankagadun* [The Ever-Ringing Belfry]. Beirut: Sevan, 1960.

Schumann, Robert. *Tagebucher, 1827–1838*. Edited by George Eismann. Leipzig: Deutscher Verlag für Musik, 1971.

——. *Tagebucher, 1836–1854*. Edited by Gero Nauhaus. Leipzig: Deutscher Verlag für Musik, 1987.

Schumann, Robert and Clara. *The Marriage Diaries of Robert and Clara Schumann*. Edited by Gero Nauhaus. Translated by Peter Ostwald. Boston: Northwestern University Press, 1993.

Shahverdian, A. *Komitas i Armianskaya Musicalnaya Cultura* [Komitas and Armenian Musical Culture]. Yerevan: Haybedhrad, 1956.

Simoniants, A. *Komitas Vartabed*. Boston: Published by the author, 1969.

Stuermer, H. *Two War Years in Constantinople: Sketches of German and Young Turkish Ethics and Politics*. Translated by E. Allen and H. Stuermer. New York: George H. Doran, 1917.

Tahmizian, Nigoghos. *Komitase yev Hay Zhoghoverti Yerazheshdagan Zharankutyune* [Komitas and the Musical Heritage of the Armenian People]. Pasadena, CA.: Trazarg, 1994.

Terlemezian, R. *Komitas*. Yerevan: Academy of Science of Armenia, 1992.

Turner, Trevor H. *A Diagnostic Analysis of the Casebooks of Ticehurst House Asylum, 1845–1890*. Cambridge: Cambridge University Press, 1992.

Yolian, Isabela. *Komitas*. Yerevan: ARMSSR Academy of Sciences, 1969.

## ARCHIVES

Tchobanian, Archag and Margaret Babaian. Letter, 11 September 1926. Doc. 70. Komitas Archives. Charents Museum of Literature and Art, Yerevan.

Gosdanian, D. "Im hishoghutyune Komitas Vartabedi masin" [My reminiscences of Komitas Vartabed]. Doc. 81. Komitas Archives. Charents Museum of Literature and Art, Yerevan.

Khrimian, M. Letter, 14 January 1902. Doc. 67. Komitas Archives. Charents Museum of Literature and Art, Yerevan.

Komitas. Autobiographical Papers. Doc. 71. Komitas Archives. Charents Museum of Literature and Art, Yerevan.

——. Letter to Mariam Tumanian, 1904. Doc. 4. Komitas Archives. Charents Museum of Literature and Art, Yerevan.

——. Letter to Garabed Gosdanian. Doc. 15. Komitas Archives. Charents Museum of Literature and Art, Yerevan.

——. Letter to Garabed Gosdanian. Doc. 17. Komitas Archives. Charents Museum of Literature and Art, Yerevan.

——. Letter to Garabed Gosdanian. Doc. 19. Komitas Archives. Charents Museum of Literature and Art, Yerevan.

——. Letter to Gabriel Menevishian, 16 April 1898. Komitas Archives. Mkhitarist Book Depository, Vienna.

——. Letter, 1914. Doc. 1369. Komitas Archives. Charents Museum of Literature and Art, Yerevan.

——. Letter to Margaret Babaian, June 1907. Doc. 1507. Komitas Archives. Museum of Literature and Art, Yerevan.

Schmidt, Richard. Doc. 65. Komitas Archives. Charents Museum of Literature and Art, Yerevan.

* * *

Certificat de Visite apres décès. Medical file of Komitas [Gomidas]. Archives of l'Hôpital Villejuif, Paris.

Cololian, Paul. Report, 6 April 1919. Medical file of Komitas [Gomidas]. Archives of l'Hôpital Villejuif, Paris.

Commitment form no. 46.273. Medical file of Komitas [Gomidas]. Archives of l'Hôpital Villejuif, Paris.

Copie des certificats medicaux, asile de Ville-Évrard. Medical file of Komitas [Gomidas]. Archives of l'Hôpital Villejuif, Paris.

Guiraud, Paul. Report, 31 July 1922. Medical file of Komitas [Gomidas]. Archives of l'Hôpital Villejuif, Paris.

Lwoff, Dr. Report, 6 August 1922. Medical file of Komitas [Gomidas]. Archives of l'Hôpital Villejuif, Paris.

Medical File of Komitas, from Maison Spéciale de Santé Ville-Évrard. Docs. 2 and 19. Société d'Etudes et de Recherches Historiques en Psychiatrie, Paris.

## DSM

American Psychiatric Association. *Diagnostic and Statistical Manual of Psychiatric Disorders.* Washington, D.C.: American Psychiatric Association, 1952.

——. *Diagnostic and Statistical Manual of Psychiatric Disorders.* 2nd ed. Washington, D.C.: American Psychiatric Association, 1968.

——. *Diagnostic and Statistical Manual of Psychiatric Disorders.* 3rd ed. Washington, D.C.: American Psychiatric Association, 1980.

——. *Diagnostic and Statistical Manual of Psychiatric Disorders.* 4th ed. Washington, D.C.: American Psychiatric Association, 1994.

## MISCELLANEOUS

France. "Lutte contre les maladies mentales" *Code de la santé publique*. 900–907.
Tashjian, S. Letter, 17 January 1995. Sydney, Australia.
Injejikian, Hasmik. "Sayat Nova and Armenian Ashugh Musical Tradition." Master's thesis, McGill University, 1990.

# Index

ARMENIA BETWEEN THE OTTOMAN AND

Principal towns, rivers and railways. Towns marked i

N EMPIRES AND PERSIA CIRCA 1914

of specific interest to Komitas's biography.